On Eagles' Wings

On Eagles' Wings

An Exploration of Strength in the Midst of Weakness

EDITED BY
DAVID J. COHEN AND MICHAEL PARSONS

WIPF & STOCK · Eugene, Oregon

ON EAGLES' WINGS
An Exploration of Strength in the Midst of Weakness

Copyright © 2008 Wipf and Stock Publishers. All rights reserved. Except for brief quotations in critical publications or reviews, no part of this book may be reproduced in any manner without prior written permission from the publisher. Write: Permissions, Wipf and Stock, 199 W. 8th Ave., Suite 3, Eugene, OR 97401.

ISBN 13: 978-1-55635-127-3

Manufactured in the U.S.A.

To Noel Vose

Founding Principal of the Vose Seminary (formerly the Vose Seminary
of Western Australia);
past President of the World Baptist Alliance;
scholar, colleague, pastor and friend.

An extraordinary man of God whose life demonstrates
the strength and grace of Jesus Christ.

Contents

Foreword by Derek Tidball (London School of Theology) ix
Preface xi
List of Contributors xiii
Abbreviations xiv

1. New wings for a molting eagle: Isaiah's bold message to exiled Israel

   David Wyn Williams 1

2. A prophet in motion:
   The counterpoint of speaking, acting and reflecting

   David J. Cohen 15

3. The "destabilized" God: Community without walls

   Merryl Blair 36

4. Obi-wan Kenobi, Neo, and Mark's narrative Christology

   Michael F. Bird 51

5. The scandal of weak leadership: Paul's defense of ministry

   Evelyn Ashley 63

6. The powerless leader: A biblical ideal or a contradiction in terms?

   Mary Evans 78

7. Martin Luther: A theologian forged by trial

   Mark D. Thompson 93

8. John Calvin on the strength of our weak praying

   Michael Parsons 105

9 In the power of the Lamb—and of the Lion
   Power and weakness in the early theology of Karl Barth

   Michael O'Neil 121

10 God's vulnerable strength: omnipotence as love

   Clark Pinnock 139

11 David and Foucault: Extreme violence and innocent suffering in a post-September 11 world

   Brian Holliday 154

12 Turning Teflon™ into Velcro™: Making words stick in an image-based culture

   Stephen McAlpine 169

13 Preaching in weakness: Reflections on the self in preaching

   Brian S. Harris 190

14 Strength in weakness: Developing this paradox through preaching and leading

   Michael J. Quicke 203

Bibliography 221

Foreword

At the heart of the Christian faith lies the paradox of the relationship between weakness and strength. Seen in the vulnerability and power of God, it is most sharply focused in the cross and resurrection of Jesus Christ. All believers, with Paul "want to know Christ—yes, to know the power of his resurrection and participation in his suffering" (Phil 3:10). But if this paradoxical way of living is required of all Christians, it presents itself as a particular challenge to those in leadership within the church.

Leadership is usually associated with the exercise of power and secular role models are lauded for their strength. Weakness is associated with failure and an inability to achieve results. Recent trends have acclaimed "successful" leadership in growth and in mega-churches. Evidence suggests many pastors seek to imitate such models often without success. This is sometimes because they are adopting a leadership style for which they are not personally equipped and which works itself out negatively at the very least in their driving the flock and at worst in power abuse. This has too often only led to frustration on the part of all concerned. Where church leaders have capitulated to secular ideas of leadership they leave the biblical teaching about weakness and servant-hood lying bloodied and battered on the floor as a nice but impractical ideal. Yet other church leaders seek to accommodate the biblical teaching about weakness and servant-hood, more by adopting, albeit unconsciously, a strategy of compartmentalising. In the pulpit they are strong and authoritative, sheltering behind the words of Scripture but pastorally, one-to-one, they are weak, diffident, and even apologetic as they confront the complexities of real-life reality. Yet others exhibit a feebleness they mistake for what Scripture calls weakness which results in them in reality abdicating the leadership role altogether, but struggling to keep people very happy.

There must be a better way! There is, and this collection of essays helps to chart the way forward, without settling all the issues or prescribing a managerial technique that will ensure we avoid all the traps. Like

Foreword

spokes on a wheel these papers radiate from one hub, the hub that concerns the paradox of weakness and strength. Almost half the essays engage with Scripture. They display scholarly competence, theological imagination and a keen sense of practical application. The questions, of course, are not new, and the next chapters help us to reflect on the issue through the experience of Luther and Calvin. A third group of essays explores the theme from the perspective a recent theology. While some heavyweights are brought into the picture (Barth and Foucault), and controversial issues are confronted (the Openness of God debate), wonderful application and imagination is demonstrated in handling the contemporary issues of violence and image. Two essays on strength and weakness as they apply to preaching and leading in the local church appropriately bring the book to a conclusion.

One of the features of this book is the international nature of the team of contributors. Perhaps special attention ought to be drawn to the fact that nine of the writers are from Australia and New Zealand. My recent travels left me with the impression of a very lively (and able) community of evangelical scholars "down under" and a sense that more of their work should be available to the global evangelical community. So I am especially glad to commend this work. It is at least another small step in the right direction of overthrowing the hegemony of British and American theology.

As I have read the essays I have found them worth savouring, both as a pastor and a theologian. They invite us not to rush through but stop and reflect on our own styles of leadership. They have a personal and spiritual impact as well as being a worthy academic contribution to discussion.

If Paul's experience, as set out in 2 Corinthians, is in any way a paradigm of ministry, rather than being the exceptional record of an apostle, then we cannot afford to neglect this topic, as, with a few notable exceptions, we have been tempted to do in recent years. After decades of hyping charismatic superstars and of admiring large church celebrities, this will help us to return to God's strange, but constant and non-negotiable, ways where strength is exhibited in weakness and wisdom is channelled through folly. They will help us to experience in our leadership the constant tension of cross *and* resurrection-shaped discipleship.

Derek Tidball
Principal, London School of Theology
July 2007

Preface

Much contemporary discussion concerning Christian leadership places significant emphasis on strength as a key characteristic for those who find themselves in, or seek, such a role in ministry. From a variety of perspectives this book challenges our perceptions of personal strength in leadership and even our understanding of God's own vulnerability in relationship with us. The nature of strength in ministry is discovered most significantly in an acknowledgment and embracing of personal weakness. The Christian leader's vulnerability within the context of relationship with God can be the place from which empowered ministry emerges to flourish on eagles' wings.

The contributors to this book follow this biblical paradigm with scholarly competence and enthusiasm. As editors we are grateful for their willingness to contribute to such a project. It has been interesting to observe the coherence in the volume despite the diverse backgrounds and research interests of the authors. Perhaps this says something about the truth and significance of the central conviction that strength is found *in* weakness, not simply despite it.

We are also grateful to the editors of Wipf and Stock for publishing the work and to Clark Pinnock for suggesting that route to publication. Thanks, too, to Derek Tidball for his generous reading of the entire text and his Foreword to the volume. We are both grateful to our wives and families for their continued encouragement of our research and scholarly endeavours—without them this volume would not be the volume it is!

Finally, a word regarding the dedication. We have both known Noel Vose for some years as a colleague and as a friend. He has been a tremendous advocate of Christ in Western Australia and throughout the world. In his eighties now he still reflects and demonstrates the kind of strength we envisage here in these essays. This book is a small thank you to God for his life-example and ministry among us. It also marks the beginning of a new era for the Vose Seminary of Western Australia as it is renamed Vose

Preface

Seminary this year in honour of Noel Vose's role as founding principal of the College.

David Cohen, Australia
Michael Parsons, England
2007

Contributors

1. David Wyn Williams, Lecturer, Old Testament, Harvest West Bible College, Perth, Australia.
2. David J. Cohen, Head of Biblical Studies, Lecturer in Hebrew Bible, Vose Seminary, Perth, Australia.
3. Merryl Blair, Lecturer in Old Testament Studies, Churches of Christ Theological College, Melbourne, Australia.
4. Michael F. Bird, New Testament Lecturer, Highland Theological College, Dingwall, Scotland.
5. Evelyn Ashley, Lecturer in New Testament, Vose Seminary, Perth, Australia.
6. Mary Evans, Vice-Principal and Senior Lecturer in Biblical Studies, London School of Theology, Northwood, UK.
7. Mark D. Thompson, Academic Dean and Senior Lecturer in Theology, Moore College, Sydney, Australia.
8. Michael Parsons, Director of Postgraduate Research at Vose Seminary, Perth.
9. Michael O'Neil, Senior Pastor, Lesmurdie Baptist Church, Perth, Australia.
10. Clark Pinnock, Professor Emeritus of Theology, McMaster Divinity College, Ontario, Canada.
11. Brian Holliday, Director of Dayspring, Centre for Spirituality, Perth, Australia.
12. Stephen McAlpine, Pastor and Freelance writer, Crowded House, Sheffield, UK.
13. Brian S. Harris, Principal, Lecturer in Pastoral Theology, Vose Seminary, Perth, Australia.
14. Michael J. Quicke, C.W. Koller Professor of Preaching and Communication, Northern Seminary, Warrenville, IL.

Abbreviations

ATA	Asia Theological Association
BibInt	Biblical Interpretation
CBQ	Catholic Biblical Quarterly
CD	Karl Barth, *Church Dogmatics*
CC	Christian Century
CNTC	Calvin's New Testament Commentaries
CTR	Calvin Theological Review
EJT	European Journal of Theology
EQ	Evangelical Quarterly
HBT	Horizons in Biblical Theology
HTR	Harvard Theological Review
IBMR	International Bulletin of Missionary Research
Inst	John Calvin, *Institutes of the Christian Religion*
Int	Interpretation
ITQ	Irish Theological Quarterly
JBL	Journal of Biblical Literature
JETS	Journal of the Evangelical Theological Society
JNSL	Journal of Northwest Semitic Languages
JSOT	Journal for the Study of the Old Testament
LTJ	Lutheran Theological Journal
LW	Luther's Works
NIB	New Interpreter's Bible
NT	Novum Testamentum
NTS	New Testament Studies
RE	Realencyklopä die für protestantische Theologie und Kirche
RefJ	Reformed Journal
RevExp	Review and Expositor
SBET	Scottish Bulletin of Evangelical Theology
SJT	Scottish Journal of Theology
TB	Tyndale Bulletin

Abbreviations

TrinJ	*Trinity Journal*
VE	*Vox Evangelica*
VT	*Vetus Testamentum*
WA	*D. Martin Luthers Werke: Kritische Gesamtausgabe, Schriften*
WATr	*D. Martin Luthers Werke: Kritische Gesamtausgabe, Tischreden*
WTJ	*Westminster Theological Journal*
ZNW	*Zeitschrift für die neutestamentliche Wissenschaft*

1

New wings for a molting eagle

Isaiah's bold message to exiled Israel

David Wyn Williams

INTRODUCTION

Faced with a recalcitrant congregation, church pastors—no matter how dynamic their preaching, or how insightful their biblical exegesis—would do well to reflect on the task that faced the prophet of the exile who we have come to call, in the absence of a more accurate name, Second Isaiah.[1] With the Holy City in ruins, the House of God destroyed, and the unconditional promise to David of a perpetual dynasty in shreds,[2] the prophet was commissioned to preach, not only to the dying remnants of a generation that had witnessed the fall of Jerusalem, but to a new generation born in exile. A generation that knew as much about Marduk as it did about Yahweh; a generation that if it heard the ancient stories of salvation at all, heard them as rumors or faint echoes

---

1. Second Isaiah, or Deutero-Isaiah, is the name given by critical biblical scholars to both the perceived author of Isa 40–55, and to that section of the book. The critical position is that while much of Isa 1–35 was authored by Isaiah of Jerusalem in the eighth century BCE, Isa 40–55, and at least some of 1–35, was authored during the Babylonian exile, from 587 to 539 BCE, by an author who was aware of the Isaianic tradition. Most of Isa 56–66 seems to have been authored during the post-exilic period, from a Judean base. The final form of the text can be described as "a symposium, or a seminar," Tull, "One Book," 279–314.

2. See 2 Sam 7.

of traditions that at one time may have been easy to believe.[3] But in exile, stories of the Exodus, of the revelation of Yahweh on the mountain, and of the conquest of the Promised Land, might have seemed like fairy tales.[4] For in exile, to a generation born without the trappings of covenant with Yahweh, the Babylonian gods seemed justified in claiming that they were mightier than the Hebrew deity.[5]

Against this backdrop, the prophet of the exile was commissioned to speak a new word to God's despondent people—but his was a message that would take some believing, even at the height of Israel's religious devotion: your savior, the shepherd that Yahweh has anointed to liberate you from exile, is the same Persian king who is marching against Babylon from the east; he is coming to destroy this mighty city and end this once-mighty dynasty—but in the process he will liberate you from exile, and you will return home to rebuild the devastated city.

One prophet, three tasks: to convince the exiles that Yahweh, despite all the evidence to the contrary, had not forgotten them; to convince them that Cyrus the Persian king would not erase them from history, but had indeed been anointed by Yahweh to be their salvation; and to convince them to leave Babylon in order to make a long and difficult trek across the desert, to a city that stood in ruins.

The hardest task of all, however, was to convince Israel that in this entire process, the exiles would witness and would be a witness (would *proclaim* as well as being the *evidence* of their proclamation) of Yahweh the Redeemer, the one, true living God—and that it would fulfill this role not from a position of strength, but from a position of weakness.

There are lessons for the contemporary Church in how the prophet appeals to a people fed up with their lot and scared of what is to come, and in the radical content of his message to a community devastated by judgment, and in bondage to disbelief.

---

3. That so much religious literary activity was carried on through the exilic and post-exilic period, and that the priesthood continued in a form throughout the period (see Ezra 2:36–58), indicates that the religious life of the Jewish people did not cease during the exile despite the absence of the temple.

4. "The exiles understood their physical well-being, on the one hand, and their pessimistic spiritual condition, on the other hand, as a sign of being neglected by God and, even more than that, as a signal of God's disappearance from the historical stage," Gitay, *Prophecy and Persuasion*, 52.

5. Ibid., 52.

New wings for a molting eagle

SECOND ISAIAH'S POLYPHONIC APPROACH

The poem of Isaiah 40:27–31 marks the beginning of the prophet's dialogue with exiled Israel; a dialogue that begins in a strongly disputational tone and continues in that tone until Isaiah 48:20, when the prophet, having argued all points of his commission, exhorts the exiles to flee Babylon, and to do so proclaiming the redemption of Yahweh. However, the tone, or form, of disputation that scholars have identified as dominating this section of Second Isaiah is not the only "voice" to be heard. A multiplicity—or polyphony—of voices contributes to the dialogue in order to appeal to Israel in ways other than argumentation.[6] The voice of lament, for example, appears briefly as an echo of Israel's own complaints against Yahweh, which even in exile may have retained some of the formal aspects of the community's worship from pre-exilic days. One hears also the voice of praise (as in 44:24–28), by which the prophet appeals to Israel in generic hymnic forms, apparently to remind the exiles not only of the ongoing praiseworthiness of Yahweh, but that they are the very people elected by Yahweh to utter such praise. Repeatedly, one hears the voice of salvation (as in 43:1–7), a pastoral voice, that reminds the exiles they are not alone, and that Yahweh's goal is their liberation.

All these voices are introduced by Second Isaiah in 40:27–31, where they establish a dialogical pattern by which the prophet hopes to evoke in the people a fresh expectation of Yahweh's salvific power, and a regenerated knowledge of themselves as Yahweh's elect. First we hear a voice of dispute, as Second Isaiah double-voices a complaint that Israel has appar-

---

6. The observation that the text of Second Isaiah features a polyphony of "voices" in an ongoing dialogue is one way of respecting the generic distinctions of different textual units identified by form critics, while also taking seriously the final form of the text, in which the juxtaposition of these units generates a dialogical whole. This hermeneutic employs the theories of Soviet literary critic Mikhail Bakhtin, who observed that language was shot through with numerous "other" voices—e.g., ideological, cultural, or political voices that infused all utterances. He called these voices "heteroglossia": "At any given moment of its historical existence, language is heteroglot from top to bottom: it represents the co-existence of socio-ideological contradictions between the present and the past, between differing epochs of the past, between different socio-ideological groups in the present, between tendencies, schools, circles and so forth, all given in a bodily form. These 'languages' of heteroglossia intersect each other in a variety of ways, forming new socially typifying 'languages,'" Bakhtin *Dialogic Imagination*, 291. Recognizing the presence of heteroglossia helps the exegete avoid imposing rigid generic categories on the text. It also provides a fresh way of considering how generic types contribute to our understanding of any particular unit.

ently uttered against Yahweh in exile[7]: "My way is hidden from Yahweh, and my cause is disregarded by my God." (v. 27). The prophet's strongly polemical tone gives the poem its force: "Why do you say, O Jacob, and speak, O Israel? ... Have you not known? Have you not heard?" (vv. 27ab; 28a).

Next we hear a voice of praise in response to these rhetorical questions. It is still the prophet who speaks, but he does so in a new form—that of the hymn: "Yahweh is the God of *forever*, he's the maker of the ends of the earth" (v. 28ab). Finally, we hear the voice of the pastor, speaking words of comfort and salvation. The voice originates in what scholars call the salvation oracle. It is heard through the whole second half of 40:27–31, indicating that the disputational tone that begins the poem is not for its own sake; that the prophet disputes Israel's lament in order, ultimately, to comfort the people.

The prophet's words of comfort have a specific content: Israel's present state of weakness is no accident of history, but an aspect of the very "cause" (mišpāt) they believe Yahweh has disregarded.[8] Their weakness is a precondition of their dependence upon Yahweh, from whom alone they will find renewal. This message is encapsulated in the image of an eagle (v. 31b)—not one that is soaring on powerful wings (an interpretation that, while flawed, has been favored by the major translations and

---

7. "Double-voicing" is another of Bakhtin's key theories and is best understood as a specific use of heteroglossia. Bakhtin describes it as "another's speech in another's language, serving to express authorial intentions but in a refracted way," Bakhtin, *Dialogic Imagination*, 324. Double-voicing serves two speakers, and expresses two intentions, simultaneously. In the example of double-voicing in Isa 40:27, Israel's lament retains its own integrity as the utterance of a despondent people—but it also serves as the basis of the prophet's dispute, and in his utterance the original lament takes on a different, accusatory tone. Says Bakhtin of such double-voiced discourse: "All the while these two voices are dialogically interrelated, they—as it were—know of each other and are structured in this mutual knowledge of each other. Double-voiced discourse is always internally dialogized," 324.

8. The word mišpāt—variously translated "judgment" (KJV), "justice" (ASV, NASB), "right" (RSV, NRSV, NJB), "rights" (ESV), and "cause" (NIV, JPS, REB)—is used more than one way by Second Isaiah, though the application to Servant Israel-Jacob of the role of bringing mišpāt to the nations in 42:1–4 is undoubtedly meant to double-voice Israel's lament here, where the word seems to denote the course of Israel's history. As Beuken argues, Israel understands its own neglected mišpāt to be determined by the nations instead of its God (Beuken, "Mišpāt: The First Servant Song," 11). The application of the word in the Servant discourse of Isa 42:1–4 suggests "right order," as in a society that is operating according to the righteous will of Yahweh. For this interpretation see Whybray, *Isaiah 40–66*, 72.

subsequently proliferated in popular theology) but one that is molting and unable to soar.

It is a key image and its correct interpretation in the context of the poem is essential, not only for the Judean exiles, but also for the postmodern church—since when Second Isaiah later describes Israel as a witness (43:10, 12) and as a servant (41:8–16; 42:1–9; 42:18–43:7; 43:8–44:8; 44:21–23; 48:20–22), it is with the backdrop of the molting eagle in view. Israel's purpose will be to witness from a position of weakness (indeed, as one who is blind and deaf, 43:8–10), and to serve from a position of humility (42:1–4). Unless the prophet establishes these parameters from the start then Israel will continue to strive for a form of human strength that, while possibly granting them freedom from exile, could never equip them for the service to which Yahweh called them. The contemporary church faces the same risk. In our efforts to establish ourselves as a community that is seen to be soaring, in truth we may be living in denial of our true calling, which is to witness to the redemption of God from a position of weakness and hopeful expectation.

A DIALOGICAL READING OF ISAIAH 40:27–31

The "voice" that opens Isaiah 40:27–31 is that of dispute, as noted already. In the first of a series of parallel couplets that comprise the poem, the prophet names the target of his discourse, and poses these questions: "Why do you say . . . Why do you speak?"[9]

The tone of disputation dominates Isaiah 40 from verse 12 on,[10] but in verse 27 it is directed specifically to Jacob-Israel for the first time.[11] This has the dual effect of spotlighting the audience that has been in the background up to this point, and of arresting Jacob-Israel in his despon-

---

9. Note that "say" (*'mr*) parallels "speak" (*dbr*), as "Jacob" parallels "Israel." This pattern of parallelism is continued through the poem. While dbr is accurately translated with "speak," some translations attempt to reflect the extra force of the word and/or the tone of lament, e.g., "assert" (NASB), "complain" (NIV), "declare" (JPS), "repeat" (NJB).

10. Melugin describes it as an "interrogative style," Melugin, *Formation of Isaiah 40–55*, 91.

11. Westermann says the purpose of the disputations from v. 12 on is realised by this unit, which is about addressing Israel's despondency (Westermann, *Isaiah 40–66*, 59). However, Childs counters, "The focus of the final form of the text does not revolve around the anthropocentric complaints of Israel, but rather the focus is unremittingly theocentric," (Childs, *Isaiah*, 307).

dency, with a question that demands a response.¹² Dispute will not be the dominant voice of this poem, but that it is the first voice suggests that Jacob-Israel's weakness is not limited to its empirical fragility. Jacob-Israel has become spiritually hardened in exile. Second Isaiah will make the point a number of times that the nation is blind and deaf (42:18–19), like the wooden idols they have begun to worship (45:9–25). This is no more an accident of history than the events that led to the exile; it was precisely the commission of Isaiah of Jerusalem (First Isaiah) to harden the hearts of the people, to make their ears deaf and their eyes blind (Isa 6:10–13). The people will benefit from knowing this, since the God who can make such things happen can also turn them around.

The use of the dual name, Jacob-Israel, is common in Second Isaiah (41:8, 14; 42:24; 43:1, 22, 28; 44:1, 5, 21, 23; 45:4; 46:3; 48:1, 12; 49:5, 6), and serves several functions. It double-voices the use of the name by First Isaiah, where it can denote the entire nation (Isa 9:8) or the remnant group of those who will survive God's judgment (Isa 27:6). In naming the exiles Jacob-Israel Second Isaiah is re-awakening their knowledge of themselves as the elect of Yahweh; despite their reduced state they bear a name that has a long history. It is not insignificant that this history includes the traditions of an ancestor who, like the exiles, went from Canaan to Mesopotamia and returned to the land of his birth following a time of hard service.¹³ For the exiles the name may also evoke the memory that Jacob was given the name "Israel" after being crippled by God, as they are now.¹⁴ But here the emphasis seems to be on evoking in the exiles an awareness that they are the nation, Jacob-Israel, who will later be addressed by Yahweh as "my servant" (41:8). Despite their feelings of abandonment and hopelessness, they not only bear the name, and therefore the ongoing history, of a nation that fell to judgment (foreshadowed in Isa 10:20; 14:1), they are the new Jacob that will take root and blossom and put forth shoots (Isa 27:6).

The second "voice" to be heard is that of Israel's lament, expressed in another parallel couplet: "My way (drk) is hidden from Yahweh, and my cause (mišpāṭ) is disregarded by my God" (v. 27cd). The lament is heard in a refracted way, however, in the double-voiced discourse of the prophet

12. Jacob-Israel is addressed in the masculine singular in the MT, but in the feminine singular in 1QIsaᵃ.

13. See Sommer, *Prophet Reads Scripture*, 133; and Blenkinsopp, *Isaiah 40–55*, 194.

14. See Gen 32:22–32. See also Seitz, "The Book of Isaiah 40–66," 6:355.

who utters the lament only to dispute it. At no point have we heard the direct utterance of Jacob-Israel. While the words of Jacob-Israel's complaint are common to the psalms of lament,[15] this specific lament is not found in the Psalms or Lamentations, signaling that it was probably not a formalized lament spoken during the exilic community's worship. This seems all the more likely since the words, if double-voiced accurately by the prophet, are not directed towards Yahweh at all. In the original utterance of the despondent exiles, Yahweh is spoken *about*. Spykerboer points out that the form of the lament matches its content: "He [Yahweh] is not addressed and he stands aloof."[16] The people no longer hope for a response from Yahweh, so they direct their complaint to his prophet, as the Exodus generation did to Moses (e.g., Num 11:1–6).

The content of the lament echoes the words of 40:14, where Yahweh's "path of justice (mišpāt)" and "way (drk) of understanding" are spoken of as being beyond anyone's counsel. The arrangement of the units that comprise Isaiah 40:12–31 was likely a complex process.[17] In the final form, however, a number of word repetitions between the units indicate some intentional juxtapositioning. The echoing of mišpāt and drk in the prophet's double-voicing of Jacob-Israel's lament casts a cynical shadow over the community's complaint. Jacob-Israel's lament, seen in the light of the prophet's earlier disputations regarding the unfathomable greatness of Yahweh, highlights the exiles' self-centeredness. They complain that God has disregarded the course of their history—essentially that he has been unjust and is not doing what he is meant to[18]—when the exilic community's attention should have been on *his* justice and *his* way. As Clifford points out, the attitude demonstrated by the community here is the opposite of waiting on Yahweh.[19]

Yet even voiced by the prophet, the despondency of the exiles can be heard clearly; and we can sympathize with their position. Why would they not feel abandoned and rejected? In the Psalms the oft-heard complaint is that God has hidden himself from his people, but here the complaint goes beyond that—God is *unable* or *unwilling* to see his people's need. This

---

15. E.g. Ps 30:7, 38:9, 44:24, 69:17.
16. Spykerboer, *Structure*, 53. See, also, Childs, *Isaiah*, 311.
17. See Melugin, *Formation of Isaiah*, 92.
18. Goldingay, *Message of Isaiah*, 68.
19. Clifford, *Fair Spoken and Persuading*, 83.

accusation is the ground of the ongoing trial scenes of chapters 41–48, in which Yahweh claims to be the one, true God who sees all things, even the future, in contradistinction to blind Israel, the dumb idols, and their foolish makers. There is no room for sympathy in the prophet's discourse to Jacob-Israel—the people's lament is unfounded, and ultimately unhelpful—and is disputed summarily.

As noted above the disputational voice is not heard for its own sake. Begrich suggests that the prophets took up the form of the disputation because they repeatedly found themselves dealing with objections, defending their point of view, and having to convince opponents.[20] But here the form is not rigid. After double-voicing Jacob-Israel's lament the prophet speaks in a voice of praise.

Verse 28 begins with another parallel couplet, again in a disputational tone—"Have you not known? Have you not heard?" But the dispute immediately becomes a voice of praise, to Yahweh as the God of forever, and the creator of the ends of the earth. The questions are loaded with irony, since the prophet knows full well that Jacob-Israel is blind and deaf, and neither knows (40:21; 42:25; 43:10; 43:19; 48:6–8) nor hears (41:26; 42:18, 20, 24; 44:1), which are signs of both his sin (Isa 1:3) and his judgment (Isa 6:9, 10). But the prophet's purpose is not to shame the exiles, but to shift their attention from themselves and their weakness, to Yahweh and his strength. Muilenburg expresses this well: "The burden of the statements is to call the bluff of the audience's empiricism even as the latter has called the bluff of the prophet's theology."[21] Having captured the attention of Jacob-Israel with the disputational double-voicing of their own lament, the prophet now reminds them of Yahweh's permanency, and his lordship over time and space, by using language that evokes in them not their communal lament, but their communal praise. It is an emotional appeal, to a God they know, but have neglected to remember. As Westermann says, the prophet "speaks to the nation's heart."[22]

The permanence of God—and his ability to predict future events, indeed, to marshal the forces of history—and his sole claim to lordship over creation, are important themes throughout Isaiah 40–48 (41:20, 27;

---

20. Begrich, *Studien Zu Deuterojesaja*, 49.
21. Muilenburg, "Book of Isaiah," 5:69.
22. Westermann, *Isaiah 40–66*, 61.

42:5; 43:1, 7, 10, 15; 45:7; 45:8, 12, 18; cf. 54:16).[23] It is no surprise that both themes are introduced here at the heart of the prophet's disputational discourse. Yahweh's claim will become the driving force of his disputations with the nations and their idols (e.g., 41:21–29; 44:8, 9–20). But it is also the foundation of Jacob-Israel's security and hope (Isa 42:5-6). The voice of praise that is introduced in 40:28 is a direct challenge not only to Jacob-Israel's perception of Yahweh, but also of himself. If Yahweh is blind, then Israel is lost. If Yahweh is truly the Lord of time and the creator, even of Chaldea, then Israel cannot be lost. As North says, "He controls the history of all peoples; how much more the drk and mišpāt of Israel?"[24] The use of the participle (bôrē') to denote Yahweh as creator emphasizes his ongoing creative activity.[25] This is important to Second Isaiah, for whom the redemption of Jacob-Israel from exile will be like a new creation (44:3).

The prophet's praises of Yahweh in grand terms continue with the pointed statements that he does not faint (yi'ap) or weary (yîgā') (v. 28c), and that his understanding (tbûnātô, echoing 40:14) cannot be plumbed (v. 28d). The first statement introduces terms that will be double-voiced in verse 30 with reference to the young—by it the prophet draws a sharp distinction between the inexhaustible strength of Yahweh, and the fragility suffered by the youngest (and strongest) of people. The second statement serves two functions—it counteracts Jacob-Israel's lament, but also foreshadows the main thrust of the disputations to follow.

From verse 29 another "voice" is introduced, and it dominates the whole second half of the poem, indicating that the prophet's purpose all along has been to address Jacob-Israel in these terms. It is a voice that evokes the salvation oracle, a pastoral voice that seeks not to dispute, but to encourage. The introduction here of a voice that comforts, on the back of one that has first sought to dispute, then to praise, sets the pattern for chapters 41–48, where disputation speeches will be interspersed with both hymns of praise and oracles of salvation. Here, as there, the purpose is to address two discrete concerns of the exilic people: that Yahweh is *unable* to save his people, and that Yahweh is *unwilling* to save his people.[26] The

---

23. "The capacity to establish providence over history is something God's rivals cannot do," Seitz, "How is the Prophet Isaiah Present?" 182.

24. A similar point is made by Muilenburg, "Book of Isaiah," 5: 445.

25. See, also, Schoors, *I Am God*, 257: "As an eternal God he is eternally creating."

26. Watts rightly adds a third concern, which falls outside the purview of this essay—that Yahweh's choice of Cyrus is not acceptable to the people. See Watts, "Consolation or

prophet's words praising Yahweh in verse 28 answer the first concern; his pastoral words from verse 29 onwards answer the second.

Hence, the tone becomes more intimate—the appeal is not to a confrontation, or praise of a God who is Lord of time and space, but to heartfelt trust in Yahweh's willingness to come alongside the despondent and weary. The disputational voice that began the poem, and that will continue throughout the following chapters, was necessitated by very real doubts among the exiles concerning Yahweh's power and will:

> Traditionally the lament psalm and its answering assurance of salvation were not concerned with Yahweh's ability to deliver ... But the exile had raised doubts about Yahweh's power, against which Deutero-Isaiah directed his disputation and trial speeches.[27]

The prophet's key statement in this poem is uttered here, in verse 29: Yahweh—the Lord of time and space, whose strength does not diminish and whose understanding cannot be plumbed—gives strength to the weary, and to those with no strength he multiplies strength. Three different words for strength signify the power of Yahweh, in contrast to the lack of it in the weary—not to highlight Yahweh's transcendence, but to demonstrate how the Almighty stoops low to raise up the broken.

The imagery of verses 30–31 substantiates the claim made concerning Yahweh in verse 29. The parallel couplet of verse 30 sharpens the contrast between Yahweh and those humans one least expects to weary (yīgāʿû, echoing the verb in v. 28c, and the adjective in v. 29a)—the young. The prophet points out that not even youth is a guarantee of strength. The image of young men falling exhausted is intensified in the Hebrew by the use of the infinitive together with the verb k̲šl (kašôl yikkāšēlû, "utterly stumble"[28]).

The waw that is prefixed to the Hebrew verb translated as "grow weary" at the beginning of verse 30a is rendered "even" by most of the major translations, and anticipates a contrasting statement, as in "Even youths get weary, but ...." The contrast comes in verse 31a, with the introduction of wĕqôyē yhwh ("those waiting on Yahweh"). In other words, there are those who rely upon their own strength, and there are those who

---

Confrontation?" 38.

27. Seitz makes a similar point: "The speech intends to drive home matters about God that Israel already knows but has forgotten, and its final purpose is to lift up, to increase strength, to bolster and rejuvenate" (Seitz, "Book of Isaiah," 342).

28. North, *Second Isaiah*, 90.

wait on Yahweh. The verb here is qwh, and can be translated as "to hope". It signifies a waiting that is hope-filled—not an aimless waiting for an event that may not happen. Those who wait, hopefully, on Yahweh, would not accuse him of being ignorant of their need—they would be anticipating his activity. North's interpretation is helpful. He says that waiting does not represent prayer, since it is humans who are at the receiving end of the waiting denoted by qwh: "There is always in it the suggestion of the tension, and hopeful expectancy, of waiting."[29] Goldingay says it denotes "an attitude of confident, well-grounded expectation and trust."[30]

"Those waiting on Yahweh" has four predicates, arranged in two parallel couplets. The parallels in the second couplet are easy to see: "They will run and not be weary" (yîgāʿû, echoing 28a and 30d) neatly parallels "They will run and not be faint" (yîāpû, echoing 28d, 29a, 30a). The sense is also clear—while the young utterly stumble, those who wait hopefully for Yahweh will not.

We might expect the lines of the first couplet to parallel each other in a similar way, since this has been the pattern throughout the oracle. But this is where the major translations seem to have encountered problems. The first predicate is simple enough: "They will renew strength." The verb translated "renew" is ḥlp̄ and here connotes change. The emphasis clearly is on the exchange of weakness for strength. But the second predicate is not so clear: yaʿălû ʾēber kannešārîm yārûṣû is translated literally as "they (those who are waiting on Yahweh) will go up pinions like eagles." The hifil form of the verb ʿlh can mean either "grow" or "cause to ascend"—so, "they will grow wings like eagles," or "they will rise up (on) wings like eagles." Most of the major translations follow the second rendering. The LXX, Vulgate, JPS and NJB translate more in line with the first, as do a number of commentators, such as Blenkinsopp: "They will grow new pinions like eagles."[31]

The question is which translation best parallels the first predicate, with its emphasis on renewal? As mentioned at the beginning of this essay, "they will rise up (on) wings like eagles" is a splendid image, but empha-

---

29. North, *Second Isaiah*, 90–91.

30. Goldingay, *Message of Isaiah*. See, also, Blenkinsopp, *Isaiah*, 194: "Biblical Hebrew differentiates between waiting as a neutral activity, something to be endured . . . and waiting with hope and the anticipation of a positive outcome (*qwh*), which is what is meant here by waiting for Yahweh."

31. Blenkinsopp, *Isaiah*, 189.

sizes strength rather than renewal. Muilenburg refers to the image as "a marvelous figure of the reality and power of faith."[32] Its parallel, however, does not highlight the power of faith, but the process of renewal.

"They will grow pinions like eagles," on the other hand, probably takes its meaning from a popular belief that eagles regained their youthful plumage when they molted (see Ps 103:5). Although North calls this idea "fanciful," it has some merit.[33] The image of Jacob-Israel in a stage of molting, yet awaiting regrowth and renewal, fits not only the parallel predicate in the line above, but also sits well with the dialogical strategy outlined in this essay. The prophet's purpose has not been to convince Jacob-Israel that he is mighty, or even that he could be if only he had the faith, but to help him acknowledge that he is weak—but that this weakness is not out of line with the will of Yahweh, his mišpāt for Israel. Just as the eagle must molt before regaining its youth, so Jacob-Israel must suffer a time of weakness in order to be renewed not by her own strength, but by that of Yahweh.

The prophet first disputed Jacob-Israel's lament in order to wake the exiles from their self-centered despondency. He sang Yahweh's praises in order to remind the exiles that their God is not an idol made of wood, but the Lord of time and space and that God is the Creator whose creative activity has not ceased; that Yahweh is the one who does not get weary when all about him do, and that he draws alongside those who *are* weary. In their weakness he gives them hope for renewal and vigor that come not as a result of their faith, but precisely because of the attitude of expectant hope that is directed towards Yahweh. As Stuhlmueller says,

> Israel will renew her strength by looking hopefully to Yahweh in this her tense moment of trial. She will find Yahweh, as the prophet here announces in hymnic style (v. 28), eternally with her, sustaining her within her weakness . . . endowed with knowledge beyond scrutiny.[34]

In other words, the strength comes from the hope—and the hope is sure because it looks forward to renewal that is certain, because it comes from Yahweh. It is here that the exhortation to the prophet to comfort Yahweh's people (see Isa 40:1) finds its goal.

32. Muilenburg, "Book of Isaiah," 5: 445.
33. North, *Second Isaiah*, 88–89.
34. Stuhlmueller, *Creative Redemption*, 150–51.

New wings for a molting eagle

THE DIALOGUE CONTINUES

A case could be made that Second Isaiah's message for exiled Jacob-Israel was for a particular people in a particular historical moment. However, even on a literary level, the message of the prophet of the exile remains open to the future.[35] A dialogical text cannot be finalized, since by its very nature it expects a response—and there is no response in the final form of Isaiah that closes off the text. From a theological point of view "those who wait on the Lord" describes anyone in any given moment—whether exiled Israel or the persecuted church. Certainly, the apostle Paul understood the message that God the redeemer reveals himself in weakness, not strength, to be applicable beyond the particular history of exiled Israel.[36]

On the basis of his message in Isaiah 40:27–31, Second Isaiah sought to convince Jacob-Israel that he would be a witness to the remarkable redemption of Yahweh, and ultimately would serve his purpose in bringing God's mišpāt to the nations. This was possible only from a position of total dependence on the strength of Yahweh. Among communities that continue to read Isaiah as inspired scripture, this lesson is no less pertinent. Some sections of the church are struggling for survival in situations not dissimilar to that of the Judean exiles. For them the message of hopeful waiting is highly relevant. But it is no less relevant to those sections of the church that are comfortable, and perhaps a little overly-pleased that they are soaring like the eagle.

The correct interpretation of this key image of Isaiah 40:27–31 is vitally important for the contemporary church. An image that should suggest renewal—and the strength that is derived from hopeful waiting on God—is easily interpreted in a way that focuses on the end result: the eagle in its splendor. This not only misses the point of the prophet's discourse, but could be used to justify a striving for majesty and strength, when sitting in "weakness" is what is called for. Whybray writes, "The wings of an eagle are an obvious symbol of great strength."[37] But that is not the purpose of the imagery here. Nowhere in Second Isaiah does Israel become majestic or even strong—it remains the witness whose redemption glorifies not itself, but its redeemer. If the church is to see in Isaiah 40:27–31 a lesson that can be applied to its own contemporary situation,

---

35. For the "unfinalisability" of dialogical texts, see Newsom, *Book of Job*, 23.
36. See, for example, 1 Cor 1:20–31.
37. Whybray, *Isaiah 40–66*, 60.

then its emphasis must be on where the text itself places it, rather than on its own preferred reading. That emphasis is on weakness, not strength.

2

A prophet in motion

The counterpoint of speaking, acting, and reflecting

David J. Cohen

INTRODUCTION

MINISTRY CAN BE TAXING and testing, whatever environment in which leaders find themselves serving. The contemporary call often seems to demand strength as a personal quality to form the basis for effective leadership. While strength can be an admirable quality in any leader, its nature, its need, and its source, raise some important questions in the realm of Christian ministry and leadership. The book of Jeremiah presents a portrait of ministry which is remarkable in many respects, not the least of which is the presentation of a prophet who manifests and acknowledges the frailty of humanity, yet still offers an empowered prophetic voice. Jeremiah chapters 11 to 20, in particular, bring the nature of the prophet's ministry leadership into sharp focus. They reveal a significant process through which the prophetic figure discovers a self-evidently empowered ministry against astounding odds.

These chapters provide a collection of speeches by Yahweh interspersed with the so-called "Confessions" and a number of symbolic actions.[1] All this, embedded within a complex literary structure, offers a rich

---

1. Notwithstanding the fact that these passages (Jer 11:18–12:6; 15:10–21; 17:14–18; 18:18–23 and 20:7–18) are often referred to as confessions, laments or complaints I will refer to them as prayers of distress.

textual counterpoint unmatched in other biblical material.² Rarely do we find such an intriguing combination of God-speech, action, and reflection. These are articulated side-by-side and emanate from a story which extends from the internal ruminations of God and Jeremiah, the prophetic figure, to ultimately encompass historical ramifications for the nation. This coalescing of God-speech, action, and reflection presents images of a process critical to our understanding of what empowered ministry can look like in the midst of human vulnerability and weakness. Despite the figure of Jeremiah struggling with his task to the point of desolation, we observe a resilience which marks the continuance of a remarkably difficult prophetic ministry.

The literary movement found within these chapters affirms the necessity of an authentic relationship between God and the person in ministry. Deepening of this divine–human relationship does not emerge from any one particular character or source, but rather the dialogical counterpoint between the three—God, the individual, and the community. The vulnerable prophet is confronted with God and an unfaithful community. The text as a whole gives readers an insight into the counterpoint between these three entities that provides both the environment and resulting impetus for ongoing empowered prophetic ministry.

So how can this dialogical counterpoint be defined? Even a cursory reading of chapters 11 to 20 reveals a number of voices that interact with each other. In particular, three distinct voices are clearly evident. God, who struggles with an unfaithful people and the implications of divine justice; the prophet, who struggles with his sense of call to the prophetic ministry and his personal vulnerability; and the prophet's community, which seems oblivious to the voice of judgment and often speaks with derision towards the prophet. This dialogical counterpoint compels the prophet and God to both act and, ultimately, reflect. As part of this process the nature of God, the prophet, and the community becomes clearer while allowing the expression of the visceral nature of the relationship between all three.

---

2. The individual psalms of lament would be the closest to these prayers of distress found elsewhere in the Hebrew Bible. However, Boorer in "The Prophetic Ministry?" 5–30, states that "it sees the lament form as having been taken up and used in the literary context for a different purpose, that is, as a means of portraying the prophetic office within the specific situation portrayed in the literary context." Diamond, in *Confessions of Jeremiah*, also suggests that, "The formal analysis of the confessions continues to confirm their strange quality of continuity and discontinuity with lament psalms."

A prophet in motion

To begin with, a brief survey of some more recent research on Jeremiah chapters 11 to 20 will provide a helpful departure point for this exploration. Thinking about the book of Jeremiah generally, and Jeremiah chapters 11 to 20 in particular, has evolved significantly over the last one hundred years. Of particular note is the pioneering study of Baumgartner who first identified the lament form of Jeremiah's prayers of distress found in chapters 11 to 20.[3] In light of this literary description other scholars have sought to take the discussion in a variety of directions.[4] In summary, these range from an emphasis on the biographical portrayal of the character Jeremiah to a concentration on the broader theological themes that permeate the text.

Three significant issues emerge from this wide ranging discussion. These provide a foundation from which to explore the dialogical counterpoint I am proposing. First, while it is difficult to defend an exclusively biographical reading of the historical character of Jeremiah it is fair to assume that the story, as it unfolds, emanated originally from real people facing real situations. McConville states, "It needs no demonstration that the figure of Jeremiah plays a more prominent role in the prophecy that bears his name than any other prophet does his."[5] While not necessarily arguing for or against the historicity of Jeremiah, what McConville does emphasize is the very human experience of the Jeremianic character. Whoever we envisage the character of Jeremiah to be, the text requires it to be someone. He cannot simply be an imaginary figure.

Having stated this, it would be unwise to limit our perspective on chapters 11 to 20 to a historical figure.[6] The second issue scholars have highlighted is that the prayers of distress signify an accepted form of expression that extends beyond any one individual or community. In other words, the form of individual lament found in these chapters is an acceptable and necessary expression of distress. Furthermore, the lament is shaped as prayer and, in the case of Jeremiah, represents a prophetic utterance directed towards God. This is, of course, in contrast to

---

3. Baumgartner, *Jeremiah's Poems*.

4. A helpful summary of scholar's research and conclusions can be found in Boorer, "The Prophetic Ministry?" 6.

5. McConville, *Judgment and Promise*.

6. Biddle, *Polyphony*, 115, notes that "Jeremiah preserves a virtual chorus of voices in dialogue, some presumably contemporaneous with one another, some from widely dispersed historical and social settings."

typical prophetic speech that is God-speech redirected to the community through the prophet. As McConville states, "The portrayal of Jeremiah, by his utterances and by the account of his experiences, becomes a paradigm of the life of Yahweh with his people."[7] The converse could also be argued; it becomes a paradigm of the life of people *with* Yahweh.[8]

It is also significant to note the use of poetic language in these chapters, particularly in expressing distress. The power of Hebrew poetry to create images and express emotions cannot be underestimated. It provides an ideal medium for the expression of thoughts *and* feelings offering a multifaceted view of the person in focus.[9]

The third issue has been the concentration on a specific theological perspective, or perspectives, espoused particularly in the prayers of distress as well as generally throughout chapters 11 to 20.[10] While specific, but overarching, theological themes are no doubt present in these chapters a close reading of the text also reveals a rich seed bed of diverse theologies and, in some cases, what might be characterized as competing theologies. These theologies arise out of and, to some degree, are dependent on the dialogical counterpoint identified within these chapters.

With this background in mind, and the acknowledgment that Jeremiah chapters 11 to 20 have been subject to significant redactional shaping, it remains for us to explore the nature of this dialogical counterpoint and its relevance for understanding the task of ministry today. There is no suggestion here that the sequence of God-speech, action, and reflection in these chapters necessarily reflects a chronological or prescriptive order. However, this is an attempt to deal with the literary sequence and explore the dynamics it suggests.

These chapters can be divided into five movements, each containing divine speech directed to the prophet, a response from the prophet, and a reflection in the form of a prayer of distress. The three "voices" (God,

---

7. McConville, *Judgment*, 65.

8. It could be argued that these are both precisely the same. However, here I am suggesting that the relationship from the human side is also dependent on perspective and perception at any given time in addition to any preconceived theological overlay.

9. For further exploration of the nature and efficacy of Hebrew poetry see particularly Alter, *Art of Biblical Poetry* among a number of significant works on the subject.

10. For example Boorer, 'Prophetic,' 6–7, who sees the confessions as a justification of Judah's destruction and exile, or, Diamond, *Confessions*, 162, 183, 191, where theodicy is the favored theological focal point.

prophet, and community) can be heard through these elements articulating the dual themes of human weakness, in conjunction with an awareness of divine presence. While I intend to examine each of these movements in turn, the goal is not to view them as independent from each other. On the contrary, the dialogical counterpoint pervades the whole section, as do the twin themes of human weakness and divine presence. The five movements are as follows:

- Movement One
    - Jeremiah 11:1–17   –God-Speech
    - Jeremiah 11:18–12:6   –First Prayer of Distress
- Movement Two
    - Jeremiah 12:7–17   –God-Speech
    - Jeremiah 13:1–27   –Prophetic Action—God-Speech
    - Jeremiah 14:1–15:9   –God-Speech
    - Jeremiah 15:10–21   –Second Prayer of Distress
- Movement Three
    - Jeremiah 16:1–13   –God-Speech—Prophetic Action
    - Jeremiah 16:14–17:13 –God-Speech—Divine Action
    - Jeremiah 17:14–18   –Third Prayer of Distress
- Movement Four
    - Jeremiah 17:19–18:4   –God-Speech—Prophetic Action
    - Jeremiah 18:5–18   –God-Speech—Divine Action
    - Jeremiah 18:19–23   –Fourth Prayer of Distress
- Movement Five
    - Jeremiah 19:1–20:6   –God-Speech—Prophetic Action
    - Jeremiah 20:7–18   –Fifth Prayer of Distress

FIRST MOVEMENT (JER 11:1–12:6)

The first God-speech in chapter 11 clearly sets out the broad theological paradigm of relationship between the people of Judah and Yahweh. It is focused on the covenantal nature of the relationship which is deeply rooted in the history of this people.[11] The section begins with Yahweh

---

11. Jones, *Jeremiah*, 181–82, suggests that Jeremiah "... saw such hope in the promulgation of Deuteronomy that he espoused it... On the other hand 8:8 shows that Jeremiah saw through the activity of many of the scribes whose responsibility it was to interpret

being portrayed as the more powerful of the covenant partners typical of Ancient Near Eastern Suzerainty covenant structures. However, the weaker partner—in this case Judah, represented here by the figure of Jeremiah the prophet—is not voiceless. Jeremiah's words may be few but they are still uttered. However, his words are, at this point, simply an affirmation of Yahweh's invoking of the covenant's consequences.[12] The prophet's voice is in dialogue as Yahweh engages with him. The second part of the speech changes in tone to one of judgment and while Jeremiah is still in focus as the addressee, there is now no verbal response from him. Yahweh, as the stronger covenant partner is the one pronouncing divine judgment, yet the prophet is the one who will proclaim the message on Yahweh's behalf. The joining of voices will culminate in the joining of forces as the prophetic message is proclaimed to an audience apparently unwilling or unable to hear.

Abruptly the movement is punctuated with an intensely personal prayer of distress. This is the dialogical counterpoint to the God-speech still resounding in the reader's ears. While Yahweh's concerns are directed towards the nation, the prophet reflects on the inward struggle with the sense of disempowerment resulting in personal distress. This prayer is psalm-like in its form and personally reflective in its content. It has the essential elements of individual lament[13] but, unlike its counterparts in the Psalter, is clearly connected with a particular prophetic figure who is reflecting on a specific experience of life. This prayer of distress provides a voice for the disempowered prophet; an opportunity to express his distress and the opportunity to call for divine action. As with some lament psalms, the prophet's dilemma manifests itself, in part, as a question of theodicy.[14] In fact, the prophet characterizes himself as being "like a gentle lamb led to the slaughter" (11:19, NRSV). It could be that there is a note of challenge embedded here in the imagery used. Has Yahweh deceived

---

Deuteronomy but who exploited it and so made it into a lie."

12. Cf. v. 5. The difficulty here is in determining exactly what the prophet is affirming. Holliday, *Jeremiah 1*, 348, sees the parallel with Deuteronomy 27:15–26 as Jeremiah affirming the cursing of Judah as a result of covenant disloyalty.

13. See Craigie, *Jeremiah*, 177, who specifies invocation, complaint, prayer and divine response. Of course, the last listed here is not typical of individual laments found in the psalms.

14. See, especially, Diamond, *Confessions*, for a discussion on the nature of theodicy in Jeremiah 11–20.

the prophet in some way? Is this God able to act or not? Will the prophet prevail despite his sense of disempowerment?

The "enemy's" voice enters at this juncture, providing a third line of counterpoint with the voice of Yahweh and the voice of the prophet. The voice of the enemy is articulated by the reflective prophet possibly as an expression of despair, possibly as a launching pad for the resulting imprecatory appeal. Clearly this is an authentic presentation of the struggle for the prophet with both the God he seeks to serve and the enemies who seek to destroy him. Despite the fact that he stands on the side of Yahweh, the supposed powerful covenant partner, the prophet feels compromised and in danger of a premature demise. Yet confidence is still expressed in Yahweh's justice. The drawing together of the three voices—that of Yahweh, the prophet, and the enemy—in a reflective prayer of distress appears to lead to a sense of ongoing empowerment for the task. On the one hand the prophet clearly believes that Yahweh "will be in the right" 12:1 (NRSV).[15] On the other hand, regardless of how events unfold, there is no retreating from stating his case. As O'Connor observes, "He [Jeremiah] lays his case before God. 'Why does the way of the guilty prosper?' he asks. God replies that things will get worse."[16] This first movement ends with Yahweh graphically describing the prophet's worsening situation. However, the prophetic ministry does not end at this point. It appears that implicit in Yahweh's words is a call for the prophet to rely on his God. Despite this ominous forecast, in reality Yahweh has heard the prophet's voice and will ultimately respond.[17] Perhaps now the prophet can continue in some sense reassured, empowered, and a little less naïve. The counterpoint between Yahweh, the prophet, and the enemy causes reflection and some level of meaning-making for the prophet while opening up a way forward in action.[18] However, before any action on the prophet's part, Yahweh speaks again.

---

15. Habel, *God of Jeremiah*, 35, highlights "the capacity of Jeremiah to confront his God—a God who is not only close but also accessible and vulnerable."

16. O'Connor, "The Prophet Jeremiah," 138. Von Rad, "The Confessions," 341–42, states here that "God lifts the veil for a moment and opens a perspective on riddles and mysteries of an incomparably difficult nature, but without giving the slightest hint of explanation."

17. In fact, Avioz, "The Call," 435, states that "Jeremiah expects God to revenge the blasphemy of His name, but he is also waiting for God to defend Jeremiah as his messenger. A vindication of the prophet will eventually lead to the vindication of God; it will be the result of God's action against Jeremiah's adversaries."

18. Carroll, *When Prophecy Failed*, 124, describes this process as "dissonance giv[ing]

SECOND MOVEMENT (JER 12:7–15:21)

The second movement begins with a progression of two God-speeches (12:7–17). However, the adjacent positioning of the prophet's prayer of distress at the close of the first movement and these God-speeches marks both a contrast and a mirroring. The contrast is a shift of perspective from the prophet's self-reflection to a divine response, which is now divine lament. The mirroring here is emphasized by the close proximity of the two laments. In fact, Fretheim argues that

> When one considers the prophet's laments alongside the divine laments, readers can see that the prophet does not simply mirror the laments of God but incarnates that divine word.[19]

The prophet may well lament his precarious position as Yahweh's spokesperson to the people of Judah, but Yahweh here pronounces and laments the abandonment of the relationship with the people of Judah. Inherent in this God-speech is an expression of both divine justice and divine suffering. This is no cold, calculating end to the relationship but rather a clash between Yahweh's mercy and justice precipitated by the people's unfaithfulness. These words provide a divine assurance to the prophet that despite the prayer of distress and dire predictions concerning his fate, God is present. Here the focus is clearly on Yahweh's sense of alienation from the people. The description of the desolation of the land seems to mirror the desolation of the people's hearts. The lament of Yahweh appears to mirror the lament of the prophet. Both distressed, yet for differing reasons.

In the first speech (vv.7–13) two significant themes appear contiguously. The first emphasizes the identity of the people in relationship with Yahweh as *naḥălāṯî*, which is translated as "my inheritance" (NRSV) or "my heritage" (NJB), while the second graphically describes how that inheritance has been abused and that Yahweh's anger will result in decisive action. The shift from the first person singular possessive ("my") to the third person plural ("they") in these verses emphasizes the tension within the divine–human relationship. The second speech (vv. 14–17) extends the theme of *naḥălāṯî* but this time with a slightly more conciliatory tone. The ultimate goal is to bring these people back to the land and engender loyalty

---

rise to hermeneutic".

19. Fretheim, *Jeremiah*, 189.

A prophet in motion

to Yahweh in line with the covenantal paradigm.[20] Again, the dialogical counterpoint is evident in this movement from the distress filled prayer of the prophet to the lament of Yahweh. In addition, there is also an internal counterpoint *within* the speeches of Yahweh between the voice of judgment and the voice of compassion. The text is moving at two levels. These speeches immediately following the first prayer of distress highlight the vulnerability of both Yahweh and the prophet in grappling with the situation.

The dialogical counterpoint between Jeremiah and Yahweh in chapter 12 leads to a symbolic action. Yahweh's voice and the voice of the prophet intersect as words become activity.[21] The symbolic action is motivated by words from Yahweh (13:1, 3 and 6). The text, as read, has no difficulty in portraying the distressed prophet as now acquiescent towards Yahweh's demands. The message, words to this point, become solidified in action and the counterpoint between Yahweh and the prophet, at times rather dissonant, now works harmoniously.[22] In addition to the action, an explanation of the symbols is also provided, offering a degree of meaning-making to the prophet, and perhaps the audience. The prophet is not left to his own interpretive prowess and the distress of Yahweh is publicly on show as the most intimate of clothing items, a loincloth, is used to illustrate both the presence and disintegration of intimate relationship. These actions are a significant part of the second movement as they assume that the prophet is empowered enough to perform these tasks. In other words, this is an empowerment for ministry that emerges from a divine–human dialogue about a seemingly hopeless situation. The counterpoint between the voice of the prophet and the voice of Yahweh has provided the impetus for Jeremiah's work to continue. God's presence is again evident and efficacious.

---

20. Brueggemann, *Commentary on Jeremiah*, 126, observes that the other nations " . . . are invited in and judged by the standard covenantal forms." This is indicative of a more universalistic program present in the prophetic message. However, it emphasizes the similarity of the parameters of relationship be it Yahweh with Judah or other nations.

21. In discussing the actual nature of this action Carroll, *Jeremiah*, 83, says, "Whether the performances are to be regarded as an ancient form of Hebrew (street) theatre or as acting in a more general sense must be left open because we have no evidence to warrant firm conclusions." Notwithstanding Carroll's comment there seems little reason to doubt that it involved physical action of some kind.

22. Thomson, *Book of Jeremiah*, 71–76, has a helpful discussion on the nature and purpose of symbolic action. He highlights the connection between word and action while cautioning the reader that, "It must be insisted that in the symbolic actions the prophets were not dealing in magical actions. . . . The power of both the prophetic word and the symbolic action derived from Yahweh alone."

Emerging from this ominous symbolic action dramatizing Judah's demise is the voice of Yahweh, again pronouncing judgment and also some sense of hope at the same time. Yahweh's dilemma is reflected in the word the prophet is to speak. While judgment must come (vv. 12–14) there still appears to be hope of averting disaster (vv. 15–17) before a return to an inevitable demise (vv. 18–17). Again, the prophet not only proclaims the intentions of Yahweh but also reveals the divine turmoil such intended action precipitates. So here the counterpoint is harmonious between the prophetic voice and Yahweh's voice, in coexistence with internally dissonant divine voices.

This movement begins with a lamenting God-speech expressing these dissonant internal ruminations punctuated in the text by a clear symbolic action pronouncing Judah's demise. Despite this rather dark message, glimmers of hope emerge in the latter part of chapter 13. However, the mood swiftly moves back to one of despair where Judah's end is expressed as a *fait accompli* in chapter 14 and the first part of chapter 15. The voice of Jeremiah is silent here and in fact the prophet, as a participant in the scene, fades into the background until he is commanded not to pray (14:11) but to speak to them (14:17). Here the voice of the prophet is intentionally silenced, at least in regards to prayer. Yahweh seems decided on the question of Judah's fate. There is now no room for compromise on Yahweh's part. Judah's God has spoken conclusively. The divine voice is now assured and the prophet is actively compliant.

This second movement also culminates in a prayer of distress (15:10–21). The voice of the prophet emerges in the text from the pronouncement of a definitive judgment on Judah. In the midst of Yahweh's ruminations concerning judgment the prophet reflects on *his* total despair at the task before him. This prayer highlights the coexistence of the divine and the human. Neither is independent from the other; one provides a counterpoint to the other; sometimes harmonious, sometimes dissonant. While the purposes of Yahweh extend beyond the individual prophet, they also incorporate the individual prophet as part of the way forward.

This second prayer of distress plunges deeper than the last as it reaches beyond the immediate prophetic task, the prophet bemoaning his own birth and existence. Almost immediately the counterpoint is evident as Yahweh's voice responds to the prophet's despair. Yet the words of response are paradoxical for the prophet. At a theological level, O'Connor argues that "The purpose of the confession is to provide credentials of legitimacy for Jeremiah's prophecy."[23] While this is a valid conclusion the prayer also functions at an existential level for the prophetic figure of Jeremiah. There may be a theological justification for his predicament; however, this does not ameliorate his feelings of despair. Again, the concerns of the prophet present a legitimate voice in dialogical counterpoint with Yahweh's voice.

In contrast to the first prayer of distress the complaint element is rather short-lived. The divine response is swift, greater in volume and, in this instance, interspersed between, rather than separate from, the words of the prophet.[24] This prayer again emphasizes the dialogical nature of the relationship between Yahweh and the prophet. In other words, the reflection on life and ministry is found here in the context of conversation with Yahweh. Clearly, from the response Yahweh is reinforcing the idea that the prophet works with, rather than independent from, Yahweh in the prophetic task.[25] This voice explicitly requests divine action (vv. 15–16) emphasizing an assumed partnership and also the challenge of presumed innocence on the prophet's part.

As with the first prayer of distress, a renewed empowerment for ongoing prophetic ministry appears to emerge from this reflection. This comfort and strength for the ongoing task again results from both the dialogue itself and also the reinforcing words of Yahweh for the task at hand.[26] However, Habel highlights the precarious nature of the prophetic ministry, stating that "He [Jeremiah] felt privileged to bear God's name and speak God's word. But the result was personal isolation and agony."[27] All this ambivalence is expressed, in spite of the fact that the section ends with an oracle of salvation (vv. 19–21).

Taken in isolation, this prayer of distress offers an insight into the dissonant thinking and experience of the prophet. However, against the backdrop of Jeremiah 12:7 onwards we gain an insight into the broader

---

23. O'Connor, *Confessions*, 42.

24. So, the Hebrew at this point. Note that the interpretive difficulties when comparing LXX and MT in vv. 10–14 are summarized helpfully by Miller, "Book of Jeremiah," 6: 696.

25. The usage of the preposition "*l*" in the first phrase of the v. 11 is interesting. The NRSV translated the phrase as "Surely I have intervened in your life for good" and also provides the alternative ending: " . . . with your life." Either translation of the preposition is allowable but both emphasize divine involvement with a slightly different nuance.

26. See especially vv. 19–21.

27. Habel, *God of Jeremiah*, 31.

context in which this distress is experienced. As Yahweh struggles with the consequences of the covenant relationship for an unfaithful people and the prophet acts out the prophetic message, so the human struggle with the divine also becomes clearly evident. Yet out of this feeling of desolation the prophet still emerges empowered and the ministry continues.

THIRD MOVEMENT (JER 16:1–17:18)

The beginning of the third movement marks a deeper incursion by Yahweh into the personal life and experience of Jeremiah. The God-speech commands the prophet's celibacy and describes its function as a symbolic action. The state of relationship for the prophet reflects the state of the relationship between the people and Yahweh. McKane concludes that

> In this account of Jeremiah's loneliness we have an exilic interpretation which establishes a parallel between the style of the prophet's life and the fate of the community from which Yahweh has withdrawn his *shalom*.[28]

Once again the experience of the prophet, articulated in the second prayer of distress (15:10–21) and immediately followed in the text by a commanded symbolic action (16:1ff.), reflects a counterpoint of both words and action between the prophet and Yahweh. This, combined with the preceding symbolic action and prophetic words, assumes that both the prophet and the people could clearly understand what Yahweh is trying to communicate.

The counterpoint is enriched as the people enter, albeit hypothetically at this point, into the conversation between God and prophet. Their ignorant response is preempted by Yahweh asking the question first and also providing the response for Jeremiah (vv.10–13). Here we have an example of reflection and meaning-making that engages the broader theological picture being presented in Jeremiah the book. Yahweh may lament the inevitable consequences of covenant disloyalty and Jeremiah may lament the predicament of prophetic ministry, but for transformation to be a possibility the wider community of God's people must be meaningfully engaged. It then becomes a question of whether or not that community

---

28. McKane, *Critical and Exegetical Commentary on Jeremiah*, 367.

is listening.[29] Again this emerges from the counterpoint between multiple voices in the text.

Perhaps surprisingly, in this portrayal of the people's ignorance and a total loss of hope for the community as a whole a clear note of hope strongly resounds (vv.14–15). It may be tempting to ignore or excise these verses from the text.[30] However, this is another theme to add to the counterpoint of voices here. This is the voice of hope, a voice rarely heard in Jeremiah; perhaps the voice of the exilic community searching for meaning in their situation. This is, very simply put, hope in the midst of judgment. Clearly it is a reminder of the past and a prompter for the future. The Exodus is in view here as the paradigm for divine action in response to the people. Given the tone immediately prior to this note of hope, it suggests that Yahweh will rescue and return the people in spite of themselves. Interestingly, there is no mention here of repentance as a prerequisite for this return.

While the remainder of chapter 16 continues in the form of a God-speech pronouncing judgment there is another interesting counterpoint to the divine voice. Verses 19 and 20 have been understood in various ways.[31] Clearly it is a prayer uttered in response to the words of judgment evident throughout this movement in the God-speeches. In this case, it articulates the nature of humankind in contradistinction to that of God. The final verse of chapter 16 seems to reinforce this distinction with a continuation of the God-speech, emphasizing both divine power and also the significance of the relationship between humankind and God. Thus the juxtaposition of judgment and hope here highlights the way in which both can actually coexist. In fact, it could be argued that they *need* to coexist, highlighting in this case the prophet's need of God and source of empowerment for ministry.

Chapter 17 continues as a God-speech, which again emphasizes the imminence of judgment. Adjacent to this is a further God-speech that is reminiscent of some wisdom literature (e.g., Ps. 1). Here is the divine voice

---

29. The interrogatives used in v. 10 belie what Brueggemann, *Exile*, 153, describes as, "The ultimate sins [which] are autonomy and self-sufficiency ... evidenced in not listening."

30. See for example Bright, *Jeremiah*, 109, et al.

31. Carroll, *Jeremiah*, 347, provides one such perspective suggesting that the section is "a loosely constructed poem made up of the prayer of the pious individual, the words of the heathen approaching Yahweh, a generalized reflection on the making of gods and a divine saying."

stressing the significance of the human response to God, the ramifications of which are evident for both the people of Judah and the prophet. Wisdom provides a further voice to the texture of the movement. In typically wisdom-like language, "Cursed are those who trust in mere mortals . . . whose hearts turn away from the LORD" (17:5b NRSV) and, "Blessed are those who trust in the LORD" (17:7 NRSV), the human response described here is focused on the individual rather than the community. The response is one of the heart; inward not primarily outward. However, this voice of wisdom is theologically ambiguous for the prophet who continues to struggle with a sense of injustice. Jeremiah has already laid his case before Yahweh claiming this very thing in the first prayer of distress. Here (vv. 14–18) he presents his case a second time as a protestation of innocence. The nation may have been unfaithful but has Jeremiah? Surely not! So the voice of the prophet reflects openly and honestly on his predicament in the light of what "wisdom" would suggest.

Even a cursory reading of this prayer exposes a great sense of need, but also an attitude of resignation. As O'Connor states, "Jeremiah's spirit continues to plummet downward but he speaks unwaveringly to God."[32] However, in spite of the struggle here the prophet is not alone. His voice is not unheard but, rather, it is a voice in dialogue with Yahweh. Despite his protestation of innocence the bulk of this prayer is a plea for help in the form of personal well-being and imprecation against the prophet's enemies.[33] While the injustice is certainly *felt*, here it is also *expressed*. This prayer provides a reflective hiatus for the prophet and the hearer or reader of the text. Is life always, or ever, as clear-cut as the portrayal of wisdom in chapter 17 or is life a constant struggle to understand God, human nature, and the relationship between the two? No answer is provided to the dilemma at this point. Even Yahweh is now silent. However, the dialogical counterpoint evident within this movement as a whole validates the feelings of the prophet and allows for the candid conversation to take place. It also paradoxically allows for the prophet to move on in spite of his circumstances. The prayer of distress, by definition, acknowledges relationship with Yahweh and the notion of a God who hears the cry of humankind. Again this forms the basis for continuing empowered ministry.

---

32. O'Connor, *Confessions*, 136.
33. In fact, over half the prayer is constituted in this way.

FOURTH MOVEMENT (JER 17:19–18:23)

As with the third movement the fourth begins with a God-speech that commands Jeremiah to preach a very public sermon. Though there is no specific response from Yahweh to the prophet's expression of distress in vv. 14–18 this could in fact be viewed as such. In light of the prophet's plea and the depth of his concern for his own sense of disempowerment the text leads us immediately back into the prophetic task laid out before Jeremiah. In fact the God-speech here becomes a speech of the prophet as he is commanded to preach a sermon to the people. At this point, the voice of Yahweh and the voice of the prophet coalesce in harmony again into the public word. There is no clear indication as to why the Sabbath appears to be singled out.[34] However, the sermon placed here clearly demonstrates a continuance of the prophetic ministry. Perhaps surprisingly, it emerges not from a moment of great victory for the prophet or his God, but rather from the midst of a prayer of distress that voices anxieties, doubts, and lacks a direct divine response.

Chapter 18 begins with another command from Yahweh to perform yet another symbolic action (vv. 1–4). However, unlike previous symbolic actions, the prophet is an observer of the process this time. The counterpoint between Yahweh commanding and the prophet responding in obedience is enriched by the image of the potter and the clay (beginning at v.6). Here the activity of the potter speaks in two ways. Initially it is symbolic of how Yahweh has molded the "house of Israel" (v.6) but later in the section the imagery is used to describe how Yahweh is molding "evil against you" (v.11). Clear meaning is attributed to the symbol in these two contrasting ways. The prophetic message and empowerment for the prophet again emerges from the dialogical counterpoint between divine speech, prophetic reflection, and symbolic action to proclaim the prophetic message.[35]

Perhaps, rather surprisingly, the community is allowed a voice (v. 12) in the face of this divine pronouncement. This is directly challenging the

---

34. Miller, *Book of Jeremiah*, 710, notes that this focus on the Sabbath echoes the Decalogue. It is possible that this is indicative of the post-exilic focus on Sabbath-keeping as a significant practice. It could also highlight the covenantal paradigm overarching all these events.

35. Ibid., suggests that "The story of the potter and its elaborated interpretation is a medium for reflection upon divine sovereignty and freedom. The passage means to assert both realities." Here we have an underlying counterpoint of divine voice against divine voice. The existence of both is not ignored, nor is it denied. It is simply stated.

divine pronouncement. It is unclear at this point exactly how the response should be understood. It could be an outright act of defiance or it could be more an expression of resignation. Either way, it provides further impetus for the divine speech and prayer of distress to follow and offers a brief insight into the reflection of the community on the prophet's message. It is obvious from this exchange that the prophet's message may have gone unheeded, but it has not gone unheard.

The continuation of the God-speech again shifts from one focused on judgment to one of reflection on the nature of the relationship between the people of Judah and Yahweh.[36] It laments the current state of the relationship. This community is alienated from Yahweh through their own unfaithfulness in the relationship and now their voice turns towards the prophet himself. The divine voice seems to be ignored at this point; the people preferring to direct their energies towards the prophet. Here again the prophet finds himself in a position of disempowerment, not because of divine action but as a consequence of divine action.

The prophet's voice heard in the fourth prayer of distress emerges from the brash interchange of perspectives in the text between the people and Yahweh. Of all the prayers of distress, in Jeremiah 11 to 20, this contains the greatest proportion of petition or plea.[37] The counterpoint between the three parties has forced the prophet to a point of desperation. In the midst of perceived powerlessness, with despair seeming the only option, the prophet reaches out in prayer to a God he still believes is present. At this most critical point of despair no response from Yahweh is forthcoming. Yet the prophet's sense of injustice and powerlessness must be expressed, and is expressed, within the context of the relationship. On this issue Carroll states, "The continued suffering of the innocent is the vindication of the wicked, hence the necessity for a transformation of roles and fates."[38] This brings to a close the fourth movement at a point of seeming despair for both Yahweh, on account of the people's lack of repentance, and the prophet, on account of his lack of personal security. Despite this grave situation and the lack of response from Yahweh the prophet expresses hope that God is present

---

36. The only statement of judgment in this section is the final statement in v. 17.

37. O'Connor, *Confessions*, 57, concludes that "this confession continues the shift away from angry complaint and accusation of the first and second confessions toward increased confidence in Yahweh."

38. Carroll, *Jeremiah*, 381–82.

A prophet in motion

in his situation, that God will act on his behalf and again, remarkably, the prophetic ministry to continue.

FIFTH MOVEMENT (JER 19:1–20:18)

The fifth movement begins as decisively as the last. However, the God-speech commanding action here is different. Unlike the requirement of a sermon to be preached (17:19ff.) the prophet is now commanded to go and buy an earthenware jug and smash it in the people's presence as a symbolic action representing the intended action of Yahweh towards the nation. Again the contrast between the prayer of distress immediately preceding these events and the nature of Jeremiah's actions could hardly be greater. With his life under threat and questions about whether divine justice indeed exists, the prophet takes his life in his hands, responds to Yahweh's call and very publicly pronounces the message. The use of pottery in the symbolic action provides a contrast with its previous use in chapter 18 as a prophetic image. Here the vessel is not molded, nor is it re-shaped, rather, it is obviously formed and complete only to be destroyed.

Once again the voice of the prophet, the voice of Yahweh and the symbolic action are presented in harmony while the people are silent in the text. The action culminates with its proclamation being made "in the court of the Lord's house" (v.14) being reminiscent of the Temple sermon of chapter 7. Here the voice of Yahweh is being proclaimed in the place of Yahweh to the unfaithful people of Yahweh. The prophet, seemingly at a point of despair at the end of the last movement, is found empowered and functioning again as the prophetic voice he was called to be.

However, the prophet's despairing position is reinforced as another voice speaks. This is the voice of the enemy, in the person of Pash'hur the priest. It is counter to the voice of the prophet and counter to the voice of Yahweh. The reader might expect Jeremiah, reminded of his precarious position, to be resigned to his demise and feeling reluctant to say anything that might put him in deeper trouble, if that was possible. However, his voice still at one with Yahweh, he pronounces divine judgment on this priest, the priest's family, and reemphasizes the judgment of Judah. Somehow, the prophet has found his most powerful voice in the midst of his utter despair as he speaks the prophetic message in concert with Yahweh. It is significant that this empowerment is not purely an internal strength or resolve. It emerges from the clear recognition of Yahweh's presence and presumably the impetus of the original prophetic call. The conflict between Jeremiah and Pash'hur demonstrates more than a clash of human voices or opinions, of course.[39]

The rest of chapter 20 (v. 7 ff.) brings us to the culmination of the fifth movement, which is clearly a final prayer of distress. Again the contrast could hardly stronger. One moment in the text the prophet is at one with the voice of Yahweh, the next, this same voice is not only heard as it speaks independently of Yahweh but also clearly against Yahweh. One might imagine that after such a progression of speaking, acting, and reflecting recounted in the previous chapters, even given the four prayers of distress so far, that the prophet would now feel in a position of relative empowerment. However, the last prayer of distress speaks of just the opposite; Yahweh enticing and overpowering. No doubt these are some of the most graphic portrayals of human emotion directed towards God as the prophet reflects on his predicament.

Much discussion has taken place as to the exact nature of the prophet's accusations against Yahweh described in v. 7, without a clear consensus.[40] However, Habel states, "It is doubtful if anyone in the Scriptures makes an uglier accusation against God than this. The language is overtly sexual."[41] Even if Habel is overstating the fact somewhat, it emphasizes the severe nature of Jeremiah's sense of helplessness and hopelessness. However, his voice is not silenced by the prophet himself, by redactors, nor by Yahweh. It is allowed to be freely expressed in explicit detail. In a more forceful way, the accusations are a recapitulation of the case put to Yahweh in the first prayer of distress. However, as with the previous two prayers of distress the divine voice falls silent.

Despite this, the voice of the prophet is not completely despairing. It moves from complaint to a strong affirmation of confidence. This affirmation includes a clear vow of praise (v. 13). Perhaps the reader might find it helpful to end on this positive note. However, the prayer then moves dramatically to express a sense of utter desolation. This desolation is not just concerning the prophet's role and immediate situation but is a despair

---

39. Another example of this can be observed in Amos 7:10–17. It highlights the tension that emerges when divine justice confronts human unfaithfulness within the paradigm of the covenant relationship.

40. Clines and Gunn, "'You Tried to Persuade Me,'" 20–27, provide a helpful summary and discussion of the issued involved.

41. Habel, *God of Jeremiah*, 33.

A prophet in motion

of life itself. The final section of the movement is a type of cursing poem (vv. 14–18), which seems totally out of character with what has immediately preceded it. O'Connor categorically states that, "The cursing poem of chapter 20 is not a component of the last confession."[42] Though this may be correct, the juxtaposition of the vow of praise and the cursing poem in the text still exists. Remarkably, the voice of hope and the voice of despair, found together in the voice of the prophet, reveal a genuine struggle for authenticity in the human relationship with the divine. It also demonstrates a reflective attempt to come to terms with divine justice and the prophet's call to ministry. Again this prayer, by definition, is an acknowledgment of the divine *in* the circumstance and evidently the prophetic ministry continues from this point in the text.

Although this prayer of distress brings the major section of chapters 11 to 20 to a close it does not mark the end of the prophet's ministry. Perhaps surprisingly, the prophetic ministry continues and history unfolds as pronounced by the word of Yahweh and the word of the prophet. The counterpoint of voices reveals a disempowered prophet who presents an empowered personal message and an empowered prophetic message in the midst of despair. The dialogical counterpoint has, in part, provided the seedbed for a prophetic ministry to flourish from the depths of weakness and despair.

REFLECTIONS

While few, if any, would claim to be engaged in a ministry of Jeremianic proportions, a number of observations from this section of Jeremiah provide a helpful, although perhaps somewhat unpopular, foundation for understanding what empowered ministry can look like in today's world. Of course, it could be argued that Jeremiah should not be taken as an example of normative ministry. However, even a cursory look at individuals functioning effectively on God's behalf to bring about change throughout the biblical text and church history often suggests that their experience was not completely different from that of the prophet.

Clearly, the prophetic figure of Jeremiah demonstrates one who is fully engaged with the whole experience that ministry on God's behalf involves. This experience can encompass anything from desolation to consolation. The prophet doubts himself and God at various times in his

---

42. O'Connor, *Confessions*, 157.

experience, feels constantly under personal threat and questions the very nature of the God on whose behalf he speaks. In other words, the text as we have it does not paint an idealistic picture of ministry being constantly victorious, self-fulfilling, accompanied by the comforting voice of God, and receptive to the community at large. Rather, we have a picture of a person who feels weak and vulnerable and is willing to say so in rather explicit ways.

These observations, of course, raise a question about what provides Jeremiah with the sense of resilience that sees him continue in the prophetic ministry, despite utter desolation at times and continual opposition. If we take chapters 11 to 20 as a whole the recurring pattern of God-speech, action, and reflection in the form of prayers of distress provide part of the answer. It did not appear to be enough for this prophetic figure to possess a sense of a call to ministry, although this was no doubt important. Yahweh's communication with the prophet and the resulting dialogical counterpoint was of paramount importance in assuring the prophet that God was in fact with him. Empowered ministry needs a sense of call to ministry, but also a sense of God's voice in dialogue with the one ministering. While few in ministry might claim to hear the audible voice of God, there is the sense in which we do hear what God is saying and engage in the communication of it to those around us. We also speak to a God who has spoken. Therefore, it is naturally affirming and empowering for us to hear before we attempt to speak, and to be able to respond to that voice with words of our own. This response to the divine must necessarily include expressing feelings of personal vulnerability in an honest way. Of course, all this assumes the divine presence *with* the one ministering.

The action in which the prophet engages is divinely motivated, as all ministry ought to be. Action, together with words, were challenging to both prophet and community. They were not often words of conciliation and comfort for Jeremiah and their communication called for great courage. The prophet lived his message rather than simply speaking it. However, despite the inevitable reaction of the people, the prophet literally stood by Yahweh's words to the people as an empowered figure even though he may not have *felt* powerful. This is perhaps the greatest challenge of Jeremiah to our understanding of what empowered ministry might look like. A logical reading of the book of Jeremiah would be to acknowledge his weakness and vulnerability. Some would say a ministry that had no future. Yet the text portrays a ministry that continued against all odds and without any semblance of a positive response from the community. Without the prayers of distress one may imagine that this is a prophet of immense internal fortitude and resolve. However, the prayers of distress, in particular, suggest otherwise. In the face of personal weakness and vulnerability an internal strength emerges. As the fears, doubts, and anger are expressed in dialogue with God the vulnerable prophet mysteriously gains a renewed resolve.

The prayers of distress provide a final necessary piece to the jigsaw of truly empowered ministry and help, in some ways, to define the nature of this illusive internal strength seen in the character of Jeremiah. They recount with astounding language the "weak" prophet before his God and record a form of reflective prayer that provides the prophetic figure with a liminal space. This leads to an engagement with personal distress and the possibility of meaning-making resulting in the strength to continue in ministry. It is questionable whether this prophet would have prevailed at all without the experience being articulated through the prayers of distress. The dialogical counterpoint evident throughout chapters 11 to 20, and particularly in the prayers of distress, demonstrates an authenticity that acknowledges the presence of God, even when God appears not to be present. Even though God does not seem to act on the prophet's behalf in the immediate situation, the opportunity for reflection encourages the prophet's resilience and he prevails.

There is no doubt that authentic ministry is often tough and at times feelings of weakness abound. The image of Jeremiah suggests that this vulnerability needs to be acknowledged and engaged with through a process of listening to the divine voice, acting in response, and reflecting on the experience. This reflection may, at times, take the form of lament and is done with an appreciation that God is with us, Emmanuel, in spite of the circumstances. The dialogical counterpoint of the divine voice, our voice, and the voice of community together with action and reflection creates a rich texture through which authentic faith and ministry can not only prevail, but also flourish in unimaginable ways.

3

The "destabilized" God

Community without walls

Merryl Blair

INTRODUCTION

THIS STUDY ARISES FROM two motivating interests: one, in the nature and role of metaphor; the other, in the question of how God might be present in the struggles of life. The nature of metaphor to resist definition, and hence to open up interpretation, is a healing antidote to political and religious systems that seem bent on defining, closing down and dividing. The power of metaphor expresses what is only faintly knowable by using words that create a world full of wide open spaces for interpretation: that which is all-powerful is also child-like; interpretive space defies boundaries, and is as fluid as the sea. This study explores a text (Hosea 11) that presents such a fluid metaphorical world, in which the suffering God is seen as less than secure in God's own characterization, thus allowing freedom for exploration and growth on the part of both God and God's human partners.

Metaphor, simply, has been widely regarded as speaking of one thing in terms of another.[1] However, metaphor is more complex. Each word used, even in such a simple transaction, comes with a range of possible

---

1. For example, "the man is a wolf"; in this simple transaction "man" is the tenor (that which is really being spoken about) and "wolf" is the vehicle (that which is used to describe, or throw light on a particular aspect of "man."

The "destabilized" God

meanings that work together to allow a richness of interpretation. In addition, the context in which even the simplest metaphorical formulation is used will support, direct and enhance meaning. Hence, it is better to speak of metaphor in terms of the "interanimation of words."[2] This suggests that metaphor is constructed by the use of words that work together to present a rich, imaginative "world" in which new possibilities of being can be explored.[3]

Hosea 11 is an intricately structured unit that builds a metaphorical world through the interanimation of words. The poem displays a clear rhetorical purpose that is supported by the particular choice and arrangement of words (that is, structuring by rhetorical devices such as framing).[4] It achieves its purpose in a variety of ways, which can be set out clearly. The poem confronts the reader with an inadequate "world," and destabilizes this world by raising commonly known themes and using them in unexpected ways. It constructs a metaphorical world from a common domain of experience to allow a meeting place between speaker and audience, from which a new way of being can be imagined. These particular words, in this particular structure, are necessary to construct this metaphorical world because they interanimate each other through association of story, memory, historical reality, and common human experience.

It is helpful to present a translation of the passage, demonstrating the structure by placing the words in the order in which they occur in the Hebrew. In this translation, English words are joined by a hyphen to indicate the single Hebrew word of origin. Similarly, in order to indicate repetition, the same English word will be used to translate each occurrence of a Hebrew root, if possible. If not possible, the Hebrew root will be indicated in brackets. Key repetitions are indicated by italics.[5]

---

2. A term used first by I. A. Richards in 1936, and refined by Black, *Models*. See also, Soskice, *Metaphor*.

3. The word "world" is somewhat paradoxical. It suggests a closed system, which metaphor can never be. The meaning intended by its use in this study is the sense of solid ground, yet ever-receding horizons and expanding space, which make up a stable-yet-unstable space within which one can imagine a way of being, and hence live towards that imagining.

4. There is not the space here for a detailed rhetorical critical reading of the text, but rhetorical critical tools have been used to examine how particular devices such as repetition, framing, personification, metonymy, etc, have been used to construct the metaphorical world.

5. The translational difficulties in Hos 11 are well documented. This translation has

On Eagles' Wings

STANZA 1

1. When a-child was-Israel *I-loved-him*
   and-out-of-Egypt I-called my-son.

2. They-called them
   so they-walked with-them.
   To-the-Ba'als they-sacrificed,
   and-to-idols they-burned-incense.

3. But-[it-was]-I-myself [who] taught-to-walk Ephraim,
   taking [them] by-the-arms;
   Yet-not they-knew that I-healed-them.

4. With-cords humane I-drew-them,
   with-fetters *of-love*;
   And-I-was to-them as-[those-who]-lift an-infant
   to their-cheek,
   and-bent down-to-him to-feed (*'okîl*) him.

STANZA 2

5. He-returns-*to-the-land of-Egypt*,
   and-*Assyria* he-himself is-his-king;
   for they-refuse *to-return*.

6. And-whirls the-sword through-his-cities
   and-destroys his-defences;
   and-it-devours [*'ăkālah*] because-of-their-schemings.

7. And-my-people are-bent-on to-turn-from-me;
   and-to-god-above [?Ba'al] they-call
   He-himself *altogether* not lifts-them-up.

STANZA 3

8. How can-I-give-you-up, Ephraim?
   surrender-you, Israel?

---

made particular choices among the various possibilities on the basis of what best fits the over-all metaphorical construct (for example, choosing "infant" rather than "yoke" in v. 4). However, the alternative translations do not greatly affect the metaphorical construct ("yoke" still presents a picture of tender care, in the context, that supports the image here of a loving parent).

The "destabilized" God

> How can-I-give-you-up like-Admah,
> treat-you like-Zeboiim?
> Changes-itself within-me my-heart,
> *altogether* aroused [is]-my-compassion.

9. Not I-will-execute my-fierce anger,
not *turn* to-destroy Ephraim;
For God am-I-myself, and-not-a-man,
in-your-midst the-Holy-One
and-not I-will-come into-the-city.

STANZA 4

> After YHWH they-shall-go;
10. like-a-lion he-will-roar.
Indeed he-himself will-roar,
and-they-will-come-trembling his-sons from-the-West.
11. They-will-come-trembling like-a-bird *out-of-Egypt*,
and-like-a-dove from-the-land *of-Assyria*;
And-I-will-return-them-to-their-homes.

—Proclamation of YHWH.

The underlying common domain of experience in this passage is that of *kinship*. References to "sons" (*bnî*, v.1; *bānîm*, v. 10) frame the passage, but an abundance of more subtle language reinforces this as the broad field from which meaning is constructed. Within this domain, various areas are highlighted at different points, depending on the affect required. Drawing from the domain of kinship, the metaphorical construct is *Israel is a disobedient but beloved child, and YHWH is a grieving parent.*

PERSONIFICATION AND METONYMY

As metonymy is mainly used in this poem in the service of personification, the two need to be considered together. "Israel" or "Ephraim" is at once the whole nation, past, present and future, and a beloved but wayward child. This image is constructed initially by the use of words directly drawn from the domain of childhood ("child," "my son," and "his sons"), which are used in conjunction with "Israel," specifically presented as the name of the child at the beginning of the poem, and its parallel, "Ephraim."

In all, there are eight references to "Israel," "Ephraim," "child," and "son" throughout the poem, four in the first stanza and four in stanzas 3 and 4. This particular metaphor (*Israel/Ephraim is a child*) is then reinforced by related concepts: teaching [a child] to walk (v. 3), lifting [a child] to the cheek, and bending down to feed [a child] (v. 4).

Hence, from the general domain of kinship, one particular aspect is highlighted: that of childhood, with its attendant nuances of value and dependency. These nuances carry over into verses 8 and 10 by implication ("give you up," "surrender you," "treat you," "following after," and "trembling," all suggesting helplessness on the part of the addressee) and by association ("Ephraim"/"Israel" already having been established as the name of the "child"). The emotional impact of these verses, which project the outcome of the punishment threatened in the preceding verses, is increased by the suggestion that it is the fate of a beloved child under discussion.

The introduction of the vehicle "child" automatically draws in the closely related field of parenthood. If Israel/Ephraim is the child, the parent must be the subject of the possessive pronouns ("*my* son"; "*his* sons"), namely YHWH. This is assumed, rather than stated, but many verbs denoting parental activity reinforce the metaphorical construct *God is Israel's/Ephraim's parent*: "I loved him," "I called" (v. 1); "I taught to walk," "taking by the arms" (v. 3); "I drew them," "I was to them," "I bent down to him to feed him" (v. 4).[6] Supporting this construct by loose association

---

6. Smith in "Kinship", 41, states that "In the realm of love between humans, the root ʾhb is first and foremost a kinship term," referring to feelings of attachment between members of a family (see, for example, Gen 22:2; 24:67; 25:28; 29:18, 20, 30; 37:3, 4; 44:20; Ruth 4:15; 1 Sam 1:5; 18:20, 28; 1 Kgs 11:1–2). Brenner expands on the wide range of applicability of the term in the Hebrew Bible (including friendship and sexual activity), but agrees that Hos 11:1–4 suggests YHWH's paternal/maternal love. See Brenner, *Intercourse of Knowledge*, 14, n.14. Eidevall, *Grapes in the Desert*, 167–74, among others, points out that it is difficult to pinpoint the vehicle domain in vv. 3 and 4, and sets out an argument for these verses using the metaphor of "shepherd," rather than "parent-child." The difficulties with translation have already been discussed. Even if the shepherd metaphor is accepted, it would still support the parent-child metaphor. See, for example, Nathan's parable in 2 Sam 12, in which the little ewe lamb "was like a daughter to him" (2 Sam 12:3). Matthews and Benjamin, *Social World*, 169f., discussing the similarities between the role of the monarch and that of the father in ancient Israel, point out the common metaphorical depiction of the king ("father" of the nation) as "shepherd." Also of interest is their discussion of sexual language in harvest songs, particularly in reference to the Hymn to YHWH the farmer/lover in Isa 5:1–7 (45f). In other words, for the Hebrew people, there appears to have been a close association between the domains of kinship and farming/herding, the latter being commonly used as a source domain for the former.

is "I healed them" (v. 3). Alongside these verbs are various other concepts that reinforce the notion of parental care: "humane cords," "fetters of love" (v. 4). Repetition of the verb *'hb* ("love") in v. 4 interanimates with the repeated root *bn* ("son") in verses 1 and 10, to narrow the focus of such a wide-ranging verb to the family context. The occurrence of "his sons" in verse 10, followed by the reference to "returning them to their homes," reinforces the metaphor of parental care through reference to the domain of the animal kingdom, prevalent in this stanza. "Returning them to their homes" returns the poem to the imagery of the first stanza, which describes the activity of a home, the natural context of a child.[7]

As the *Israel is a child* metaphor has been seen to carry over into verse 8 by association rather than by direct use of terminology from that domain, so the *God is parent* metaphor works in a similar fashion: the one who is considering the possibility of giving up/handing over the child must be the parent; the natural feelings of a parent for a child (described here as *nḥm*, "compassion") are therefore brought into consideration, and must have an effect on the outcome of God's deliberations in this stanza.

The only stanza that lacks any language from the child–parent domain is the second. This changes the source domain to that of war, mainly by implication through the references to Egypt and Assyria (v. 5), and to the sword (v. 6). Each of these is metonymic: "Egypt" stands for oppressive overlords of the past (hence "return . . . to Egypt" equals "return to slavery"). At a deeper level, "out of Egypt" stands for Israel's myth of origin. Its placement at the beginning and end of the poem suggests both the power and the fragility of this myth. On one hand, Israel is an entity because of this myth (being called out, saved from slavery, removed from exploitative imperial structures); on the other hand, Israel's position is always tenuous, because Egypt (as a symbol of imperial power and exploitative ideology) always exists and threatens Israel's existence, both from external sources and from within Israel's own structures.[8]

---

7. Dearman, "YHWH's House," 97–108, points out that "[s]pouses and children in ancient Israel, as in virtually all pre-modern societies, found their primary identity in the family, rather than through their individual social roles . . . held together under the primary social unit known as the family/household." Arguing against too narrow a reading of the gender-specificity of metaphors in Hosea, he suggests a reading of the various metaphors in terms of "YHWH's household."

8. Keefe, *Woman's Body*, 208f., notes that Hosea reverses the myths and symbols of identity related to the Exodus event throughout the book. The themes of reversal are set up at the very beginning with the naming of the children (Not-my-people, Not-pitied)

"Assyria" is both a literal presence within the world of the book, and a metonym for military power that threatens Israel's identity. Assyria does not belong to the myth of origin, but symbolizes the possibility of Israel's loss of identity.[9] The metonym "sword" provides a graphic image of the powers that threaten Israel's identity, encompassing the destructive violence of soldier and weapon. This destructive power is made vivid by the verbs used in verse 6. Although *ḥlh* appears to read best here as "whirls" (from the root *ḥwl*, whose meanings include "writhing in pain/labor"), it could also be drawn from the semantic field of "sickness," "weakness," (*ḥlh*) bringing in connotations of suffering and disease. "Whirls" allows for a more macabre image (a "dance of death"), which takes on a darker meaning when it is reinforced in the next colon by the parallel verb "destroys." The field of the root *ḥlh* includes the sense of "completion," in this case, complete annihilation. The third colon then adds another shade of darkness with the verb *'kl* "devour," with its harsh repetition of the consonants *l* and *k*, and its connotations of ravenous, all-consuming destruction (as in 2:14 and 13:8, in which the subjects of the verb are "wild animals" and "lion"). The harsh gutturals of these verbs serve to highlight the harshness of the metonym "sword." Overall, this verse presents a vivid and chilling illustration of the domain of war and destructive conquest.

The rhetorical result of presenting Egypt and Assyria as metonyms in this stanza is twofold. First, Israel, by implication, is imagined as a conquered, enslaved people, whose only relationship for most of the stanza is to its conquerors. While there is a literal element to this image (Israel will in fact be conquered by the powerful Assyrians), the metaphorical element is equally important. It introduces a contrasting domain to that developed in the first stanza: in the kinship domain, Israel was presented as the beloved child of a loving, nurturing parent; now, in the war domain, it may be the victim of vicious, devouring conquerors. The framing of this stanza highlights the two contrasting domains of relationship. In the

---

and with the startling claim "I am not there for you." Hoffman, "North Israelite," 169–81. Hoffmann argues that the status of the Exodus myth was well-established prior to Hosea, as it has reached such a high theological status in the book of Hosea, which views the Exodus as a typological myth, rather than a mere historical event.

9. All of the references to Assyria in the Book of Hosea are linked with the idea of futility, either on the part of Assyria as a savior for Israel, or on the part of Israel or its worship practices. Perhaps the most telling reference is 9:3, where going to Assyria and eating unclean food is a consequence of not being allowed to remain "in the land of YHWH." De-creation, for Israel, is loss of land and religious symbols.

opening (v. 5), the only possessive pronominal suffix is attached to the political and (in this context) military noun, "king" ("Assyria—he-himself is his king"). In verse 7 the possessive pronominal suffix returns to the domain of kinship. "*My* people" attains great poignancy in this position, following immediately after the three-fold destruction described in verse 6. The relationship introduced by "my people" is, ironically, one of alienation ("are bent on turning from me . . . to Ba'al they call").

Second, the joint metonyms Egypt and Assyria re-introduce Israel's myth of origin (associated, in stanza 1, with love and nurture) and instantly undermine it through reversal. Instead of associating Egypt with a rather sentimental narrative of salvation and journey to a special land, it is associated with violent removal from the land, destruction within the cities (the places of safety) and even total annihilation ("devouring"). The effect of this is to suggest that Israel's existence is null and void. Creation, for Israel, has been reversed. In summary, Israel's relationship with the loving, nurturing parent has been replaced by a relationship with a violent military power and Israel's self-identity has been destroyed.

A final metonym that needs consideration in this poem is "Ba'al" (v. 7). References to "Ba'al" are relatively rare in Hosea, perhaps surprisingly, so the use of the term (and "the Ba'als," v. 2) is significant. Keefe notes that when a specific Canaanite god is referred to in the book of Hosea, the term "Ba'al-Peor" is used.[10] Otherwise, references to "Ba'al" or "the Ba'als" appear to be closely associated with idols, especially the Yahwistic bull icon of official religion.[11] Links between the idols—especially the bull icon, and "Beth-Aven," Hosea's sarcastic appellation for the royal sanctuary—suggest that references to the Ba'als are critiques of the official cult of the northern kingdom, and of the ruling class centered around the cult. In Hosea 11, the ineffectiveness of the Ba'als echoes the ineffectiveness of the rulers referred to elsewhere (7:7, "All their kings have fallen/none of them call on me"; 8:4, "They made kings, but not through me/they set up princes, but without my knowledge").[12] If "Egypt" and "Assyria" are metonyms for slavery and violent domination from external sources, "Ba'al"

10. Hos 9:10; 13:1. Keefe, *Woman's Body*, 125.

11. For example, 2:8; 4:17 (in a context that refers to Beth-Aven and, possibly ironically, likens Israel to "a stubborn heifer"); 8:4 (which links the making of idols with the royal cult); 10:5 (parallels "the calf of Beth-Aven" with "their idolatrous priests"); 13:2 ("People are kissing calves").

12. Hos 8:4 continuing with a diatribe against the calf of Samaria.

appears to be a metonym for the corruption within Israel's own political and religious systems, which are destructive by being ineffectual.[13]

SIMILE

The final stanza of this poem employs two similes that operate on at least two levels. Within the stanza, they introduce fields of meaning from different domains, giving a dense tapestry of interrelated pictures. Within the whole poem, they support the main metaphor of kinship.

The first simile compares YHWH to a roaring lion. This arises from the source domain of the animal kingdom, specifically wild animals. This domain normally introduces the common experience of fear, which is how it is used elsewhere in the book: YHWH is compared to a lion who will "tear" and "carry off" (5:14); to a lion, leopard, bear, and wild animal who lurks in ambush (13:7) and will "devour" and "mangle" (13:8). Eidevall draws attention to the use of this imagery in the psalms of lament, where the "enemy" is often portrayed as a lion that waits to tear apart the supplicant.[14] Hence, outside this chapter, this simile presents YHWH as a threatening predator, Israel's enemy. The sense of threat is supported and extended towards a sense of awe by the verb *hrd*, "tremble," which is associated with the response to a theophany.[15]

The second simile, "his children . . . like a bird/like a dove," is introduced by the repeated verb "tremble." This simile also appears elsewhere in the book: describing Ephraim as "like a dove, silly and without sense" (7:11); and threatening the loss of "Ephraim's glory," which will "fly away like a bird" (9:11). In the latter passage, the culmination is loss of progeny and expulsion from the land. In bringing together these two similes, with their connotations of the destructive power of a lion and the aimless fluttering of a fearful bird, the poem draws on common experience to set up a conventional picture (terrifying predator, terrified prey) that is immediately undercut. First, when this lion roars, the ones who "come trembling" are not described as prey, but are called "his sons," returning the reader to the beginning of the poem ("my son") and the metaphor *Israel is a beloved*

13. Note the similarity between 7:7 ("All their kings have fallen/none of them calls on me") and 11:7 ("To Ba'al they call/but he does not raise them up at all").

14. Eidevall, *Grapes in the Desert*, 181. See Pss 7:3; 10:9; 17:12; 22:14, all of which are individual psalms of lament.

15. Cf Exod 19:16,18, in which first the people, then the mountains themselves, "tremble."

child. Second, they come trembling "out of Egypt" and "from the land of Assyria." Instead of being scattered and cast out to wander landless, they are returned in a manner reminiscent of the Exodus ("out of Egypt," vv. 1 and 11) to "their homes."

Thus simile supports the metaphorical construct in a surprising way, by reversing expectations within the stanza. YHWH, who is elsewhere presented through the vehicle of threatening, destructive wild beast, is instead shown by the same vehicle to be the powerfully protective parent presented in the first stanza, who can again bring the child out of Egypt/Assyria (slavery/conquest) and settle it in a home. Israel, who has been depicted as silly, directionless and exiled, is instead reminded of its status as "child," with a firm place in the family home. This whole stanza uses simile to introduce, and then overturn well-known fields of meaning, and surprisingly uses the domain of the animal kingdom to reinforce the overall metaphorical construct drawn from the domain of human kinship: *God is a parent who is strong and protective.*

REPETITION AND THE LANGUAGE OF MOURNING

Having explored the metaphorical construct of God as parent/Israel as child in stanza 1, and touched briefly on the occurrence of this metaphorical domain in stanza 3 (mainly imported via the metonymic use of the names "Israel" and "Ephraim"), it is important to consider more closely the interrelated domains within stanza 3, especially in verse 8. The vehicle used to depict the tenor, YHWH, is not made explicit. Rather, a subtle and complex vehicle is created through the use of juxtaposed verbs and metonyms within a particular rhythmic structure, leading to the description of a mental and emotional process occurring within the "heart" of YHWH which supports the metaphorical construct of *God as a grieving parent.*

The questions which begin verse 8 arise from several domains of experience, with overlapping fields of meaning. The rhythm is that of the dirge, or *qinah*, hence one source domain is that of death and bereavement. The repeated introductory phrase, "How can I," recalls various similar instances of divine questioning, including Hosea 6:5. Terence Fretheim suggests that divine questions such as these indicate a God who is open to risk, and who becomes vulnerable.[16] More remotely, but nevertheless

---

16. For further discussion of the function of divine questions, see Fretheim, *The*

supportive of this domain, the question "How can I give you up?" draws in the question posed by the prophet in 9:14: "Give them, O Lord—what will you give?" The answer that follows is "a miscarrying womb and dry breasts." The "gift" in that instance is the death of "cherished offspring of their womb" (9:16). All of these elements—*qinah* metre, divine questions, dirge vocabulary, and intratextual reference—support the construction of the metaphor *God is a grieving parent*.

Attached to the rhetorical questions are the four proper nouns, Ephraim/Israel and Admah/Zeboiim. The metonymic use of Ephraim/Israel to represent "child" has been discussed above. The names Admah and Zeboiim are also metonymic in this setting. In Genesis, they were two of the "cities of the plain," located along the southern border of Canaanite territory (Gen 10:19). In this Hosean setting, the names of the cities stand metonymically for the inhabitants who were proverbial for overwhelming sinfulness, leading to their destruction by YHWH. By association, the names Admah and Zeboiim refer to the wider field of recipients of YHWH's punishment for sinful behavior (including Sodom and Gomorrah).[17] In using the names in parallel with Ephraim/Israel, Ephraim/Israel are drawn into the field of *sinful populations deserving of YHWH's destruction*. The wider metaphorical picture is thus drawn, by implication, through carefully interwoven fields of reference: Admah and Zeboiim were "overthrown" (*hpk*); Ephraim/Israel may possibly be treated like Admah and Zeboiim; Ephraim/Israel is a beloved child; YHWH has previously threatened to destroy Ephraim's precious children (9:16). However, the *qinah* rhythm and lament language suggest grief, not anger, as the dominant emotion on this occasion.

Verse 8e and f reinforces the vehicle of grieving parent by intratextual and intertextual allusion, while not using specifically parental imagery. The parental domain, as stated earlier, is carried over into the stanza by the use of the names "Israel" and "Ephraim" (the "child," whose "parent" is God). The appropriate response to the destruction of a precious child is lament (v. 8a, b, c and d). Now, in verses 8e and f, we see the effect that this posited destruction has upon the innermost being of the "parent": as the cities were *hpk* "overthrown," so YHWH's heart is *nhpk* (translated in

---

Suffering of God, 53–59. Divine questions that appear to open up the future occur in Hos 6:4; Jer 5:7,9; 9:7,9. Other instances of "How can I" as part of a dirge are found in 2 Sam 1:19; Jer 9:18. Cf. also Ps 137:4.

17. Deut 29:23; cf. Wis 10:6.

this study as "changed," but it is important to recognize the underlying sense of "overthrown").[18] The metaphor gains support from the use of the phrase "my compassion (*nḥûmāy*) is completely aroused (*yḥd nkmrû*)," which once again points back to 9:14 with a play on words between *nḥm* and *rḥm* ("womb," described in 9:14 as "miscarrying"). Janzen's illuminating discussion regarding the translation of this phrase draws attention to intertextual allusion to other occurrences of the verb *kmr*.[19] In Genesis 43:30 and 1 Kings 3:26, it is linked with *rḥm* to describe "a surge of positive feeling" towards family members (brothers in the former, child in the latter) in emotionally fraught situations. Although the accompanying noun is changed here to *nḥm*, there is support for detecting an underlying domain of kinship in this phrase, especially highlighting the aspect of parental (motherly, "womb") love, with its attendant anguish at the threatened death of a child.[20]

Hence, the movement within this verse is a dramatic one. It opens with the metre and vocabulary of a dirge, alludes to an earlier threat of miscarriage and death of precious offspring, and paints an unmistakable picture of present threatened destruction of the child. This builds up to the climax of verse 8e, where an "earthquake" takes place in God's being, and intertextual allusion points to the anguish of a mother over the threatened death of a child. The decision that occurs in verse 9 cannot be read separately from this careful build-up without completely disrupting the rhetorical power of the stanza.

THE CHARACTERIZATION OF GOD

God's characterization radiates from the phrase "For God am I-myself, and not a man." All metaphor must be read paying attention to how the vehicle *is like* the tenor, and also how it *is not like*. This assertion calls for

18. Gen 19:21, 25, 29; Deut 29:22; Jer 20:16; Lam 4:6; Amos 4:11 all use this verb in connection with the destruction of the "cities of the plain." Also Jonah 3:4, threatening the "overthrow" of Nineveh. Janzen points to the use of the verb, both in the *qal* and *niphal* stems, to describe an intense emotional change (made explicit of Saul in 1 Sam 10:6, "and you shall be turned into another man"—Janzen's translation.) Janzen, "Metaphor," 28–29. Brueggemann, *Old Testament Theology*, 39–41, and Eidevall, *Grapes in the Desert*, 179, both comment on the picture presented here of YHWH's inner being depicted as a landscape in the throes of earthquake.

19. Janzen, "Metaphor," 29.

20. Note also that *BHS* suggests a more probable reading of rḥmy here, supported by some Syriac and Targum MSS.

careful attention to be given to the surrounding metaphorical field, to distinguish between "is like" and "is not like." To be ʾl, "God" is to be different from ʾyš, "man," but also to be alike, kin.²¹ *God is* loving and committed to the relationship of kinship; *God is not* tied to systems of honor that require vengeance, as a man would be. This paradoxical sense of difference yet likeness is supported in the following colon, "in your midst the Holy One." "In your midst" reverts to metaphor, suggesting YHWH as physical presence, and especially (in the wider context of the poem) the immanent physical presence of kinship. While this particular expression is not used elsewhere in Hosea, it is reminiscent of the threat of absence in 1:9; "in your midst the Holy One" reverses this threat by stating that *God is* present. "The Holy One" suggests that the essence of being "God" goes beyond any common domain of human experience.²² "Holiness" suggests otherness, transcendence (absence), but is paradoxically experienced in presence. "If God is in our midst, he cannot come back to destroy us, at least not without destroying himself."²³

A second contrast is drawn that helps characterize God by examining what God *is not*. Five emphatic pronouns are placed throughout the poem in a way that invites comparison. "I-myself" (ʾnky) characterizes God as teaching the child to walk. In contrast, "he-himself" (hwʾ) is king, characterized by Assyria (that is, violent, despotic, destructive). "He-himself" is also Baʾal, "altogether" ineffectual and unable to save Israel. At the

---

21. There is much scholarly discussion regarding whether this should be taken generically, "human," or as gender-specific. Eidevall, *Grapes in the Desert*, 180, n. 90, argues for the former, preferring to stress "the radicality of this utterance, which transcends all kinds of anthropomorphism, male and female alike." However, the metaphorical construct has not separated "being God" from all aspects of "being human" (for example, nurturing and teaching are acceptable likenesses; God can be parental, but not Baʾal, "Lord," in the sense of being allied to the royal cult with its overtones of political corruption). Only some aspects of being human are specifically rejected: military violence such as that of Assyria, and ineffectiveness such as that of man-made idols are unacceptable likenesses. Reading ʾyš as gender-specific heightens both the sense of *is like* and the sense of *is not like*. Landy, "In the Wilderness," 49, draws attention to 2:18 [16], in which YHWH states that Israel will call him) yšy, "my man," rather than bʿly, "my Baʾal"; this contrasts with 2:4, where YHWH declares that he is not Israel's ʾyš and she is not his ʾyšh

22. See Landy, *Hosea*, 24, for a discussion of the paradox of presence and absence in Hosea (among other paradoxes present in the book). For example, the naming of a child, indicative of welcome into a family, is simultaneously a statement of alienation in chapter 1. The book can be read as a study of the problem of presence and absence, or kinship and alienation.

23. Landy, *Hosea*, 143.

The "destabilized" God

end of the poem, because "I-myself" decides to be "God, not a man/the Holy One in your midst," "he-himself" (now God) will roar like a lion and bring the children home.

DESTABILIZATION AND CONSTRUCTION OF THE METAPHORICAL WORLD

It has been argued that a poetic text can construct a metaphorical world in which destabilization of previously held assumptions can occur, and a new world imagined, for the purpose of bringing about a difference in living. The metaphorically constructed world of Hosea 11 first destabilizes hegemonic structures (such as monarchy, honor/shame sociological patterns, and empty or automatic religious institutions) and constructs a world that is essentially family space. This has implications for how the people of God are called to live in community. If God cannot dwell within rigid sociological, political or religious structures, neither can the people of God. There are several important aspects to be considered here.

First, the family metaphor presents a world that is resilient. The family endures for generations, changes and adapts, allows for various degrees of intimacy and distance, and expects roles to change as members mature and change. There are no "happy ever after" stories within a family, just further episodes in a long, evolving history. The community that takes this as a model is flexible.[24] There is no rigid threshold beyond which one no longer "belongs." Rather, there are stories that are passed down through the generations, nurturing each succeeding generation and allowing identity to form through a sense of love and belonging.

Second, the family has no particular test of membership. The stories of the Hebrew Bible present differing views on the issue of belonging, but there is a vigorous strand that argues for a form of kinship that has nothing to do with adherence to particular rules, or with bloodlines. Rather, kinship is between those who act with loyalty, love and compassion, bringing divine activity into the human realm and evidencing "the Holy One in our midst." This model of community examines the requirements of law and honor, and puts them aside in favor of continuing relationship, no matter how painful this process.

---

24. Flexibility is represented in Hosea 11 by the verb "to turn." The angry God who would return Israel to Egypt refuses to turn to destroy, and so returns the children to their homes.

Finally, this family model preserves a space in which it is safe for both God and human partners to test self-identity, and to test relationship. This is not a space defined by walls, but by ground. The feet stand solidly on love and compassion, but the walls keep expanding and crumbling. The image of salvation in Hosea 11 is simple but profound: bringing the children home. There is space within the home for nurturing and growth, for invitation and reconciliation. The suffering God allows this space, as this God painfully gives up room to allow the messiness of human reality to exist. The destabilized God, paradoxically, is the ground of community.

4

Obi-wan Kenobi, Neo, and Mark's narrative Christology

Michael F. Bird

INTRODUCTION

As a Generation-Xer I confess to loving the science-fiction epics *Star Wars* and *The Matrix*. It is evident from their box office takings alone that these two movie sagas captured the attention of audiences with their spectacular visual effects and the triumph of their central character over temptation and evil. In this sense both *Star Wars* and *The Matrix* could be said to fit loosely into the genre of a "messiah" movie. What I find interesting is the way in which the heroes in both movies overcome evil. The dark hordes are not defeated through the application of superior violence, but they are overcome through weakness, sacrifice, and even death. In *Star Wars* episode IV, there is a scene where Obi-Wan Kenobi faces off to Darth Vader and warns the malevolent Vader that if he strikes him down he will only succeed in making him more powerful. As Luke Skywalker and his friends escape to the Millennium Falcon, Obi-Wan casts one last glimpse at Luke, gives Vader an I-know-something-you-don't-know smirk, and finally lowers his guard allowing Vader to strike him cleanly. Obi-Wan's body mysteriously evaporates and, from the Netherworld, Obi-Wan is able to guide and direct his young apprentice in the battle against the evil Empire, resulting in the death of the emperor, the triumph of the alliance, and the eventual redemption of Darth Vader/Anakin Skywalker as well. Similarly, in the final and climactic battle between Neo and Agent

Smith in *The Matrix: Revolutions*, Neo willingly allows Agent Smith to destroy him and so enables the Machines to eradicate the viral Agent Smith, thereby inaugurating the regeneration of the Matrix.

What does this have to do with the Gospel of Mark? In short, Mark's Gospel has similar traits in that it is the Messiah story *par excellence*. The Gospel of Mark is about the defeat of evil, political and cosmic—not through the application of superior force and coercive violence, but through faithfulness, weakness, powerlessness, sacrifice, humiliation and death. The Gospel of Mark sets forth a redefinition of true power, but also issues a challenge to the existing power structures of the day, be it of Rome, the Herodian client-rulers, or even the Parthians in the east. The Roman emperor was also known as "Lord," "Savior," and a "Son of God," but he was a twisted parody of the real thing and often a malevolent tyrant who had usurped the authority that was not rightly his. In contrast to the propaganda and politics of the Greco-Roman world where *might makes right* (see e.g., *The Odes of Horace*), Mark would have us believe that strength is personified in weakness, fear is overcome by faith, terror is triumphed by hope, liberty is found in service, honor attained through shame, and power (that is *true* power) manifests itself in the depths and ignominy of powerlessness. The Gospel of Mark is a dramatic story that turns the assumptions of its audience on their heads, inverts them, subverts them, and finally replaces them with the good news that Jesus is the Son of God, his kingdom is the true kingdom, and his power is redeeming. Mark, the master of irony that he is, brings all this to the surface in his story of the suffering Son of God.

Therefore, the purpose of this study is to examine the contours of Mark's narrative Christology, where Jesus is both the Spirit empowered Son of God and the rejected and crucified Son of Man. I argue that these themes find their dramatic resolution in the architecture of the Marcan story where Jesus's crucifixion is in reality another expression of his power by expressing the saving reign of the kingdom through his redemptive death on the cross.

MAPPING MARK'S STORY

Mark's Gospel does not begin with the reflective poetry of John's prologue, or with the formal literary etiquette of Luke's preface, or even with the apologetically driven genealogy of Matthew. No, Mark begins with a burst of light and a roar of thunder designed to capture our undivided attention to his subject matter concerning "Jesus Christ, the Son of God" (Mk 1:1). It is as if, as Tom Wright says, you are sound asleep and then someone suddenly wakes you up by splashing you with cold water in your face because something crucial is happening.[1]

The focal point of the Marcan narrative is Jesus. The opening accounts seemingly evoke the question: who is this man and why does he do what he does (Mk 2:7; 4:41; 8:27)? If Jesus is Mark's central character, then "kingdom" is one of Mark's central themes and it is the relationship between the actor (Jesus) and the action (inaugurating the kingdom) that brings us to the inherent tension within the Marcan storyline. Jesus commences his ministry in Galilee by announcing that "the kingdom of God is near, repent and believe in the gospel" (Mk 1:15). The background to this "gospel" is Isaiah 52:7, where the prophet announces the coming victory and the future reign of Yahweh who will deliver his people from exile and bondage and return them to their own land to live in fellowship with him. When Jesus declares this "gospel" of the "kingdom" we are left with more questions than answers: what kind of king is here, what kind of kingdom is coming, what kind of victory awaits? The kingdom of God is, in some sense, analogous to the presence of God in strength to save and redeem his people,[2] but how is this power manifested?

It is tempting to say that in Mark 1–8 Jesus is depicted as the miracle working Son of God and then in Mark 9–16 he is the suffering Son of Man. This is only half-true. The first half of the Marcan Gospel clearly accentuates Jesus's messianic credentials—the dynamics of his kingdom ministry through various exorcisms, healings, miracles—while the latter half of the Gospel propels him towards the cross. But from the very beginning we encounter in Mark's story an underlying motif that includes a convergence of the kingdom and the cross, power and powerlessness, *dumamis* and death, glory and suffering, regalia and rejection, victimization and vindication. While the opening chapters present Jesus as the miracle working Son of God, concurrent with that, but beneath the surface, is the developing narrative thread that Jesus will be crucified. Mark's objective is to demonstrate that the kingdom has come and is coming, not despite the cross, but through it.

1. Wright, *Mark for Everyone*, 1.
2. Cf. Chilton, *God in Strength*.

WHAT KIND OF KINGDOM?

The kingdom of God is perhaps best described as the saving reign or rule of God now being manifested by Jesus and awaiting to be implemented in its fullness. Thus, in Mark's eschatology, the kingdom is both present and future, now and not-yet. The present or "now" aspect of the kingdom is related to Jesus's ministry of healing and miracles. These are described as mighty deeds or acts of power in several places (Mk 6:2, 5, 14). In fact, Jesus radiates *dunamis* ("power") that positively affects those who come near him (Mk 5:30). What is more, the kingdom of God is said to come "in power" (Mk 9:1). This verse is particularly important as it is encases a key motif of Mark, the relationship between the cross and the kingdom.[3]

For example, John the Baptist prepares the way for the coming deliverer who we are told will "baptize you with the Holy Spirit" (Mk 1:8), which may itself be idiomatic for, *he will plunge you into the fiery breath of Yahweh*.[4] Whereas John's baptism is preparatory, the future baptism administered by the "stronger one" will be purifying and empowering. Ironically, the next time that we hear of baptism in the Gospel of Mark it pertains to Jesus's baptism concerning his death (Mk 10:38–39). The "stronger one" will experience his own baptism of powerlessness in a torturous and inhumane execution.

In Mark 2:18–22 we encounter the enigmatic narrative about the sudden departure of the bridegroom that foreshadows Jesus's coming death. The pericope makes a furtive connection between Jesus's death and the coming "day of the Lord" (cf. Amos 5:18–21, 27). The coming "day" when the bridegroom is taken away will be the "day of the Lord" and marks the coming of Yahweh as King where there will be salvation for the elect and judgment for the enemies of God's people. This "day" is seemingly identified with Jesus's passion and that is when the disciples shall fast and mourn.

At the Last Supper, Jesus gives his disciples a symbolic meal, which explains the nature of his forthcoming death in salvific terms. It is a meal that evokes a story about the exodus, the new exodus, the coming of God's kingdom, and these are mysteriously manifested in the martyrdom of the Messiah. The words of Jesus reported by Mark, "This is my blood of the covenant, which is poured out for many" (Mk 14:24) links Jesus's death

---

3. Cf. Bird, 'Crucifixion,' 23–36.
4. Cf. Dunn, *Baptism*, 8–14.

with the coming kingdom. The cogency of the link is that the concept of covenant is correlative to the kingdom of God as both espouse God's lordship and saving activity.[5]

At his trial, Jesus' statement to the High Priest in Mark 14:62 that "you will see the Son of Man seated at the right hand of the Power, and coming with the clouds of heaven" is not a reference to his *parousia* or second coming. The remark is reminiscent of Daniel 7:13–14 and is a bold and audacious statement that Jesus, the messianic representative of Israel, will be vindicated, enthroned and exalted to a position of authority reserved exclusively for God.[6] Richard Hays writes,

> Daniel 7:13–14 is without question a vision of ascent and enthronement of a human figure representing Israel's vindication and triumph over the kingdoms symbolized by the beasts in the preceding visions. When, in Mark's story, Jesus quotes Daniel to claim this role for himself, the high priest quite understandably judges his words to be blasphemy, because Jesus is foretelling that he will share the divine throne with the Ancient of Days. The parallels in Matthew 26:24 ("*from now on* you will see the Son of Man seated at the right hand of the Power") and Luke 22:69 ("*from now on* the Son of Man will be seated at the right hand of the power of God") are even more clearly to be understood as references to enthronement rather than a future return from heaven.[7]

In the midst of weakness and victimization, Jesus makes a provocative claim that in his sufferings and humiliation that he is actually being enthroned as God's vice-regent.

This portrait of the kingdom being established in Jesus's death is confirmed by the crucifixion narrative in Mark 15.[8] The whole passage is dominated by the theme of Jesus as King.[9] The word *basileus* ("king") is used six times and exclusively of Jesus (vv. 2, 9, 12, 18, 26, 32). The mocking titulus "King of the Jews" expresses a stark irony since, as Messiah,

---

5. Taylor, *Gospel*, 546. I must unfortunately disagree with Scot McKnight (*Jesus and His Death*, 293–321) on the authenticity of the reference to "covenant" at Jesus' quasi-Passover meal with his disciples. It is precisely the association of covenant and kingdom that makes such a mention of covenant in the sense of "new covenant" from Ezekiel and Jeremiah as plausible on the lips of Jesus.

6. Cf. Wright, *Jesus*, 524–28.

7. Hays, "Why do you stand?" 121.

8. What follows is indebted to Bird, "Crucifixion," 29–30.

9. Cf. Matera, *Kingship of Jesus*.

Jesus is the true King of Israel. Jesus proclaims the kingdom of God and yet what we find at the end of the story is the announcement of the kingship of the crucified.[10] At the cross Jesus is called a "Son of God" by the centurion (Mk 15:39) which was a designation for a King in both Jewish and Roman religions (cf. e.g., 2 Sam 7:14; Pss 2:7; 89:26–27). In fact, the whole crucifixion process parallels the triumphal procession of victorious Roman generals returning to Rome from their campaign and receiving acclamation for their glorious exploits. The salute by the Praetorian guard, the acclaim of Jesus, the purple robe, the long drawn out journey along the *Via Dolorosa*, the requisition of a bystander to lead the sacrificial victim, the co-regents on either side of the triumphator—the parallels are provocative and overpowering to Greco-Roman readers. The crucifixion of Jesus is, in fact, the enthronement of Jesus and a manifestation of God's saving power.[11] In the words of Paul Barnett, "Mark wants us to understand that, incredible as it may seem, 'the kingdom of God' actually begins with the crucifixion of 'the king of Israel.'"[12]

Returning now to the enigmatic statement in Mark 9:1 ("Truly I tell you, there are some standing here who will not taste death until they see that the kingdom of God has come with power"), the overall context of Mark should lead us to identify this saying—not with the Transfiguration or with Pentecost, but with Jesus's death.[13] That is where the kingdom comes with power, in the very midst of disempowerment, degradation, and death.

WHAT KIND OF KING?

The Gospel according to Mark is that Jesus is the Christ, the Messiah. His narrative aim is to persuade his audience to accept this perspective. He is fully aware of the shame and scandal of the cross, and his story of Jesus seeks to assuage the misgivings that his readers/auditors may have about a crucified Messiah. For Mark, Jesus is the Christ not despite the cross,

---

10. Boring, "Kingdom of God in Mark," 144.
11. Schmidt, "Mark 15:16–32," 1–18.
12. Barnett, "Mark: Story and History," 34.
13. The context supports this as Mark 9:1 is preceded by the first passion prediction and the necessity of carrying one's own cross in Mark 8:31–38, while in Mark 9:7 the divine voice from the cloud exhorts the disciples to listen to Jesus, including his poorly received passion predictions.

but precisely because of it. Thus, Mark's Gospel can be characterized as an apology for the cross.[14]

A generation ago it was common to think that Mark's Gospel is designed to refute a *theos anēr* or "divine man" Christology where Jesus is merely a wondering miracle-worker.[15] This is problematic on several accounts.[16] First, there was no uniform pattern of a divine man and such figures, including Plutarch's Alexander and Philo's Moses, were not distinguished by working miracles. Second, some of the so-called divine man figures set up for comparison with Jesus (e.g., Apollonius of Tyana) postdate the Gospels by some three hundred years. Mark is not trying to correct a theology of glory with a theology of suffering, or to refute a "divine man" Christology.[17] To the contrary, for Mark, Jesus' suffering *is* his glory. Larry Hurtado comments,

> Mark does not sentimentalize weakness and suffering over against some supposed "divine man" Christology; instead the author enables Jesus's miraculous power and obedient suffering to illuminate each other.[18]

It is perhaps in Mark 10:41–45 where we see most clearly that Mark portrays Jesus as the exemplary King who serves and suffers for his people. Given the disciples' expectation for the arrival of an earthly and political kingdom, the two ambitious Zebedee boys try to beat the pack for the choice places of power and prestige in the new re-ordering of power that will come into effect when Jesus is installed as King in Jerusalem. Jesus rebuffs their request, since participating in his glory will mean participating in his baptism, which is a coded reference to his death (Mk 10:37–38).[19] Jesus then attacks the standard evaluations of power and greatness extant in the Greco-Roman world. He exhorts his disciples not to lord over others or to tyrannize others. That is the way of Rome, of Caesar, but not the way of the Kingdom. Jesus urges his followers to renounce the quest for

---

14. I explore this theme more fully in my "Jesus is the Christ," 1–14.
15. Cf. Weeden, "Heresy," 145–58.
16. Witherington, *Christology*, 160–61.
17. Weeden, "The Cross as Power," 115–34.
18. Hurtado, *Lord Jesus Christ*, 290.
19. In this sense Mark's view of Jesus' death as his glory is in accordance with the Johannine perspective of Jesus's death as a constituent element of his glorification by the Father (Jn 7:39; 12:16, 23).

power and to discover greatness in service and seek priority in humility. Jesus is, in effect, stating that the Gentiles

> are Daniel's beasts, raging across human history with their oppression and bloodshed, their unbridled acquisitiveness and tendency to violence in the pursuit of gain. Why should anyone want to be like them?[20]

He sets before them his own example: "For the Son of Man came not to be served, but to serve and to give his life as a ransom for many" (Mk 10:45). In both ideal and example, Jesus is the Servant King who represents a stark alternative to the self-deified monarchs of Rome or the puppet potentates of Palestine, both of which looked after their own interests and relentlessly pursued their own self-aggrandizement.[21]

POWER IN POWERLESSNESS

As a reader/auditor is taken through the Marcan Gospel it is apparent that Jesus is a person of almost unparalleled power. This power includes a charismatic power to draw followers (Mk 1:16–20; 2:14–15) that matches the appeal of the greatest of philosophers to call disciples.[22] Jesus also has power and authority over the demons (Mk 1:21–28, 34; 3:11–12; 5:1–20; 9:14–29), nature (Mk 4:35–41; 6:45–52), and even death (Mk 5:21–43).[23] Yet despite the awesomeness of his power, Jesus somehow ends up on the cross in miserable weakness. The reasons for this are given in the passion predictions, in the ransom *logion*, and in the words spoken at the Last Supper (Mk 8:31; 9:31; 10:33–34, 45; 14:22–25). Jesus's death is "necessary" (Mk 8:31), redemptive (Mk 10:45), and "it was written" (Mk 9:12; 14:21). Thus Jesus's death is determined in the divine economy of salvation and will achieve the long hoped for new exodus and redemption from the bondage of sin.[24]

There was no more hideous cruelty than death by crucifixion in the ancient world and crucifixion was a piercing symbol of Roman power that declared the absolute sovereignty of Caesar over his subjects. Crucifixion

---

20. Bolt, *The Cross from a Distance*, 66.
21. Cf. Kaminouchi, "*But It Is Not So Among You.*"
22. E.g., Diogenes Laertius, *Lives of Eminent Philosophers* 2.48 tells of Socrates meeting Xenophon and saying to him "follow me."
23. Cf. Bolt, *Jesus' Defeat*, on Jesus's power over death in particular.
24. Watts, *Isaiah's New Exodus*, 258–87.

implied that "you are our property and we will do with you as we will" and yet Jesus willingly subjects himself to it with a view to establishing, once and for all, the kingdom of God. The cross that expresses the zenith of disempowerment, degradation and death becomes the vehicle for the kingdom's salvific power. It is by renouncing power to save oneself that the power to save others is unleashed with formidable force. This is observed in the climax of the crucifixion account in Mark 15:31–32 where the High Priest and Scribes mock Jesus because he is not "powerful" enough (*ou dunatai*) to save himself, and therefore, not a king (*basileus*). However, the same power that pillaged the demonic realm and stilled the storm on the Sea of Galilee is now displayed in the apex of human weakness and suffering. In a strange irony, it is in Jesus's outright refusal to save himself with an awesome display of heavenly power that will implement the salvation of others by ransoming their sins. It is also this very salvation that proves that Jesus is King (cf. Isa 33:22, "The Lord is our King, He will save us").[25]

In reference to the loud cry of Jesus in Mark 15:37, it is an exclamation of divine victory over evil. Thomas Weeden writes,

> In the triumphant cry of Jesus, good, reversing its plunge toward apparent defeat, emerges victorious from the cosmic battle, and seals the final judgment and ultimate destruction of evil.[26]

At the cross the defeat seems complete and all hope for victory appears vanquished, and still it is in this moment of absolute despair, humiliation, and dejection that Mark asks his audience—those who have eyes to see and ears to hear—to look on that cross and see not merely another dead Jew, but *God in strength*. The cross shows Jesus on his throne, his true display of kingly power by dying a sacrificial death, the triumph of his kingdom over Satan, and Mark so poignantly sets before us the fitness of his strength. Dorothy Lee-Pollard writes,

> Mark demonstrates that in the final analysis God's power is the power to *renounce* power. In other words, it is only through *God's* power that Jesus is able to allow himself to become power-*less* and face the necessity of the cross.[27]

---

25. Bird, "Crucifixion," 31.
26. Weeden, "Cross as Power," 130.
27. Lee-Pollard, "Powerlessness," 173–74.

MARK AND DISCIPLESHIP

The significance of the Marcan story for contemporary readers can be seen in three distinct horizons:

1. *Community Formation.* In the Marcan story Jesus calls for followers (Mk 1:16–20; 2:14–15; 8:34), Jesus calls his followers to preach the good news (Mk 3:14; 5:19–20; 13:10; 14:9) and Jesus's followers can expect opposition. On this latter aspect the intercalation of the story of the death of John the Baptist, bracketed by the sending of the disciples in Mark 6:7–29, makes the motif of opposition abundantly clear: heralds of the kingdom can end up in dungeons or dead. The same point is made in Mark 13:9–11 where the disciples can expect to be persecuted precisely because of their mission. Yet what enables, empowers, and encourages followers to continue proclaiming the kingdom amidst perilous hostility is the community of faith.

Following Jesus entails hardship and rejection, but it also involves participation in a fictive kinship where followers are part of a new family, Jesus's family. This family is forged together by a bond stronger than one's own blood relations (Mk 3:31–35). Similarly, the reward for undertaking the work of the kingdom is that one can expect to inherit brothers, sisters, mothers and children in the coming age (Mk 10:29–31). Christian community is a family community drawn together by virtue of the fact that they have a common savior and a single Lord. They form a new family that strengthens each other for service, that nourishes each other with the Word, and celebrates together the presence of the risen Lord in their midst. Although they are weak of themselves, they are strong together for Christ's sake.

2. *Spiritual Formation.* The spiritual dimension to Mark's Gospel can be neatly summarized with a quotation from Paul, "I have been crucified with Christ and I no longer live, but Christ lives in me. The life I live in the body I live by faith in the Son of God who loved me and gave himself for me" (Gal 2.20). According to Mark, disciples are those who take up their cross and follow Christ (Mk 8:34). Taking up the cross implies following Christ's example, but it is also more than that. To take up the cross means to regard one's very own identity as being inexplicably bound up with the cross and the crucified one. The cross is the letter 'I' with a line through it. Reading or hearing Mark's Gospel is a *cruciforming* experience and we are forced to decide if we will adopt the self-sacrificing ethos of

the protagonist and adopt his pattern of life, his symbols, his praxis, and his way of being Israel.[28] While the cross may be the quintessential symbol of mockery, powerlessness and scorn, for the believer it is a source of inspiration, renewal, and spiritual strength.

3. *Ministerial Formation.* In some circles the ministerial office has been professionalized and the success of the pastoral practitioner assessed in terms befitting employment in the corporate world. Senior Pastors in certain congregations act like CEOs and their staff operate as vice-presidents with various portfolios such as marketing, growth and development, administration, and human resource management.[29] Even worse, the marketing ethos often impacts the message itself and it leads to a more marketable "gospel," which either appeals to felt needs or else proclaims a Christ who is less offensive and more palatable to the spirit of the age. In which case, such a minister is not really a servant but a religious variation of a Wall Street power broker and the message of Christ crucified is emptied of its power.

What does Mark have to say about this? First, when it comes to appeal, power, and influence as the world knows, Mark tells us "but it is *to be* not so among you" (Mk 10:43). Instead, Christian leaders are to model themselves in the categories of a servant (*diakonos*) and a slave (*doulos*), not according to corporate archetypes. David DeSilva comments, "Perhaps the most important lesson Mark teaches those who minister in Christ's name is that Jesus embodied servant-shaped leadership and his representatives are to embody the same."[30] In Mark's telling greatness is found in lowliness, influence is gained in humility, esteem is attained through service and, as Paul would say, "power is made perfect in weakness" (2 Cor 12:9).

Second, Mark's incipit, "The beginning of the gospel of Jesus Christ" introduces a narrative that is dominated by the imminent death of Jesus on the cross. Jack Kingsbury goes so far as to call Mark "the Gospel of the Cross."[31] Thus, any gospel or any sermon that deliberately eviscerates the mention and meaning of the cross is sub-Christian. A gospelette will only produces Christianettes. The message of Jesus Christ as crucified and risen,

---

28. Wegener, "Reading Mark's Gospel," 462–70.
29. Cf. Piper, *Brothers*.
30. DeSilva, *Introduction*, 229.
31. Kingsbury, "Significance," 95.

in contrast, produces disciples who carry their own crosses along the highways and boulevards of our postmodern metropolis. The message of the cross may look and sound like foolishness and weakness; and yet, because God stands behind the message it is actually full of wisdom and strength.

In summary, Mark's Gospel is the greatest messiah story ever told. It is a story that may lack the stunning visual effects of *Star Wars* and *The Matrix*, but unlike these sci-fi extravaganzas it is story that we can identify with and even participate in. In following Jesus we enter the story world of Mark, a world that corresponds to our own world, and through living out that story we discover power in powerlessness and experience strength in weakness.

5

The scandal of weak leadership

Paul's defense of ministry

Evelyn Ashley

INTRODUCTION

A JOB ADVERTISEMENT READS: Pastor Required

- For a growing, charismatic church with a congregation of diverse backgrounds.
- Must have strong leadership qualities and the ability to cast vision.
- Excellent preaching skills required.
- Needs to demonstrate appropriate spiritual gifts.
- Ability to interact with the influential in society an advantage.
- Attractive remuneration package.

Have you ever seen a job advertisement like that? It is the sort of job advertisement I could imagine the church in Corinth writing. However, their apostle and pastor did not quite meet their expectations. As an apostle, Paul was not very impressive. He was not the eloquent speaker they had hoped for. Instead of providing the "strong" leadership they wanted, he treated them with gentleness. He taught about spiritual gifts, but hardly ever talked about his own experience. Rather than mixing with the influential, he insulted them. Even worse—he would not take their money!

He was an apostle who was radically different from the expectations of many in the Corinthian Church. He was not the embodiment of success, influence, power or eloquence they had hoped for. Instead, he was weak, sick, persecuted, afflicted, and suffering. To then add insult to injury, he had the audacity to tell them that his weakness was actually proof that he was genuine! How could that be possible?

What has come down to us as 2 Corinthians is Paul's defense of his model of apostleship; his insistence that the appropriate model for ministry was one where divine power was demonstrated in the presence of human weakness. This was the model because it reflected the pattern of Jesus who was "crucified as a result of weakness, but lives as a result of God's power" (2 Cor 13:4).[1]

2 CORINTHIANS 1:3-11

After the initial greeting at the beginning of 2 Corinthians, Paul launched into a benediction of praise for "the God of all comfort, who comforts us in all our distress" (1:3–4). Paul went on to elaborate on the relationship between suffering (*pathēma*) or affliction (*thlipsis*) and comfort or encouragement (*paraklēsis/parakaleō*). Far from affliction disqualifying him from being an apostle, it was, in fact, a demonstration of his apostleship. For when he was afflicted, he received God's comfort, and both were for the benefit of the Corinthians. Thus, through the opening benediction Paul provided the theological basis for a defense of suffering and affliction as part of his apostolic ministry.

As he expounded these themes, Paul gave an example of God working through his suffering in a very dramatic way. While in Asia he had experienced an affliction where he had become convinced that he would not survive, and yet God had rescued him. While this was an example of what he had been explaining about the relationship between suffering and comfort, it was much more than that. For the reason Paul gave for the experience was not so that he would be able to comfort others, but so that he would learn to "rely on God who raises the dead" (1:9).

1. I am working from the assumption that 2 Corinthians 10—13 was written after 2 Corinthians 1–9, either as part of the same letter, or as an additional letter written shortly afterwards, probably after Paul received additional information regarding the changing situation in Corinth.

The scandal of weak leadership

Here, in stark contrast to other descriptions of afflictions he had experienced in the course of ministry, Paul gave only sketchy information about the details of the event. Instead, using very intense language, he emphasized his emotional response and the theological significance of that response. This "near-death experience" impacted much of what Paul wrote in the remainder of the letter. What he had learned through this event would become the backdrop against which he would defend his ministry. Through this experience, the principle of relying on God rather than relying on oneself had been compellingly reinforced. The situation had forced him to abandon self-reliance and any pretence of self-sufficiency and rely solely on God.

2 CORINTHIANS 2:14—3:6

In 2:14–3:6 Paul described and defended his apostleship as new covenant ministry. He did this by a series of metaphors and rhetorical questions. First, Paul likened being a minister of Christ to being led as a captive in a Roman triumphal procession.[2] This presupposes having previously been conquered, and brings to mind the fate of those in such a procession. That fate was usually to be executed as a demonstration of the superior power and authority of the victor—unless the one whose procession it was showed mercy. Paul pictured himself as one being led to death for the sake of Christ.

Then Paul likened being a minister to the wafting aroma of sacrifice. Incense was burned in the context of the Roman triumphal procession, but Paul's choice of words also suggests an allusion to the aroma of Old Testament cultic sacrifices. So it was that as the apostle was such an aroma, the knowledge of God was spread abroad—with eternal consequences. It was a perfume to those who were being saved, but an awful stench to those who were perishing (2:15–16a). A comparison of these verses with 1 Corinthians 1:18 strongly supports the need for congruity between the content of message, the method of proclamation, and way of life of the one who proclaims it. This means that the message of the cross was always to be lived out by the one who proclaimed that message. How the message of the cross was demonstrated in the way Paul proclaimed

---

2. While there has been much discussion about the meaning of the verb, *thriambeuō*, the view that appears to have the strongest support is the one that understands it as referring to defeated prisoners of war being led as captives in a Roman triumphal procession.

the message is described in 1 Corinthians 1:17—it was not with eloquent wisdom.³ Paul maintained that to proclaim it in such a way would have been to empty the cross of its power; his eloquent speech, rather than the power of the cross, could have been given the credit for success. The way the paradigm of the cross was demonstrated in Paul's life is made explicit in 2 Corinthians 2:14–16. It was as he was led to death as a captive in God's triumphal procession that he became the means through which "the aroma of the knowledge of God was spread in every place"; that Paul "became the fragrance of Christ to God" (2 Cor 2:14b–15a). "It is Paul as the *proclaimer* of Christ crucified, and who as a consequence suffers, who is the aroma of Christ."⁴

The message of the cross, the manner in which it is proclaimed, and the lifestyle of the person who proclaims it, must all fit the same pattern. Thus, Paul's suffering for the sake of the Gospel, far from invalidating his standing as an apostle, actually endorsed it. It was because he suffered, because he proclaimed the Gospel in the power of God, rather than with eloquent human wisdom, that his apostleship was valid.

Neither of the images Paul used were images the Corinthians would have naturally associated with apostleship. Their criticisms of Paul suggest they would have used much more "noble" images. However, Paul used images of weakness—the image of being led as a captive and the image of being the aroma of a sacrifice—to illustrate his calling as an apostle.

But even with such "weak" images, Paul claimed to be adequate for the task (3:16b). In contrast to the apparent claims of some others, Paul's sufficiency came not from himself, but from God. He was not the victor in the triumphal procession; he was the defeated captive. His presence in such a procession was not due to his own victory or achievement, but to the victory of God. It was from a position of weakness and defeat that he became the aroma of the knowledge of God. Twice in the space of just a few verses (2:17–3:6), and in only slightly different terms, he stated that he spoke and functioned as a minister of the new covenant, as one who was sent by God, whose responsibilities were carried out in the presence of God, and who labored as he did because of his relationship to Christ. The Corinthians, themselves, were the evidence that this was the case. Thus, he carried out his ministry with confidence, in the knowledge that his competency for

---

3. *ouk en sophia logou*; lit. "not in wisdom of words."
4. Barnett, *Second Corinthians*, 153.

ministry did not come from himself, but came from God. Once again, the contrast between human power and divine power is evident.

2 CORINTHIANS 4:1–12

This same principle—that ministry can only be conducted in God's power and not in human power—is reiterated with the statement in 2 Corinthians 4:1: "Therefore, since by God's mercy we have this ministry, we do not lose heart." As Hughes comments, "It is not an achievement of human ability but a consequence of divine mercy."[5] It was through God's enabling, expressed here as God's mercy, that Paul could face the difficulties, the suffering, the persecution, that apostolic ministry brought.

This is made even more explicit in 4:7: "We have this treasure in clay jars, so that this extraordinary power might be of God, and not come from us." Paul had just given a summary of his approach to ministry—it was with integrity both before people and, more importantly, before God. With two parallel statements, he had provided a summary of the content of his message: "the light of gospel of the glory of Christ, who is the image of God" (4:4) and "the light of the knowledge of the glory of God in the face of Jesus Christ" (4:6). This is immediately followed with Paul's image of treasure in clay jars. His weakness, lack of eloquence, ordinariness, fragility, suffering, and hardships, formed a stark contrast with the unparalleled glory and power of the "treasure" he carried.

While Paul's application of the image may have seemed outlandish, the image itself would have been familiar to Paul's audience. Cheap, fragile, often unattractive, and readily discarded, clay jars were part of everyday life—much like the plastic container of today. Once again, Paul gave a startling picture of what apostolic ministry was like, an image that reinforced the concept that both suffering and divine power were integral parts of his ministry. As Garland summarizes,

> Picturing himself as an ordinary, everyday utensil conveying an invaluable treasure is as striking an image as Paul's picture of himself as a defeated but joyous prisoner marching in God's triumphal procession (2:14).[6]

---

5. Hughes, *Second Corinthians*, 122.
6. Garland, *2 Corinthians*, 220.

The second part of 4:7 forms a purpose clause: "so that the extraordinary power might be of God and not from us." Most standard translations include the words "to show that," or something similar. The treasure is contained in clay jars *to show* that the power comes from God. The assumption is that the power for ministry does come from God; the fact that the "treasure"—whether that is understood as a reference to the "light" of the gospel, the "ministry" of the gospel, or the gospel itself—is contained in the clay jars of fragile, weak human lives, simply demonstrates that. However, the "*to show that*" is not in the Greek. It simply has "so that the extraordinary power *might be* of God, and not from us" (cf. NAB, NJB)—a present tense subjunctive (*ē*) of the verb "to be" (*eimi*). If Paul wished to say "show that" it is God's power, there are several verbs he could have used, but he chose not to. Thus Savage asks the question,

> Is it possible that Paul means exactly what he says, that it is only in weakness that the power may *be* of God, that his weakness in some sense actually serves as the grounds for divine power?[7]

If Paul is understood to mean exactly what he says, this opens up an alternative interpretation. It raises the possibility that ministry could be attempted with human effort, in human power. But the reason the treasure is in "clay jars" is so that this will not be the case. The weakness and fragility of the clay jar of a human life, is so that the minister will give up any illusion of self-sufficiency and realize that ministry can only be carried out in God's power. Once again, sufficiency comes from God and the minister must rely on the "God who raises the dead."

2 CORINTHIANS 6:3–10

In 2 Corinthians 5 Paul described his ministry as a "ministry of reconciliation." This ministry was possible only because it was through Christ's death and resurrection that God had acted to reconcile the world to himself. This is yet another passage revealing that not only was it Paul's message about Christ's death and resurrection, and the right relationship with God that is possible as a result, but also his manner of proclamation of that message, and indeed his whole way of life, that followed the same pattern.

As Paul commended himself to the Corinthians (6:3–10), he did so using a well-known genre, that of the "hardship catalogue," but in do-

---

7. Savage, *Power*, 166.

ing so he did not draw attention to his own self-sufficiency in enduring hardship. Rather, the "great endurance" (2 Cor 6:4b) he displayed was the result of functioning "in the Holy Spirit" and "in the power of God," and was demonstrated in a genuine, authentic and loving relationship with the Corinthian Christians (6:6b–7a). The antitheses he used to describe his ministry (6:8–10) reflect his paradigm that viewed apostolic ministry as sharing in both the suffering and death of Jesus and God's power in raising him from the dead.

2 CORINTHIANS 12:1–10

In 2 Corinthians 12:1–10 Paul brings his comments regarding weakness to a climax. In chapters 10 and 11 he had addressed various accusations and inferences that he was "weak," and thus at least an inferior apostle—if indeed he was an apostle at all. His manner of dealing with these issues was to do what the Corinthians thought he should do—to boast of his qualifications, even though such boasting was, he said, foolishness (11:1, 21; 12:11). However, instead of boasting of his power and eloquence, he boasted of his weaknesses, including his persecutions (11:23–33; 12:9–10).

In 12:1–10 Paul dealt specifically with the matter of the relationship between ecstatic visions and qualification for apostolic ministry. He recounted his experience from fourteen years earlier, but even though it involved an exceptional revelation, he gave only minimal details about the experience, and revealed nothing at all of its actual content. Such an exceptional revelation could easily be the cause of enormous pride. In order to stop him from becoming proud, Paul was given a "thorn in the flesh" (12:7).[8] Three times he pleaded with the Lord for it to be removed, but only when he received a categorically negative reply, did he realize its true purpose: to keep him from becoming proud because of the exceptional revelation he had received. Instead of the "thorn" being removed, it would remain as a constant reminder that not only such revelations, but also his apostolic ministry, were based on God's grace, not on Paul's worthiness.

---

8. There has been a huge amount of discussion regarding what the "thorn in the flesh" might have been. The two most common views are that (1) it was some sort of physical infirmity, or (2) it was some form of opposition or persecution. While the balance of evidence seems to be slightly in favour of it being some form of physical infirmity, there is insufficient evidence to identify this "thorn in the flesh" with any certainty. For the argument in this essay the existence of the "thorn in the flesh" is important, but its precise nature is immaterial.

Unlike the "unutterable utterances" Paul heard when he was caught up to paradise (12:4), the Lord's reply to his request that the "thorn" be removed, was something that Paul openly shared.[9] The statement is traditionally translated, "My grace is sufficient for you; for my power is made perfect in weakness," although some recent translations omit the "my," which is not in the older manuscripts. However, a more literal translation is "My grace is sufficient for you; for power is brought to an end in weakness."

The history of interpreting "the power" as a reference to the Lord's power,[10] coupled with a textual variation,[11] has led to a perpetuation of the traditional translation. The majority of commentators follow the translation of the standard English versions without comment on any textual issues. Even though some more recent translations omit the "my" and a number of commentators acknowledge that it is not original, the statement is still frequently interpreted as if the "my" were there; as if it were a reference to the Lord's power. With regard to Paul's choice of verb, most commentators, if they comment on it at all, argue that Paul used the verb *teleō* (*bring to an end, finish, complete*) as if it was *teleioō* (*complete, end, finish* or *make perfect*). Exceptions to this are Lenski and Dawn,[12] who argue that the usual meaning of *teleō*, ("finished"/"ended") is the one that is intended here. Lenski opts for the translation, "For the power is brought to its finish in weakness." He does, however, still argue that it is God's power, that is, the purpose of God's power is brought to completion. Dawn follows Lenski in arguing that *teleō* should be translated "to finish" and not "to make perfect" as if it were *teleiō*. However, she differs from Lenski in that she argues that the power is Paul's power that is brought to an end in weakness.

There is significant overlap in meanings between the words *teleō* and *teleioō*. However, with the possible exception of 2 Corinthians 12:9, the meaning of "to perfect" appears to be limited to *teleiō*. Thus, if 2 Corinthians 12:9 does indeed have the meaning of "made perfect," it would appear that the verb *teleō* has been used as if it were *teleiō*. This raises the question of whether there are other occurrences of this phenomenon.

---

9. *arkei soi hēcharis mou, hēgar dunamis en astheneia teleitai.*
10. *hēdunamis.*
11. *hēgar dunamis mou en astheneia telioutai.*
12. Dawn, *Powers, Weakness*, 37–41.

The scandal of weak leadership

It is difficult to find other examples of such usage. There are none in the New Testament. There is one possibility in the LXX. The NRSV renders Wisdom 4:16 as "youth that is quickly perfected,"[13] but has a footnote indicating that it could mean "ended". As the phrase is contrasted with "prolonged old age," "youth that is quickly ended" is at least as good a translation as "youth that is quickly perfected," if not better. Outside of biblical literature, it is also difficult to find examples. One has to go back or forward several centuries to find possible examples of *teleō* being used as if it were *teleioō*, and even those are far from certain.

The evidence points overwhelmingly to the standard meaning of *teleō* being "ended, completed, finished". While a meaning of "perfected" cannot be completely ruled out, it is at best a rare usage. As elsewhere, Paul uses the verb *teleioō* and related words to express the idea of "made perfect,"[14] it seems that his use of *teleō* here was intentional.

As highlighted above, Paul began the section by recounting an experience from fourteen years earlier when he was caught up into paradise and was given an outstanding revelation. As a result of this vision, he received a "thorn in the flesh" to stop him from becoming proud. Three times he prayed for its removal, but the reply he received from the Lord was, "My grace is sufficient for you; for power is brought to an end in weakness."

The nature of the revelation meant that it would have been possible, perhaps even probable, that Paul would have become proud, and that he would have equated the outstanding nature of the revelation with his qualification, even right, to be an apostle. His qualifications, his experiences, in essence his own power, could have become the basis of his apostleship. It was to stop this that the "thorn in the flesh" was given. It was to be a constant reminder of his dependence on God, a constant reminder that his apostleship, his ministry, was not the result of his own power, but rather the result of God's power.

In the weakness of the "thorn in the flesh," Paul's power was brought to an end. "Therefore," he said, "I prefer to gladly boast in my weaknesses [rather than in the extraordinary visions], so that the power of Christ might take up residence in me." This is a further example of how the weaknesses Paul suffered brought him to the place of realizing that his own power was inadequate, and of letting go of his reliance on human re-

---

13. *neotēs telesthesia tacheōs.*
14. Phil 3:12; cf. 1 Cor 2:6; 13:10; 14:20 Phil 3:15; Eph 4:13; Col 1:28; 3:14.

sources. The "thorn" was a powerful and ongoing reminder to rely on the "God who raises the dead," a reminder that stayed with him and impacted his entire ministry.

The newcomers in Corinth presented the church with a model of apostleship that was very different from the model Paul presented. They advocated an apostleship that was strong, eloquent, boastful and forceful, and, as it fitted with their cultural expectations, this model of apostleship gained popularity among the Corinthians. By comparison, Paul's model of apostleship was at best inferior, and possibly even invalid. It was in addressing this situation that Paul discussed his exceptional vision and subsequent "thorn in the flesh." and then reported the Lord's statement, "My grace is sufficient for you; for power is brought to an end in weakness." The traditional interpretation has provided comfort for countless people over the centuries, and will no doubt continue to do so. Nevertheless, the context indicates that Paul's intention was not to comfort people who were weak and suffering, but rather to challenge those who valued power. Thus this alternative interpretation is, I believe, more likely to express the apostle's intentions in defending his apostleship in the face of accusations of weakness.

SECOND CORINTHIANS 13:1–4

The theological underpinning for Paul's understanding of weakness bringing human power to an end, and thus allowing divine power full freedom of operation, was the death and resurrection of Christ. This is made explicit in 2 Corinthians 13:3b–4:

> He [Christ] is not weak in his dealings with you, but is powerful among you, for indeed he was crucified as a result of weakness, but lives as a result of God's power. So we also in our dealings with you, share in his weakness, but we will live with him as a result of God's power.

While it was only as he concluded the letter that Paul spelled this out, it was in fact the paradigm that underlay all he had said in the letter, in particular, his defense of his apostolic ministry.

Paul's statement of his paradigm contains three interrelated statements that are structured and include significant repetition, parallelism and contrasts, especially of the "weakness"/"power" antithesis. That Christ had not been "weak" among the Corinthians had been demonstrated by

The scandal of weak leadership

their conversion, and continued to be displayed among them. But the "power" of Christ's resurrection had been preceded by the "weakness" of his suffering and death. It is apparent from this passage that Paul drew a parallel between his ministry among the Corinthians and Christ's death and resurrection. Both Paul and the Corinthians were agreed that Paul was "weak," but unlike the Corinthians who viewed such "weakness" as a disqualifier for ministry, Paul viewed it as being one with Christ's "weakness." Just as he shared in that weakness, so too would he also share in God's power in his dealings with the Corinthian congregation. It would not be the human power of eloquent speech and forceful leadership that the congregation admired in the newcomers to Corinth. Rather it would be divine power that, if they did not change their ways, would be demonstrated in discipline. Even this would be for their benefit, for as he had previously stated (4:10–12), his sharing in the weakness and suffering of Christ not only meant that he shared in Christ's life, but that they, too, shared in that life. What he had demonstrated in the way he interacted with them he now spelled out in theological terms: valid ministry must reflect a sharing both in Christ's suffering and death and in God's power in raising him from the dead.

REFLECTIONS

For the average pastor or lay leader, a search for Paul's paradigm for ministry is little more than an interesting academic exercise unless a bridge can be built between the first century and the twenty-first century. The aim here is to build at least some of the scaffolding for such a bridge. It can only be a scaffold and not a carefully constructed bridge, for the nature of the topic means that as soon as detailed instructions are formulated on how to apply Paul's paradigm for ministry, the ministry is no longer one that relies on "God who raises the dead" (2 Cor 1:9), but becomes a ministry that relies on human instructions instead. Thus each minister must learn to rely on God as they work out what sharing both in Christ's weakness and in the power of his resurrection means for their particular ministry, for it will be different for each person. It is hoped, however, that this brief discussion will stimulate the thinking so that ministers of the gospel of Christ can begin to wrestle with what functioning in God's power rather than their own power means for them.

For many in the first century, the cross, and thus ministry that followed that pattern, was a stumbling block and a scandal. It is, perhaps, the same for us, but over the centuries we have had a tendency to sanitize the cross, and thus downplay the scandal of the cross. We have made the cross the subject of art, jewelry and architecture and, to a large extent, have forgotten the horror and revulsion of such suffering and degradation.

In the Western world, at least, we have a tendency to see "scandal" not so much in the cross itself, but in leadership that follows the pattern of the cross: leadership that displays human weakness, human limitation, human suffering, and human fragility, but functions in God's power. Somewhere along the line, we seem to have fallen into the same trap as the Corinthian church. We have come to value power, control, and success. As Shoemaker comments, "The super-apostles are with us today promoting a religion of super-pastors, super-Christians and super-churches."[15] We have developed a theology of health and wealth, of professionalism and success that reflects the values of our culture. We have turned to the secular wisdom of our society to discover a pragmatic solution to church leadership and while the insights of our society are not all mistaken, they are not always congruent with what either Jesus or Paul taught and modeled. A religion that looks to the wisdom of its culture for answers is, in Paul's terms, a "different gospel" about "another Jesus" (2 Cor 11:4), for it has forgotten that the cross is the power and wisdom of God (1 Cor 1:18–25). The challenge that faces us—whether we realize it or not—is how can we rediscover the power and the wisdom of God that are revealed in the cross?

The advice of much that is written on the topic of church leadership calls for leaders to gain the best training they can, to discover their gifts, to work from their strengths, to research their target audience and tailor the approach to fit, to plan ahead, to have a vision for the future and communicate that vision to the congregation, and so on. There can be value in these strategies. Paul teaches that believers have been given spiritual gifts for the benefit of the whole church (e.g., 1 Cor 12–14), and the parable of the talents recorded in the Gospels (Matt 25:14–18; Luke 19:11–27) makes the point that the talents received should be used. But Paul's example and the argument he expressed in 2 Corinthians indicate that as much as we are called to use our gifts, talents, training and intel-

---

15. Shoemaker, "2 Cor 11:1–21", 407–11.

The scandal of weak leadership

ligence, Christian ministry and Christian leadership are to be more than that. Beerens makes the provocative statement,

> In the established church, one leads out of skills and natural abilities and natural gifts. Such things alone do not establish leadership and authority. Our ability to be suffering servants is a testimony to renewal, to renewed and redeemed leadership.[16]

The assertion that skills, gifting and training on their own are insufficient for Christian leadership, that such leadership requires one to be a "suffering servant," is one that tends to be uncomfortable for us. It was also uncomfortable for the Corinthian congregation, but it is congruent with Paul's paradigm for ministry based on sharing both in Christ's suffering and in the power of his resurrection (2 Cor 13:4).

Paul had an enviable heritage (Rom 11:1; 2 Cor 11:22), a good education and a zeal for God (Acts 22:3), but those are not the things of which he boasted nor the things in which he placed his confidence. To the disgruntlement of many in Corinth, the things of which he boasted were his weaknesses, suffering, hardships, and persecution—the things that forced him to rely on God. Perhaps there is something here for the leader in the twenty-first century to learn. As important as good training and good strategies might be, they are no substitute for reliance on God. If this was the case for Paul, then surely the same would hold true for ministers of Christ today. Dodd comes to the following conclusion,

> It is exciting to feel strong, competent and in charge, but there is no true spiritual power in this, no ability to materialize God's kingdom reality. Life-giving leadership flows from a deep dependency on the One who empowers, cleanses, guides and gives life.[17]

This parallels Paul's statements in 2 Corinthians. While we might accept this intellectually, it is difficult to embrace it in life and ministry. Our natural inclinations, as well as everything our society has taught us, point in the opposite direction. Yet this brief look at 2 Corinthians makes it difficult to draw any other conclusion. What Paul taught and lived, not to mention what Jesus taught and lived, say this is the way to experience God's power in ministry. Nouwen puts it this way:

---

16. Beerens, "Journey into Weakness," 26.
17. Dodd, *Empowered Church Leadership*, 32–33.

> The way of the Christian leader is not the way of upward mobility in which our world has invested so much, but the way of downward mobility ending on the cross . . . Here we touch the most important quality of Christian leadership in the future. It is not a leadership of power and control, but a leadership of powerlessness and humility in which the suffering servant of God, Jesus Christ, is made manifest.[18]

To be a servant leader was not easy for Paul; it resulted in much suffering and hardship. The same will almost certainly be true for us if we choose to follow Paul's—and Jesus's—paradigm for ministry. This is not the easy way, but Paul demonstrated that it is the way to effective ministry in God's power.

Servant leadership in reliance on God means vulnerability, openness, and honesty. It means that there must be a congruency between the message proclaimed and the way of life of the messenger. Like Paul, we are called to come in weakness and to proclaim "Jesus Christ, and him crucified," so that "faith might rest not on human wisdom but on the power of God" (1 Cor 2:2–5). We are not only called to proclaim the message of Christ crucified and raised, we are also called to live it.

> To come to Christ is to come to the crucified and risen One. The life-giving apostle embodies in himself the crucifixion of Jesus in the sufferings and struggles he endures as he is faithful and obedient to his Lord. So Paul preaches the crucified and risen Jesus, and he embodies the dying of Jesus in his struggles to further point to the Savior. His message is about the cross and his life is cruciform, shaped to look like the cross.[19]

This is not a popular approach to ministry. The plethora of books on Christian leadership that take a different approach clearly demonstrate this. Yet this is the approach that Paul both taught and modeled: ministry in dependence on God and following the pattern of the death and resurrection of Jesus.

No crucified life, no cruciform existence, no life-giving ministry.[20]

What Paul wrote in 2 Corinthians demonstrates that his paradigm for ministry was one of dependence on God. It was not in his strengths and

---

18. Nouwen, *In the Name*, 62–63.
19. Dodd, *Empowered Church Leadership*, 70.
20. Ibid., 67.

The scandal of weak leadership

achievements that God's power was demonstrated. Rather, it was in his weaknesses, when he abandoned self-reliance and learned in the midst of extremity to rely on God that his ministry was truly in God's power. This was Paul's paradigm because it followed the pattern of Jesus's death and resurrection. Thus we discover that in essence Paul's paradigm for ministry was the paradigm of the cross.

This is the challenge for ministers in the twenty-first century: to learn what it means to follow Paul's paradigm, to follow the way of the cross. Circumstances today are very different from the circumstances that Paul faced. It is not possible to do a "direct transfer." Rather, it is necessary to learn how to apply the same paradigm that Paul used in the first century to the twenty-first century so that we can say with Paul,

> He [Christ] is not weak in his dealings with you, but is powerful among you, for indeed he was crucified as a result of weakness, but lives as a result of God's power. So we also in our dealings with you share in his weakness, but we will live with him as a result of God's power (2 Cor 13:3b–4).

As Henri Nouwen looked forward to the beginning of the twenty-first century, he made a remarkable and challenging statement. As we now find ourselves in the latter part of the first decade of the twenty-first century, his statement continues to challenge us to reflect on how Paul's paradigm for ministry based on the death and resurrection of Jesus, might be applied today:

> I leave you with the image of the leader with outstretched hands, who chooses a life of downward mobility. It is the image of the praying leader, the vulnerable leader, and the trusting leader. May that image fill your hearts with hope, courage, and confidence.[21]

---

21. Nouwen, *In the Name*, 73.

6

The powerless leader

A biblical ideal or a contradiction in terms?

Mary Evans

INTRODUCTION

WHAT DOES IT MEAN to be a Christian leader in today's world? One of the problems in answering this question is that the nature of leadership is complex and not all leaders, let alone those who are led, have the same understanding of their role. One thesaurus lists the following synonyms for leadership: administration, direction, directorship, domination, guidance, management, running, superintendency, authority, command, control, influence, initiative, pre-eminence, supremacy, sway.[1] Some of these relate to the task, some to the "power," and some to the status of a leader. Leadership and power are often seen as inextricably linked. If this perception is correct then clearly to speak of a powerless leader is nonsensical. But are leadership and power or leadership and authority really synonymous? Or have the values of the world so overtaken the values of the church that the biblical perspective in this area has been lost?

In this chapter, I am suggesting that one of the world's values, which Christian faith turns upside down, is the relationship between leadership and both status and authority. This leads to the conclusion that powerlessness is far from being an inappropriate term to apply to biblical leadership. I will argue that the critique of secular values that we find in the teaching

1. McLeod, *The New Collins Thesaurus*.

of Jesus in relation to leadership is prefaced in the Old Testament in a variety of ways and is then developed within the teaching of the epistles. Inevitably, as the topic is so wide, this will involve something of a meander through a whole range of texts and themes. I make no apology for that. Scripture challenges all readers to identify and think through the implications of its stories and deals with many topics, including this one, in what might be seen as a meandering way!

Most Christians today would want to support the concept of servant leadership. We would generally agree that, for Christians, leadership should not be primarily a matter of either claimed authority (that is, the exercise of power by one person over another) or of status (that is, of special recognition within the community) but rather it is a matter of servanthood. It is, like the Christian life in general, a matter of giving up our rights for the benefit of others, of constantly considering those others as better than ourselves. At least that is the theory, but is this really more than a sound bite. How often do we—and the "we" here includes both those who are seen or see themselves as leaders and those who are seen or see themselves as led—take what are basically servant words, like "minister," or "deacon," or "pastor," and turn them into status words? In practice, do we simply think of a servant leader as a ruler who rules kindly? The language of servanthood (or slavehood) clearly does not fit comfortably with an understanding of leadership based on power and authority, but is it really possible to find a different model of Christian leadership for which the term "servant" is not a complete misnomer and yet which remains effective in encouraging and enabling a vibrant and well-organized church community?

OLD TESTAMENT PERSPECTIVES

Creation

The creation narratives do not focus on the question of leadership, although questions relating to who would be in charge or who was the most important or who was responsible for whom came into play as soon as sin broke into the world. Nevertheless, the pattern of creation itself could be seen as relevant. God created human beings giving them genuine choice and responsibility. Encouragement and education seem to have been an important part of his relationship with Adam and Eve—but not control. They were instructed as to what was right, but the responsibility for following or not following God's way was left to the humans themselves. In one sense, we see a deliberate self-limiting of God's power or at least a refusal to use that power to ensure that Adam and Eve (and later on Cain) made the decision that God would have wanted. Human beings were created with the responsibility for making what might be seen as godly decisions for themselves, rather than simply having all decisions made for them. Maybe, just maybe, there is an example here for those who might be assumed to have authority over other people.

The philosophy and practice of leadership

Leadership in ancient Israel differed in several ways from many of the societies that surrounded it. There was a monarchy, but the king was never given and indeed never claimed divine status. He was not given unquestionable authority either, or complete control over every sphere of national life. Sometimes kings, perhaps including Solomon, attempted to function as a one-man band but this never lasted and there was always a varied system involving prophets and priests as well as kings; each with their own set of responsibilities and their own sphere of influence. Priests were born into their role, appointments made entirely on the basis of heredity. Prophets, in general, were called by God independently of society and had no doubts about their right and responsibility to critique and if necessary criticize and condemn the establishment. Some kings were specifically anointed and appointed by God, but even in these cases public recognition was also seen as important. Lohfink argues that these checks and balances, the "distribution of the functions of power" were key concepts within Israel's constitution.[2]

> The functions must be distributed among *different* authorities—that is, no one authority is simply a delegation from a superior authority—and delegation of the separate, distributed powers must be made in accord with an antecedent constitutional law that exists for these powers.[3]

As we shall see below, "precisely such a law is found . . . in Deuteronomy."[4] Whether this move towards a balance of power was intended to prevent the abuse of authority by an individual leader, or to correct pre-existing

2. Lohfink, "Distribution," 336.
3. Ibid., 347.
4. Ibid.

The powerless leader

abuse, depends on whether Deuteronomy should be seen as a preface or a conclusion to the history of Israel.[5] In either case, it is clear that such a balance was viewed as important and that leadership in Israel was never intended to be centered on one person.

The overall attitude towards the monarchy within the Old Testament is ambiguous and we are left with a number of open questions, even beyond the obvious one as to whether the monarchy should have been introduced at all at the time it was and in the way it was. How far should kingship, in particular, and leadership in general, be seen as God's provision for dealing with specific and temporary situations and how far should it be seen as a permanent endowment, lasting for the leader's lifetime? How far is leadership based on personal authority and how far should it be? The practice in Israel was in almost every instance very much about power—who is in charge, who rules, who controls. However, behind that lies an ongoing discussion and the theory seems much more to reflect the New Testament picture of servant leadership. The good leader of God's people is the one who best enables the people themselves (both the community and individuals) to live in the light of their covenant relationship with God.[6] It seems that the reforms within Israel that had most effect were those that took care to ensure that all the people took "ownership" of what was going on. The covenant renewal ceremonies instituted by Joshua at the start of Israel's life in the land and by Ezra after the exile make the involvement of all the people explicit.[7] It is probable that Isaiah completely omits any reference to Hezekiah's reforms because they were not "owned" by the people and therefore had no ongoing effect on national life.[8] Again, the key seems to be to enable the people to make godly decisions for themselves rather than seeking to make those decisions on their behalf.

---

5. McConville provides a thorough discussion on the dating of Deuteronomy in the Introduction to his commentary *Deuteronomy*.

6. I have argued elsewhere that the books of Samuel, for example, provide an extended reflection on the nature of power and its use and abuse particularly in the leadership of Israel (*The Message of Samuel*). The introductory poem of Hannah, which reflects on the way in which God overturns the values of the world and makes the powerless powerful, and vice versa, provides the starting point for this reflection.

7. Josh 24, Neh 8–10.

8. Described in 2 Kgs 18 and 2 Chr 29, but completely ignored by Isaiah in the account he gives of Hezekiah's reign.

The ideal leader

Deuteronomy 17:14–18 provides instructions as to how kingship in Israel, once it exists, ought ideally to function. There is something ironic in the way these instructions are presented in that it speaks of the king being chosen by God and yet the whole focus is on the proper actions for both people and king to take! The God-chosen king they appoint is to be one of the people. The explicit reference here is that he is to be an Israelite, not a foreigner; but included in this is the concept that the king ought not to view himself, or be viewed by the people as anything other than one of them. The prophetess Huldah picks this up when, in response to the government officials that King Josiah sent to her to find out how they should respond to the recently found Book of the Law, she replies, "Tell the man who sent you to me" (2 Chr 34:23; 2 Kgs 22:15) even though it is very clear that she knows that this man was the king. The king had a function, a very significant function, to fulfill but there is no question that his being given this function turns him into a different kind of person. Scripture is very clear that there is no such thing as blue blood—aristocracy, whether it relates to ruling classes within society in general or within the faith-community is never more than a cultural construct. Even the king in Israel was "not to consider himself better than his people" (Deut 17:20).

The king is to avoid building up the trappings of power. Wealth, status symbols, lavish court systems and other reflections of Eastern potentates are not to be the hallmark of the Israelite monarchy. This is not what happened in practice, Solomon's kingship, for example, falls down on virtually every one of the points emphasized here, but the theory is clear. It is again ironic that Psalm 72, which reflects on the king's service of God and the people in upholding righteousness and delivering the needy, is ascribed to Solomon.

In general, the ideal king is defined not by how he should rule but how he should live. His key task is to read, understand and keep the law for himself, something that might also be seen as a key task for any Israelite! The king's primary role is apparently showing the people how to be, rather than telling them what to do. The prophetic ideal is described in very similar terms in that holy living and good theology are pictured as far more significant that exciting signs and demonstrations, even of what might be seen as supernatural power.[9] The people are given the responsi-

---

9. Cf. Deut 13:1-5; 18 and Jer 23.

bility of judging whether what the prophet says is in line with what God has already revealed and whether how the prophet behaves is how a godly person should behave—it is on the basis of those conclusions that the prophet's words are to be accepted or rejected.

Isaiah 53 as a leadership model

Throughout Christian history the servant songs in Isaiah and, in particular, those found in Isaiah 52:13–53:12 have been interpreted in relation to Christ's own ministry. It is a beautiful, powerful and poignant poem foretelling the life and work of Jesus. No Christian believer has doubts that that is true and that the passage is very appropriately interpreted in that way. But in some ways, this proper Christological emphasis has led us away from seeing it as a model for all God's servants or even all God's servant-leaders. The New Testament clearly calls us all to imitate Christ in our lives. However, perhaps because it is clear that Christ has a unique atoning function and that function is a key part of the parallels that have been identified with Isaiah 53, the call for us to imitate Christ has rarely been picked up in this context. But surely the servant-songs in general have a wider application than the Christological one. The responsibility to forward the cause of justice and righteousness, to be "a light for the Gentiles," to "release from the dungeon those who sit in darkness" (Isa 42:1–7) certainly remains part of the task assigned to God's people. It is not a very appealing prospect for God's servant leaders to see part of their role as being despised and rejected, familiar with pain, and giving up all glory for the benefit of those whose sorrows we may be called to carry. But does the example and teaching of Jesus mean that this is indeed part of our calling to follow him?

Ezekiel 33:30–32 (The "pop-star" passage)

There is no doubt that sometimes Christian leaders, and in particular "famous" preachers, do achieve celebrity status. Followers flock to hear what they have to say, in a very similar way to that of some music fans who would do or give almost anything to meet their idol or even to get into their latest concert. But the message given to Ezekiel makes the dangers of public acclamation very clear. Any leader who thinks that such acclamation, or that a massive and even apparently really appreciative audience, is any measure of effective service is deceiving him or herself. They may as well be singing pop songs. The only really valid measure of effective leadership for God's servants is whether those they lead are living lives that reflect their covenant relationship with God, lives that have been transformed by the gospel message. This is not directly addressing the question of whether or not power and authority are appropriate terms to use in relation to godly leadership. But it is relevant to the overall picture and, in particular, to the way in which New Testament ideas and ideals are already clearly present in Old Testament writings.

JESUS

His example

There is no doubt that Jesus was the leader of his followers and is to be acknowledged as the leader of his church. He was clear that the disciples were quite correct to call him Teacher and Lord (Jn 13:13). But what kind of example is he? How did he exercise his leadership? Philippians 2:1–11 tells us something of the attitude with which he carried out his ministry and explicitly calls us to imitate this. Just as Christ set aside his own glory and "made himself nothing, taking the very nature of a servant," so are we to "do nothing out of selfish ambition or vain conceit. Rather in humility [we are to] value others above ourselves . . . looking . . . to the interests of others." The element primarily stressed and that we are called upon to imitate is not authority or the way in which Jesus exercised power, but his humility. It is surely not irrelevant that in John 13 Jesus's acknowledgement of his position as their teacher and lord comes in the context of his taking the role of servant and washing their feet.

It could be argued that Jesus's refusal to have any part in the established power structures of his time, either religious or secular, also provides a model for us. It would have been possible for Jesus to have been born into a ruling family, or to use his gifts to "rise" from the ordinary working family into which he was born, into a position of power and status within the establishment. However, he resolutely turned his face against such a path and the desire for power over and reverence from "the kingdoms of the world" is shown to be a satanic temptation needing to be resisted (Jn 6:14–15; Matt 4). He did teach regularly in a synagogue setting, but not as part of the hierarchy.[10] The implication seems to be that

---

10. Matt 4:23; 9:35; 13:54; Mark 1:29, 39; Luke 4:15; 6:6; John 6:59; 15:20.

the teaching needs to be heard and received for its own sake and because of their response to Jesus as a person, not because it came from any official authority.

The pattern of delegation set up by Jesus could also be seen as a model. He chose the twelve not just to be with him and learn from him, although both of those things were important, but also to be apostles, sent out on his behalf to serve in their own right. But he did not just send out the twelve or indeed the seventy. Matthew 28:19 commissions the disciples to "go and make disciples" who will presumably be expected also to take up the same task. Jesus functioned as an enabler. His teaching was given to equip his followers to imitate him. Often this teaching came in the context of interactive discussions picking up how the disciples were faring in their own service.[11]

His teaching

What does Jesus have to say about status, power and authority in general and in relation to leadership in particular? There is far more, of course, than can be covered in an article of this breadth and length. The disciples were fascinated, perhaps even obsessed, by the concept of who was going to be in charge, who was the most important, who should be seen as having the highest status.[12] Jesus spent what sometimes seems an inordinate amount of time and effort trying to get the point across to his disciples that they were starting from the wrong premise, asking the wrong question. Let us consider a selection of incidents and sayings taken from just one gospel, that of Matthew.

The beatitudes in Matthew 5 give us a range of approaches and attitudes, which are considered blessed, and while there is nothing here that affirms those who seek power or authority, there is much that commends weakness and even powerlessness. It is the meek, the poor in spirit, the persecuted, who are blessed. In direct response to their question about who is greatest in the kingdom he told them "unless you change and become like little children you will never enter the kingdom" (Matt 18:3). Can we see implied here, "you won't even enter, let alone lead, while that question remains so important for you?" It is those who humble them-

---

11. Collinson and Hill, *Making Disciples*, provides an excellent discussion of issues relating to the way in which Jesus functioned as a discipler.

12. Matt 18:1; Mark 9:34; Luke 9:46; 22:24.

selves like a small child, with no power and no authority who are in fact the greatest.

Speaking more directly about leadership Jesus contrasts the understanding and practice found in the society surrounding them with his own example, which he expected his disciples to follow.

> "You know that the rulers of the Gentiles lord it over them, and their high officials exercise authority over them. Not so with you. Instead, whoever wants to become great among you must be you servant and whoever wants to be first must be your slave—just as the Son of Man did not come to be served but to serve" (Matt 20:25–28).

It is hard to see how he could have made it any clearer that leadership within his church was not to be about power. But just in case they really still had not grasped it, he returns to the issue in Matthew 23 where he contrasts the leadership style he expects from them with that of the Pharisees:

> You are not to be called "Rabbi" for you have only one Master and you are all brothers and sisters. And do not call anyone on earth "father" for you have one Father and he is in heaven. Nor are you to be called "teacher" for you have one Teacher, the Christ. The greatest among you will be your servant. For those who exalt themselves will be humbled (Matt 23:8–11).

Surely there is more to this than the use of particular terminology. The approach of Christ's followers to those they might be seen as leading is not to be that of a guru, a master who is to be followed without question. We are called to make disciples of Christ, not of ourselves. Nor are we to behave as if we were the parents and those we lead the children. We are not to present ourselves as the ultimate authority, a teacher whose views cannot be questioned. The concept of servant leadership clearly has a lot more flesh on it that just "ruling in a nice way".

In Matthew 19 we also have the story of the disciples rebuking those who brought children, obviously concerned that Jesus should not be interrupted by such unimportant people while he was teaching the Pharisees. Jesus clearly did not see it that way, "let the children come . . . for of such is the kingdom of heaven." Placed immediately after this account is the story of the rich young ruler, the man who had everything going for him. Jesus makes it abundantly clear that riches and social status in no way indicate that a person is necessarily going to be a key member of the kingdom community, indeed these things are more likely to be a hindrance, "it is hard for the rich" (should we add here, and those who in human terms are seen as powerful?) "to enter the kingdom." The disciples' "Who then can be saved?" shows how little they had yet understood of what Jesus had been saying to them. For them the question now seems to be "If it is so hard for such an important and significant person to enter the kingdom, what chance is there for the rest of us?" No wonder this is followed by the wonderful expression, "Jesus looked at them." Matthew clearly remembered that look! Perhaps it was a combination of exasperation and tolerance and maybe there is a hint of irony in the following phrase, "Humanly, this is impossible, but with God all things are possible." It is possible that the rich might just be able, with God's help, to set aside their dependence on riches and that Christ's disciples might just be able, with God's help, to understand what status in the kingdom of heaven is really all about!

Would Jesus look at us in much the same way as he contemplates our attitude to leadership and status? Of course, modern Christians would never use the term "Rabbi," and those from a strongly protestant evangelical tradition would never call a human leader "Father" either, but we seem to have no problem at all substituting other terms of address like "Reverend" or "Pastor" or "Vicar." Would our reasoning, perhaps that it matters that we know where people stand and it is important to show proper respect and to have it shown to us, be any more acceptable to Jesus than that of the early disciples?

LEADERSHIP AND AUTHORITY IN THE NEW TESTAMENT

Some relevant verses

Of the eighty or so references to authority in the New Testament over sixty refer to either the authority given to Jesus or to that of the secular government. Of the rest, six speak of the authority over evil spirits that Jesus gave to his disciples when he sent them out;[13] two of the authority from the chief priests given to Paul to act on their behalf (Acts 9:14, 26:10); one of the mutual authority of husband and wife over each other's bodies (1 Cor 7:4); one of a woman's authority over her own head (1 Cor 11:10); and one

---

13. Matt 10:1; Mark 3:15; 6:7; Luke 9:1; 10:19.

of the command for a woman or a wife not to exercise inappropriate authority over a man.[14] None of these speak in any way of an authority given to leaders within the Christian community. We are left with five verses. In three of these Paul speaks of the authority that the Lord has given to him. Second Corinthians 10:8 states, "For even if I boast somewhat freely about the authority the Lord gave us for building you up rather than tearing you down, I will not be ashamed of it." This could sound as if Paul was advocating authoritarian leadership. However, it is important to note that this comes as part of an appeal, which is significantly described as delivered "by the meekness and gentleness of Christ" (v. 1) and in the context of answering an accusation that his leadership was not authoritarian enough and in fact could be described as "timid." He stresses, in a manner very parallel to Jesus's approach, that his method was different from that of the world. The emphasis is on the fact that the authority he has been given, and of which he is not ashamed, is for "building you up and not tearing you down" in contrast, apparently, to those who have set themselves up as powerful figures within the church. Although he is very clear and very firm about the implications of the gospel and will brook no contradiction when those implications are threatened, it is clear that for Paul the real authority is found in the gospel itself and not in him or his leadership style. Three chapters later (2 Cor 13:10) Paul again speaks of his really wanting them to heed his words so that "when I come I may not have to be harsh in the use of authority" (whether his own or that of the gospel) but he precedes this by stating that "we are glad whenever we are weak but you are strong" and follows it by repeating his understanding of authority as relating to "building you up." It is as if Paul wants to make it very clear that he is still distinguishing himself from the power-mongering that seems to have been rampant among them.

The conclusion that Paul sees any authority as grounded in the gospel itself is confirmed by 1 Thessalonians 4:2 where he says, "[Y]ou know what instructions we gave you by the authority of the Lord Jesus." The implication is that the instructions were based on Christ's word and it is there, rather than in the person who gives the instructions, where the authority lies. I would argue that the same implication is also there in Titus 2:15 where Titus is told to "encourage and rebuke with all authority"

---

14. 1 Tim 2:12. The number of alternative possibilities given in the TNIV footnotes indicates something of the problem in translating this verse, but the fact that this is preventing rather than supporting the authority of one human being over another is clear.

The powerless leader

and not to "let anyone despise you." This relates directly to the message that he should present to the people and the things he should teach. The authority once more lies in the message, rather than in the individual who presents the message.

Having said all of that, the final verse, at least as it is translated in the NIV, does apparently support unambiguously the concept of the personal authority of those who lead over the people who are led by them. Hebrews 13:17 tells the believers to "obey your leaders and submit to their authority." However, this is somewhat misleading on two counts. First, the word translated "obey" is not *hupakouō*, the standard word for obey, but *peithō*. *Hupakouō* is almost always translated as "obey" in most English versions of the New Testament. On the other hand, *peithō*, although it can, at least in the middle or passive voice, mean "obey" is much more often translated by words more reflective of support than power.[15] The TNIV picks up on this and has "Have confidence in" rather than obey "your leaders." Second, the NIV, and this has not been amended in the TNIV, has "submit to their authority" to translate *hupeikō*. This word, found only here in the New Testament, means "yield" and therefore, by derivation, "submit" is appropriate, although the "do what they say" of some modern versions may express the sense better.[16] However, any reference to authority is completely missing from the Greek text. It is not just that a particular translation has been chosen, there is no word there to translate! It appears that the translators of both the NIV and TNIV simply take it for granted that leadership automatically implies authority and therefore have felt free to add that concept into the text. However, the reason given in Hebrews for people to support the leadership is not that they have no choice but to do so because of the leader's authority or position, but that they should choose to do so because of the leader's weakness. Leaders may (or may not) have authority but there is no doubt that they do have responsibility and are held accountable. They have a difficult job to do and it can only benefit everyone if their work is made a joy for them by the cooperation

---

15. For example in the TNIV 18 (out of 21) occurrences of *hupakouo* are translated "obey" whereas this happens for only 2 occurrences of *peitho*. Of the rest, 9 are translated as "persuade," 11 as "convince," 13 as "confidence" or "confident" and 4 as "trust". Most other versions, which choose to use "obey" in Heb 13:17 rarely do so elsewhere. In fact, the only other time the NIV uses "obey" to translate *peitho* is in Gal 5:7 ("Who cut in on you to keep you from obeying the truth").

16. NLT, CEV, cf *Worldwide English New Testament*.

of the people they lead! Indisputably, this verse encourages trust in and support of those in leadership positions but it does not sanction any claim to authority.

So then there is not a single verse in the New Testament that unambiguously supports the idea of any human leader being given direct authority over another. Relevant to this is the concept of the priesthood of all believers. This affirms that all can enter into God's presence, all can relate directly to God. If this is to be more than just another sound bite then it must also affect our understanding of leadership. It is a dangerous temptation for leaders to think that they stand in some sense as a mediator between God and other people, making it appear that the led have to go through their leader to get to God, rather than having direct access. First Timothy 2:5 makes it very apparent that to create such an impression is to usurp the position given solely to Christ himself.

The question of power

Space precludes extensive discussion on the relationship between power and weakness found in the New Testament. It is perhaps enough to note a number of verses that provide evidence for the existence of this relationship:

- "For the message of the cross is foolishness to those who are perishing, but to us who are being saved it is the power of God" (1 Cor 1:18).

- "But we have this treasure in jars of clay to show that this all-surpassing power is from God and not from us" (2 Cor 4:7).

- "But he said to me, 'My grace is sufficient for you, for my power is made perfect in weakness.' Therefore I will boast all the more gladly about my weaknesses, so that Christ's power may rest on me" (2 Cor 12:9).

- "For to be sure, he was crucified in weakness, yet he lives by God's power. Likewise, we are weak in him, yet by God's power we will live with him in our dealing with you" (2 Cor 13:4).

- "I want to know Christ—yes, to know the power of his resurrection and participation in his sufferings, becoming like him in his death" (Phil 3:10).

The powerless leader

I would argue that these verses are relevant to the question of what it means to be a Christian leader. It is beyond dispute that the New Testament sees Christians as endowed with power. They are given power to deal with and overcome the power of demons or of human governments, power to testify, power to do signs and wonders, power to live life as a Christian, and power to grasp the truth of the gospel.[17] But there is no indication that the New Testament ever presents "power" as an appropriate term for describing either the role of a leader or their relationship with those they lead.

CONCLUSION

First, it is important to note that nothing that has been said denies or denigrates the existence or the importance of leadership. There is no doubt that certain members of the community are called and gifted to take leadership roles. Any society that does not have some kind of structure and that does not allow anyone to take responsibility is unlikely to last or to stay strong for very long. However, there seem to be profound differences between the way that leadership amongst God's people and leadership in the surrounding world is, or at least should be, understood. It may be quite wrong to use Hebrews 13:17 to support authoritarian leadership, but the passage nevertheless clearly presents leaders as having both responsibility and accountability. The challenge for Christian leaders is precisely that of carrying responsibility without power, of depending absolutely on the support and cooperation of those for whom they might be responsible. Believers should follow human leaders, not because they have been given a particular position but because they are pointing in the right direction. It is not without significance that the criteria for Christian leadership found in the New Testament are almost completely based on character and lifestyle rather than on skills (e.g., 1 Tim 3). Just as for the Israelite kings, the primary role is apparently showing the people how to be, rather than telling them what to do.

We return to the point where we started. Leadership is not about status or about power, but about servanthood. Our value and the only meaningful status we have comes from the fact that we are created as human beings by God and that through his grace and through the death and resurrection of Jesus Christ we have been made holy and enabled to become as children of God. Any attempt to ascribe status within the

17. E.g., Luke 10:19; Acts 1:8; 4:33; Rom 15:19; 2 Cor 10:4, Eph 3:16–18.

church to the rich rather than the poor, to the educated rather than the uneducated, to the young rather than the old, or to the leader rather than the led is to deny the significance of our status in Christ (see Jas 2:1–7). Similarly, our attempts to see our leadership role as having power over others is to deny the power of Christ and the life of the Spirit within them as well as within ourselves.[18] The leader who does not have the power of Christ within and is not completely confident of the authority of the gospel message cannot be called a Christian leader. In that sense and that sense alone, to speak of a powerless leader is a contradiction in terms. However, in every other way, the powerless leader—who guides, enables, teaches, encourages, supports and trusts—but who does not seek to control is indeed a biblical ideal.

---

18. 1 Cor 1:17; 2 Cor 4:7; Eph 1:19.

7

Martin Luther

A theologian forged by trial

Mark D. Thompson

INTRODUCTION

IN EXAMINING MARTIN LUTHER and his contribution to Christian theology or indeed the practice of Christian ministry, two things are rightly demanded. In the first instance, the student of Luther must be willing to acknowledge and to appreciate the distance between Luther and the twenty-first century. Luther was, as Heiko Oberman loved to say, a medieval man, a medieval German man, a medieval German man who was heavily influenced by particular theological and spiritual currents in early modern European thought.[1] Skating over the difference between Luther's context and ours, pressing Luther into service of contemporary theological or ecclesiastical agendas almost inevitably involves a measure of distortion. It is all too easy to read ourselves into our account of Luther's thought and practice.

Yet just as important is a willingness to recognize the lines of similarity, continuity and even to some extent of identity, between Luther's basic concerns and those which rightly occupy the Christian five hundred years later. Luther saw himself as living in the last days. This was a profoundly theological judgment anchored in the perspective of the New

---

1. Oberman, *Luther*, xix.

Testament itself. Luther reveled in the victory of Christ while at the same time warning about the reality of trial, suffering, weakness, and defeat—a reality that would continue until that day when Christ returns to bring all things to their conclusion. Luther saw himself as an inhabitant of that age when God's glory and power are hidden under the form of the contrary, when the pattern of the cross is writ large over all God's dealings with creation. Christ has certainly been raised, but the glorious resurrection of his disciples is yet to come. Now is the time for faith and the preaching of the word of God, and the context of that vital activity is opposition, struggle and temptation from the devil. From time to time, Christians in the early twenty-first century need to be reminded that we too live in these last days.

LUTHER'S REVOLUTION

If this paradox of distance and yet identity is properly a feature of an attentive study of Martin Luther and his contribution, then it is not surprising that both perspectives should loom large as we address Luther's approach to Christian ministry in general and the life of a theologian in particular. But first we should recognize that Martin Luther revolutionized the concept of Christian ministry. Whether he intended from the beginning to do so or not is matter of continued debate, but the undoubted fact is that Christian ministry after Luther—in the Protestant churches and to some extent even in the Roman churches—was never quite the same again. This revolution is worth revisiting.

In the first place, he reoriented Christian ministry to the word of God. As far as Luther was concerned, the Christian minister is, above all else, a preacher. The Christian soul can do without everything except the word of God.[2] Of course, preaching had played a critical role in the practice of ministry long before Luther. Luther was not the first to assert its priority. Nevertheless, the dire state of much medieval preaching, the distraction of the all-embracive sacramental system and particularly the high value placed on "the sacrifice of the mass" deeply disturbed him. As he protested at table in 1533, "[A] minister is one who is placed in the church for the preaching of the word and the administration of the sacraments. But I was called to sacrifice, which is impious."[3] The church needed

---

2. Luther, *LW* 31.345.
3. Ibid., 54.100.

to be called back to Christ through the proclamation of the Gospel of Christ. Even the symbolic elements of water or of bread and wine were of little benefit unless they were accompanied by the gospel word and so became a genuine sacrament.[4] Whatever else a minister did—and there was indeed much else—this obligation stood above all others.

There was, as Luther could testify, great joy in preaching the word of God. Yet Luther knew that preaching meant daring to speak for God in God's presence and that prospect was terrifying. In that light, preaching called for humility as well as boldness. As he told Lauterbach in May 1532,

> I have never been troubled by my inability to preach well, but I have often been alarmed and frightened to think that I was obliged to speak thus in God's presence about his mighty majesty and divine nature. So be of good courage and pray.[5]

Preaching was, in this sense, not a choice but a necessity. The preacher should be bold, confident that the word he speaks will honor Christ, and yet at the same time the preacher is both exposed and vulnerable. No other word but God's word will accomplish the task and God is present as his name is invoked. Against all temptation the preacher must not see the sermon as an opportunity for self-aggrandizement or for a display of personal brilliance. The hungry bride of Christ has come to be nourished by the word of Christ. Faithfulness, simplicity, and boldness are the hallmarks of effective preaching and thus effective Christian ministry. Here is a perspective that is sometimes lost today in an age preoccupied with novelty, image, and technique. The preacher feeds the people of God in the presence of God. A concern for the honor of Christ and for the edification of the church actually led Luther to suggest in 1540, "Some day I'll have to write a book against artful preachers."[6]

Second, Luther not only reoriented Christian ministry to the word of God, he de-sacralized it, placing it firmly in the context of the Christian home. The idea of the Christian minister modeling faith in the midst of ordinary, daily life; the notion of the minister's wife and the minister's marriage, family and home as the arena in which the service of God's people might properly occur—all this was new in the sixteenth century. Thirteen centuries of tradition had obscured this possibility. But Luther

4. Luther, *LW*, 36.42–44.
5. Ibid., 54.158.
6. Ibid., *LW* 54.384.

insisted that Christians should not isolate themselves from the patterns of life God gave us from the beginning. We do not flee from the world but live in the world, bringing to it the life transforming message of the gospel of Christ. As a result of Luther's teaching and example, as well as a fresh study of the Bible on these matters, "Protestants viewed the ministry as an ethical service among spiritual equals, not a superior religious state"[7] and this transformed the practice of ministry itself in a variety of ways.

This new focus on ministry in the midst of ordinary life, rather than at a distance from it, brought with it a new engagement with the struggles of living as a Christian in the world. The joys of family life could be embraced but its inevitable sorrows added new pressures. Luther delighted in the play of his children but he would also have to bury two of them. Katie was an ideal partner and a wonderfully generous hostess, caring for the hordes that joined them for meals over the years. Yet Luther now bore the concerns of a husband. He had to think about the impact of his actions upon Katie. He knew all too well the burdens she must carry if he were taken from her. As it happened, within months of his death Katie would have to flee Wittenberg as imperial troops marched through in their attempt to stamp out Luther's reformation once and for all.

Third, and perhaps most important of all to the man himself, Luther recast the work of Christian ministry in terms of eschatology, the cosmic purposes of God worked out over the entirety of universal history and culminating in the consummation of Satan's defeat. The preaching of the parish minister was a critical element in the purposes of God to overthrow the rule of Satan and to redeem and renovate his creation. In 1538 Luther told his students, "God provided his church with audible preaching and visible sacraments. Satan resists this holy ministry in all earnestness, and he would like it to be eliminated altogether because by it alone is Satan overcome. The power of the oral Word is truly remarkable."[8] God's word cannot be defeated even though the struggle might be intense all the time until Jesus returns.

One of Luther's most salutary warnings about Christian ministry as a participation in the ongoing war between Christ and the devil was made at table in 1540:

---

7. Ozment, *Age of Reform*, 390.
8. Luther, *LW* 54.318.

> Christ fights with the devil in a curious way—the devil with great numbers, cleverness, and steadfastness, and Christ with few people, with weakness, simplicity and contempt—and yet Christ wins. So he wished us to be sheep and our adversaries to be wolves. But what an unequal contest to fight with ten or a hundred wolves! He sent twelve disciples into the world, twelve among so many wolves. I think it's a remarkable war and a strange fight in which the sheep are killed and the wolves stay alive. But they'll all go to ruin as a result, because God alone performs miracles. He'll preserve his sheep in the midst of the wolves and he'll crush the jaws of the wolves for ever.[9]

Here is neither triumphalism nor pessimistic resignation. Christ cannot but win and yet the war continues and the Christian's experience is not always one of victory. Luther commented two years earlier,

> We have to learn that a Christian should walk in the midst of death, in the remorse and trembling of his conscience, in the midst of the devil's teeth and of hell, and yet should keep the Word of grace, so that in much trembling we say, "You, O Lord, do look on me with favour."[10]

What is more, Christian ministry is engagement in the front lines and far too often "the sheep are killed and the wolves stay alive."

These three fresh perspectives—the proper context of the war between Christ and the devil, the proper arena of home and marriage rather than simply the cloister and the cathedral, the proper method of a bold proclamation of the gospel in word and sacrament rather than simply the performance of rituals and the veneration of relics—in combination meant that Christian ministry not only looked different, but could be honest about its weaknesses as well as its victories. The theology of the cross could be expounded as the heart of Christian theology. The daily struggles of the home could be faced with a new vigor borne of familiarity rather than distance. The reality of the devil could be acknowledged without fear, but also without pretence. In the final analysis, the cause of Christ was furthered "not by human strength but by the word" (*non vi sed verbo*).

The urgent tone of Luther's call for change along these lines sounds strange to twenty-first century ears, it is true. Nevertheless, at each point this transformation of the practice of Christian ministry can also be un-

---

9. Luther, *LW*, 54.379.
10. Ibid., 12.405.

derstood as a challenge to our own time. Luther well understood what we far too often forget, that toleration and a measure of respectability are not the normal experience of the servants of Christ in the last days: "Woe to you when all men speak well of you, for that is how their fathers treated the false prophets" (Lk 6:26). Luther and his companions were labeled a sect by state and church alike.[11] The gospel at the heart of genuine Christian ministry is the fragrance of life to those who are being saved, but the stench of death to those who are perishing. In response, Luther would have echoed the question of the apostle Paul, "And who is equal to such a task?" (2 Cor 2:16). But he also knew that the absence of persecution is itself the most complete persecution, an instrument of the devil that ultimately undermines faith and obscures cosmic realities.[12]

The knowledge of God in the midst of turmoil

Luther's famous words about the development of true theological understanding need to be seen in this light. "Experience alone makes a theologian," he said at table in 1532.[13] What he meant was that God is not known in isolation from everyday experience. The truth about God is not something abstract. It cannot be disentangled from life in God's world with all its fragility and frustration. God gives himself to be known in the midst of such life, most powerfully, of course, in the human life and death of the eternal Son. God is not better known by retreating from the world, but by being immersed in it.

Here, once again, Luther's discovery that the cross provides us the proper perspective on all reality, not least of all the character and purposes of God, comes to the fore. This was an important corner he had turned right back at the beginning, eschewing high-blown speculation about the essence of God and his necessary attributes and embracing instead the God-given entry point of revelation in and through the cross. A person who looks upon the invisible things of God as though they were clearly perceptible in those things which have actually happened does not deserve to be called a theologian. He deserves to be called a theologian,

---

11. Hieronymus Aleander said at the Diet of Worms: "[I]t is necessary and crucial to see to it that this subversive sect be wiped out forthwith."

12. Luther, *LW* 10.361. Cf. Oberman, *Luther*, 254–57.

13. Ibid., 54.7.

however, who comprehends the visible and manifest things of God seen through suffering and the cross.[14]

An addiction to Aristotle had led the theologians of the previous two centuries to insist on what God must be like in conformity to certain a priori definitions. Luther's rejection of scholastic theology, most especially its critical Aristotelian elements, led him to explore what God was like on the basis of how he had in fact acted in Christ. In the humiliation of the cross, the glory of God was on display in an unexpected way but one entirely in keeping with God's purposes as explained in the Old Testament. Christ's suffering was not a sign that God had abandoned him, but rather that he was the means through which God was reconciling the world to himself (2 Cor 5:19). In that harsh judgment, God's love and mercy were being played out on an unimaginable scale. The true theologian does not hunt through human experience looking for transparent demonstrations of the majesty and power of God. In line with the example of Christ, these are rather to be found in the midst of suffering, weakness, and humiliation.

Perhaps Luther's most famous comment in this connection is one made in the midst of his second series of Psalms lectures from 1520: "It is not understanding, reading or speculation, but living, dying and being damned that make a theologian."[15] Once again, the issue is experiential theology over against the more prevalent speculative mode of thinking and talking about God. God is not known in the way a mathematical equation is known or even as a famous person might be recognized from a distance. He is God *for us*. He is *our* Father. Jesus is *our* Savior. On the one hand, Luther was convinced that human beings had to be brought to the end of their resources before they could really know God in this way. So profound is the hold that pride has over the human heart that it actually prevents a genuine knowledge of God by fooling us into thinking that this knowledge is itself some kind of human achievement. Cutting away this foolishness would seem to be at least part of the explanation for Luther's scatological language—human pride needs to be brought low and the devil who feeds our pride is worthy of nothing but degradation.[16]

---

14. Luther, *LW* 31.40.
15. Luther, *WA* 5.163.28–29.
16. Oberman, *Luther*, 107–109, 155.

On the other hand, the character of God's dealings with the creation in the light of the cross needs to be understood. To speak and write of the true God, the God of the crucified Christ, means to speak and write of how God's strength is made perfect in weakness, how the glory of God is to be found in the midst of apparent defeat. This insight was not gained in the calm, cool rationality of the lecturer's study, but in the extremities of everyday existence. This is what the true God is like. He encounters us in the midst of the trial, in the heat of the action of our great struggle with the condemnation we deserve. It was here that Luther discovered there was nowhere else to go when brought low by the expectations of God's law. God himself is our only help. We flee *from* God *to* God, from God's strange work of wrath and judgment to God's proper work of rescue and blessing.[17]

Luther famously coined the word *Anfechtung* for his experience of a sense of being abandoned to God's judgment.[18] He did not believe it was a particular quirk of his own character to experience these depths so regularly throughout his life. In fact, in the midst of his *Greater Catechism* he wrote the following.

> No one can avoid temptation and enticement as long as we live in the flesh and have the devil around us; and this will not change: we must bear tribulation, yes even be in the midst of it. But that is why we pray not to fall into and drown in it.[19]

Anfechtungen are a natural part of the Christian life; they are not just the special affliction of Christian leaders and teachers. Commenting on Psalm 51 in 1538 he would say,

> A godly man feels sin more than grace, wrath more than favour, judgement more than redemption. An ungodly man feels almost no wrath, but is smug as though there were no wrath anywhere, as though there were no God anywhere who vindicates His righteousness.[20]

So, in this business of knowing God, the experiential nature of the knowledge of God, the particular form of God's dealings with his creation in the light of the cross, and the sensitivity of the godly person to their own

---

17. Luther, *LW* 13.135.
18. For more detail see Thompson, "Luther."
19. Luther, *WA* 30-1, 209.24–27.
20. Luther, *LW* 12.358.

sinfulness all come together to make weakness and trial our constant companions. God cannot truly be known in any other way. Whether a trained theologian or a young Christian neophyte, we, like Moses, are not permitted to see God's glory in any other way than through the word spoken in the midst of our own struggle. This is the word that lays bare God; this is what nourishes genuine faith. Without this experience of trial, Luther would tell the students around his table, "[O]ne does not really know what the spiritual life is."[21]

LUTHER ON CHRISTIAN MINISTRY IN THE MIDST OF WEAKNESS

Luther's understanding of the strength and power of Christian ministry demonstrated in and with its weakness must be understood in the broader context of this perspective on the Christian life and the true knowledge of God. Suffering and trial are to be expected by all faithful Christian men and women, but they take on a peculiar character in the life of the minister of the gospel as the devil tries in vain to halt the spread of that gospel and the saving purposes of Christ. Luther's own trials centered not only on his personal standing before God, but also around a question he knew came straight from the pit:

> Are you the only wise man? Can it be that all the others are in error and have erred for so long a time? What if you are mistaken and lead so many people into error who might all be eternally damned?[22]

So intense was this inner questioning that Luther told his students that when it comes "I hardly know what I am about, whether I preach aright or not."[23]

Luther knew what it was like to be described as weak by others as well. Firebrands like Andreas von Karlstadt and Thomas Müntzer broke with him in the early 1520s because he would not embrace the forceful, even coercive methods of reform they advocated. In 1522, Luther was forced to return from safe custody in the Wartburg when riots broke out in Wittenberg. As is well known, on returning he dressed himself again in his monk's robe, had his tonsure restored, and then mounted the pulpit

---

21. Luther, *WATr* 5.490.24–491.1.
22. Luther, *LW* 36.134.
23. Ibid., 54.37.

for eight successive days to preach reform by the persuasion of the word rather than by force or by law. The second of these eight *Invocavit Sermons* is justly famous. In it Luther laid bare both the weakness and the power of the ministry of the word.

> It is not in my power or hand to fashion the hearts of men as the potter moulds the clay and fashions them at his pleasure. I can get no farther than their ears; their hearts I cannot reach. And since I cannot pour faith into their hearts, I cannot, nor should I, force any one to have faith. That is God's work alone, who causes faith to live in the heart. Therefore we should give free course to the word and not add our works to it. We have the right to speak [*jus verbi*] but not the power to accomplish [*executio*]. . . . I simply taught, preached, and wrote God's word; otherwise I did nothing. And while I slept, or drank Wittenberg beer with my friends Philip and Amsdorf, the word so greatly weakened the papacy that no prince or emperor ever inflicted such losses upon it. I did nothing; the word did everything.[24]

Karlstadt wanted to tear down the altars, force people out of the monasteries and nunneries, smash the images, and stone the idolaters. Müntzer would later try by force to establish the kingdom of heaven on earth. Their impatience and contempt for Luther and his methods stung sharply but it did not entirely take Luther by surprise. He knew there have always been, and would always be, those who considered a ministry of the word and prayer to be weak and ineffectual. Had not Paul needed to confront the same disdain? "I am not ashamed of the gospel," he was prepared to write to the Romans, "because it is the power of God for the salvation of everyone who believes" (Rom 1:16). "We have this treasure in jars of clay," he told the Corinthians, "to show that this all-surpassing power is from God and not from us" (2 Cor 4:7).

In a bold move, Luther was willing to assess the ministry of others in the light of this important truth. An appreciation of the weakness and fragility of Christian ministry would prove to be a valuable counter to both the triumphalism of the fanatics of his day and the worldly grandeur of the Roman church. In a letter to Philip Melanchthon (13 January 1522) from the Wartburg, he had advised his friend to inquire of the wandering prophets who were troubling the people of Wittenberg "whether they have

---

24. Luther, *LW* 51.76–77.

experienced spiritual distress and the divine birth, death and hell."[25] A ministry that is not assaulted by the devil can be unmasked as a ministry that poses him no threat at all. But when by preaching Christ we challenge the devil's lies and place before men and women the reality of salvation and new life, we can expect opposition to intensify. Gospel ministry, too, lives under the shadow of the cross.

A CHALLENGE TO THE MOMENT

Martin Luther knew about God's power in the midst of weakness from his own experience in the monastery, in the lecturer's study, and among the churches of the Reformation. He was regularly brought low by a grinding sense of being utterly lost, compounded by the accuser's insistent suggestion that he was leading untold numbers of people to eternal doom. In those moments the only thing he could hold on to was the promise of God in the gospel. Here, in what to some seemed merely weak, ineffectual words, Luther understood that the all-surpassing power of God was at work.

Ultimately it was his study of the Scriptures, encouraged by his mentor in the monastery and given a certain urgency by his appointment to the teaching position at the University of Wittenberg, that enabled Luther to see this most clearly. He came to understand that the cross of Jesus is more than simply a talisman or even an inspiring tale of God's action in the past. The cross provides the entry point for truly knowing God, the pattern for authentic Christian living, and the shape of genuine Christian ministry. It points us away from a superficial assessment of success and failure to the way God shows his power in the world, in the midst of weakness. The Christ that Paul was determined to preach was Christ crucified (1 Cor 2:2), since he also knew that "the foolishness of God is wiser than man's wisdom, and the weakness of God is stronger than man's strength" (1 Cor 1:25).

Luther's precise challenges differ at many levels from those faced at the beginning of the twenty-first century. Christendom as he understood it is long dead. The opponents of the gospel can now call upon the arguments of Enlightenment, post-Enlightenment and even post-modern thinkers, and truths assumed on all sides to be beyond dispute in the sixteenth century are said to be questionable today. Neither reason nor an appeal to authority can expect to carry the day. Yet there is much in Luther's reflections upon the nature of God's dealings with the world, the

---

25. Luther, *LW* 48.366.

basic context of the Christian life, and the shape of Christian ministry that merits careful attention in our own very different time. Perhaps we need to be particularly vigilant that we do not simply reflect the assessment of the pagan world around us, applauding the spectacular, pursuing impact and the trappings of success, and despising the so-called weakness of an unadorned ministry of prayer and the word of God. The plethora of books on how to have a successful ministry filling Christian bookshops around the world would suggest the danger is real. But Luther wanted his students to know that things are not what they seem.

> Our Lord God fills His high office in an odd manner. He entrusts it to preachers, poor sinners, who tell and teach the message and yet live according to it only in weakness. Thus God's power always goes forward amid extreme weakness.[26]

---

26. Luther, *WATr* 3.639.39–640.2.

8

John Calvin on the strength of our weak praying

Michael Parsons

INTRODUCTION

AT ONE LEVEL, THE sixteenth century Protestant reformations were explicitly pastoral movements. Peter Matheson suggests that "the reforming process was not fundamentally about ideas in the mind or structures in church and state but indicated much more elemental changes in spiritual direction."[1] He says, further, "Biblical images are being reworked here, released and unleashed to emphasize gratuity, access, intimacy. From this perspective the Reformation can be seen as an infinitely varied, but coherent and extended, metaphor for the bountifulness of God's grace."[2] So, then, at the specifically pastoral level, those involved in "spiritual direction," those preaching, teaching and leading congregations, sought to draw people to a living relationship with a more intimate God through Jesus Christ, and also sought to enable believers to live more closely to that God on a day-to-day basis, calling for and experiencing "the bountifulness of God's grace." Small wonder, then, that the Word of God was continually emphasized and spoken, singling out for exposition among other things, biblical narratives, the commandments, and passages on prayer.[3]

There was certainly no shortage of works on prayer—many of the reformers wrote on the subject, all of them preached upon it. The com-

---

1. Matheson, *Imaginative World*, 6.
2. Ibid., 8.
3. See Parsons, *Luther and Calvin*.

mon emphases in these works, those we might term "reformational emphases," seem to have included the sovereignty of the God who answers prayer, the fatherhood of God, the importance of faith and hope in the supplicant, the central significance of Jesus Christ to the divine hearing and answering, the pivotal position of the Lord's Prayer for understanding, and so on. Naturally, the reformers had different perspectives on the theme and stressed different things, but on these key topics they seem to have agreed.

The following short essay begins by outlining some representative works on prayer by Zwingli, Luther, and Melanchthon. This will give a broader context for an examination of John Calvin's theology of prayer from the *Institutes*, Book 3, chapter 20, stressing the pervasive idea in his thought that the strength of prayer is found in an honest and vulnerable acknowledgment of our inherent weakness before a sovereign Father.

REFORMATION PRAYER

Huldrych Zwingli

In the Swiss city of Zurich, Huldrych Zwingli wrote on the subject of prayer in the context of a very self-conscious reformation. He speaks in his work *True and False Religion* of the prayers of former ecclesial practice as hypocrisy, as "an insult to God," as mercenary ("hired prayers"), concluding, that previously "the devotion of the heart has dared to sell itself as a work of merit."[4] This, in itself, is part of Zwingli's repeated contrast between faith in the divine and faith in external things.[5] Indeed, in his *Reply to Emser*, for example, he distinguishes between the faithful (that is, those who depend on God) resorting to him alone, and the unfaithful who turn from God to creatures hoping for aid from them.[6] A little earlier he had defined it at some length:

> Prayer, therefore, is the conversation which as a result of faith you have with God as with a father and a most safe and sure helper. Prayer, then, is the uplifting of the heart, not of the breath or voice to God. We pray, therefore, when the heart draws near to God,

---

4. See Zwingli, *True and False Religion*, 3.279–83.
5. See Stephens, *Zwingli*, 141–42. Also, Büsser, "Spirituality," 300–317.
6. Zwingli, *Reply*, 3.383–8. Also, Zwingli, *Exposition*, 2.238–43; *True and False Religion*, 3.282.

when it speaks with Him, when in sincere faith it seeks help from him alone.[7]

In discussing prayer as adoration towards God Zwingli states, "Adoration is ... the devoting of the heart to God, that is, to the Lord who *can* do all things and to the Father who *will*."[8] We notice in these quotations those reformational emphases mentioned above: God as sovereign and as Father, the importance of faith. However, it is also evident that he stresses above all that prayer is the individual believer reaching out of the heart in communion with the eternal God—that is, he speaks of prayer essentially as relational experience. Given the strongly theocentric character of Zwingli's theology, this existential element is quite remarkable.[9] Indeed, G. R. Potter's estimate of the reformer in this respect is that his understanding (given that it was early on in the Reformation) "was something almost original."[10]

Martin Luther

Martin Luther evidences similar teaching on prayer and certainly echoes some of Zwingli's emphasis. In an early work, *An Exposition of the Lord's Prayer for Simple Laymen* (1519), he stresses that prayer is a "spiritual good" and that the essence of true and acceptable prayer is "a lifting up of heart or mind to God."[11] Prayer from the heart is an inner longing, sighing, desiring. Again, what comes across in Luther's exposition at this point is the relational aspect of prayer; believers need to move God to mercy, but their confidence resides in the fact that the sovereign God is actually their Father ("a friendly, sweet, intimate, and warm-hearted word").[12]

Later, in 1528, we find the reformer again expounding the fatherhood of God for an understanding of prayer. In a sermon, preached in that year, he uses the metaphor of a sack that the faithful hold open before their Father, in which they receive more and more the longer they hold it open, for the Lord mercifully desires to give.[13] Another emphasis is added

---

7. *True and False Religion*, 3.281.
8. Ibid., 3.279. See also, 3.282. Also, George, *Theology*, 130.
9. See, for example, Stephens, *Zwingli*, 36, 69, 141–42; idem. "Theology," 80–99; Miller, "Huldrych Zwingli," 157–69, particularly, 160.
10. Potter, *Zwingli*, 114.
11. Luther, *Exposition*, LW 42.26, 25, respectively.
12. Ibid., 42.22.
13. Luther, *Sermon*, LW 51.169–76, specifically 51.171.

in this work—that of prayer as obedience: Luther states, "You should pray and you should know that you are bound to pray by divine command." Again, "This work I have been commanded to do and as an obedient person I must do it."[14] In fact, Luther attaches the spiritual exercise of prayer to the second commandment; it is a requirement that believers use God's name in worship and adoration—that is the positive corollary to the negative commandment concerning the wrongful use of the Lord's name. This, in itself, gives added confidence to those who would call on the name of the Lord; as God has commanded it from them, he will answer their obedient petition.

In his later work, *A Simple Way to Pray* (1535), Luther singles out the Lord's Prayer as evocative of true supplication: "To this day I suckle at the Lord's Prayer like a child, as an old man eat and drink from it and never get my fill."[15] Here the reformer is at his most practical, for example, advising believers of the importance of prayer, and of letting it "be the first business of the morning and the last at night."[16] However, the exceptional element in this work is that the reformer refuses to be tied to rules, and, noticeably, he allows space for an intimate experience of the Holy Spirit:

> [I]f in the midst of such thoughts [on reading the Lord's Prayer] the Holy Spirit begins to preach in your heart with rich, enlightening thoughts, honor him by *letting go of this written scheme*: be still and listen to him who can do better than you can.[17]

Perhaps with an eye to Paul's words in Romans 8:26–27[18] and certainly in the context of his own relational theology, Luther himself moves and directs his readers away from an empty and idolatrous rote and towards an experiential piety.[19]

---

14. Luther, *Sermon*, 170. See also, *Tabletalk*, no. 5510, LW 54.439.

15. Luther, *Simple Way*, LW 43.200. See also, *Tabletalk*, no. 495, LW 54.85; Lohse, *Martin Luther*, 106; Koch, "Luthers reformatorisches Verständis," 47–66.

16. Ibid., 43.193.

17. Ibid., 43.201–2, (emphasis added).

18. This is likely because the Apostle speaks of the Holy Spirit interceding for us and speaks of it in the context of the Spirit knowing our hearts.

19. See Hendrix, "Martin Luther's Reformation," 240–60.

Philip Melanchthon

Philip Melanchthon examines the topic of prayer in his influential work, *Loci Communes* (1543).[20] In the reformer's theological system, according to Scheible, prayer was the second pillar of the church, next only to doctrine—though, interestingly, the reformer himself speaks of it as "the chief bastion of the church" in this particular writing.[21] Characteristic of reformational theology, Melanchthon repeatedly argues that one should adore rather than investigate the mysteries of God and it is within that context of adoration of mystery that prayer is found.[22]

The reformer speaks of prayer as "this highest of all virtues," even if it remains "only a brief groan."[23] It is noticeable that the writing is at once pastoral and personal.[24] For example, he encourages prayer in times of trouble, saying, "In my own case I know that by the help of God many calamities have been mitigated." The broader context and some of the emphases can be deduced from the following short paragraph of pastoral advice,

> Let your prayer be in the Spirit, that is, not in hypocrisy, not in babbling of words, but in godly emotion of the heart, and let it be in truth, that is, in true recognition of God. Let it be directed to the true God and to the mediator.[25]

Together with these emphases on true prayer as spiritual, genuine, from the heart, in recognition of God and Jesus Christ, comes a stress on confidence, obedience, and faith,[26] and on the gospel, specifically, and on the Word of God.[27]

The scaffolding upon which he builds his theology of prayer is a list of five points that he enumerates to help his readers' understanding. The five points act like rules for what Melanchthon considers true prayer, or what he terms "a well-expressed form of prayer."[28] The five points are as follows

20. Melanchthon, *Loci Communes* (1543).
21. Ibid., 196a.
22. See Scheible, "Philip Melanchthon," 80.
23. *Loci Communes*, 196a, 204a, respectively.
24. Ibid., 200b.
25. Ibid., 205a.
26. Ibid., 196a, 196b. Elsewhere, he says that "God wants our faith to be increased by these exercises of piety," 204a.
27. Ibid., 198a.
28. Ibid., 204b.

- The supplicant must consider what God they are invoking.[29]
- It is "a very great sin" not to render worship, gratitude and requests to God.[30] That is, similarly to Luther, Melanchthon ties his understanding of prayer to the second commandment, but he appears to make less of it than his Wittenberg colleague.[31]
- We must remember the importance of the promises of God—particularly, his promises to be reconciled to us through Christ, and to supply all our needs.[32]
- Though he recognizes that faith is stronger and more evident in some than in others, faith must be added to prayer. He says, for instance, "Faith must shine forth," or again, "We must always in every petition present this faith to God." We must believe that God's desire is to give.[33]
- It is of central importance that we hold that "Prayer is the worship of God, because worship attributes this honor to God—that in our great miseries He will bring help to those who call upon Him. His name is not an empty thing."[34]

This last point reminds us that the reformers, generally, speak of prayer in the context of our weakness. Zwingli, Luther, and Melanchthon recognise that believers cry from a position of weakness to a strong, capable, and merciful God. Indeed, Melanchthon says a great deal about it. He employs the following prolonged image, for instance,

> [T]hose who have tasted our common miseries judge far differently and understand that this whole life is filled with troubles, like a city which is besieged on all sides and attacked sharply by its enemies, which now on this side and now on that side is attacked by the enemy who starts fires, tears down buildings, and can scarcely be held in check. It is a certainty that all wise men wonder why this

---

29. *Loci Communes*, 197a. Also, 207a.
30. Ibid., 197a–b.
31. Ibid., 196a.
32. *Loci Communes*, 198a.
33. Ibid., 198b, 199a, respectively.
34. Ibid., 201a.

present and still weak nature of men is burdened down with such great evils, which our nature *by its own powers* cannot endure.[35]

The italicized words indicate the image as the context for prayer: we supplicate God because without his aid we are unable to sustain life against all that would trouble us. Melanchthon returns to the image later, saying, "[W]henever you think you are living in a besieged city which is being sharply attacked on all sides, these very circumstances should instruct you to seek help."[36]

The reformer, then, speaks of "our great weakness."[37] By this he affirms both a weakness of nature and a weakness in behavior. "We have often fallen," he says, "we deserve punishments, we are unworthy of the blessings of God." He speaks of the weakness "that attaches both to our mind and our body," the fact that we are guilty, ungrateful, and he speaks also of "the stupidity of the human mind as it flees from God" (by which he refers to doubts that besiege our thinking).[38] The world, too, is full of difficulty, impinging upon us as "miseries and troubles of this life."[39] The church itself is presently subject to sin and to physical miseries, "to public and personal calamities." Indeed, Melanchthon reminds his readers of the principle that "the church must be subject to the cross,"[40] in which image he seems to include "physical torments" and the present wrath of God (noticeably, he specifies the occurrences of the plague).[41] Behind much of this lies the work and deception of Satan, himself, of course. The reformer speaks of "the tyranny of the devil,"[42] warning believers that Satan seeks to trap them in ways that cannot be described in words. Using a pertinent Old Testament narrative, Melanchthon likens the church to Daniel and his friends surrounded by lions; the church always lives in the centre of trouble, in the face of Satan's attacks.[43]

---

35. *Loci Communes*, 202a, (emphasis added).
36. Ibid., 203a.
37. Ibid., 209b.
38. Ibid., 197a, 201b, 208a–b, 198a. Also, 197b, 209b.
39. Ibid., 207a.
40. Ibid., 199a. See also, 203a.
41. Ibid., 198b, 200a–b, 202b, 207a.
42. Ibid., 207a.
43. Ibid., 202a.

Of course, this last image implicitly speaks of escape through the sovereign help of God. As Daniel received divine assistance in that hour, so does the church. There is in this a recognition of the wider context of prayer and this introduces, on the one hand, Melanchthon's emphases on the nature of the giving God, the importance of the gospel, of Christ, of the divine promises and on providence; and, on the other hand, his stress on the believer's faith, confession, gratitude, and hope. We cannot deliver ourselves. Yet, he assures us that deliverance is not an accident, it comes from our Father in response to our requests and pleading.[44]

JOHN CALVIN ON PRAYER

Intimate conversation

Calvin's ideas on prayer were already formed in 1536, though there are one or two minor revisions in later editions of the *Institutes*. According to the reformer, there are six purposes of prayer:

- to fly to God with every need,
- to set all our petitions before God,
- to prepare us to receive God's benefits with humble gratitude,
- to meditate upon God's kindness,
- to instill the proper spirit of delight for God's answers in prayer,
- to confirm his providence.[45]

Despite the fact that elsewhere he writes concerning prayer, "I lay down laws for no-one,"[46] it is, of course, well known that Calvin posits four rules for governing true prayer:

- a heartfelt sense of reverence,
- a sense of need and repentance,
- a surrender of all confidence in self and a humble plea for pardon,
- a confident hope.[47]

---

44. *Loci Communes*, 200a, 203b. See also, 201a.

45. *Inst* III.xx.3. These are listed here in the words of Beeke, "Calvin," 139.

46. Calvin to the French church in London, Geneva September 27, 1552, in *Letters*, 2.362. The complete quotation runs into what appears to be a general rule: "I lay down laws for no-one, but it were much to be desired that the sobriety of our prayers should show the reverence we feel for the name of God."

47. See *Inst* III.xx.4, III.xx.6, III.xx.8, III.xx.11, respectively. Again, summarized by Beeke, "Calvin," 140.

According to Calvin, the chief part of worship "lies in the office of prayer". The closest that he gets to defining prayer is perhaps where he claims that it is "properly an emotion of the heart within, which is poured out and laid open before God, the searcher of hearts."[48] He teaches that God desires that we "descend into our heart with our whole thought" and to "enter deeply within."[49] That is, prayer for Calvin is something that causes us to focus within, into the heart, because it is there that the Lord looks for "a sincere and true affection," one that dwells in the "secret place of the heart." His reasoning appears to be straightforward enough, "For since we ourselves are God's temple," he says, "if we would call upon God in his holy temple, we must pray within ourselves."[50]

Nevertheless, we will note below de Kroon's words that, for Calvin, prayer is "a back-and-forward movement," and so it does not simply stop at focusing inwardly to draw out that affection and true piety of the heart, as important as that is. Prayer is ultimately to be described as the heart (or mind) "lifted and carried beyond itself." Significantly, Calvin adds "in so far as this is possible."[51] In this immediate context the reformer employs a telling image, which he picks up several times in his exposition of prayer. Indeed, his first rule (in his own words) is that "we should be disposed in mind and heart as befits *those who enter conversation with God*". Later, he speaks of God's generosity in admitting us into what he calls "intimate conversation" with him.[52] Later still, he has this to say by way of pastoral advice:

> I have said that, although prayer is an intimate conversation of the pious with God, yet reverence and moderation must be kept, lest we give loose rein to miscellaneous requests, and lest we crave more than God allows; further, that we should lift up our minds to a pure and chaste veneration of him, lest God's majesty become worthless for us.[53]

---

48. *Inst* III.xx.29. See also, *Inst* III.xx.5, III.xx.31, *Comm. Acts* 10:2, *CNTC*, 6.284–5. Spykman, *Reformational Theology*, 505, speaks of the heart, in this context, as "the religious unifying center of our entire personhood," and prayer as "the disturbing of the heart before God."

49. *Inst* III.xx.29.

50. Ibid., xx.30. The comment made by Chul-Ha, "A comparison," 68, that Calvin defines prayer as petition "in a literal sense, viz. 'to obtain something' from God" appears too simple to convey the reformer's complex understanding.

51. Ibid., xx.4.

52. Ibid., (emphasis added), *Inst* III.xx.5, respectively.

53. *Inst* III.xx.16.

The metaphor of conversation with God is useful, but the reformer does not want those who read his work to get the wrong idea. God is God, after all. To him belongs glory and honor, and it is proper that we enter into conversation with him humbly, and with considerable thought and care. (See his four rules.) But, then again, as John Kelsay writes, the image does suggest "a relation in which the thoughts of at least two parties are shared,"[54] and that is an important factor in Calvin's thinking.

The person and disposition of a beggar

Two further images that Calvin employs indicate that relationship of shared thought—both convey, in different ways, a sense of weakness and vulnerability in the supplicant and a sense of strength and capability in the God to whom they turn. The first is the image of a beggar approaching someone who is immersed in riches; the other is of a child drawing near to their father. The former he uses sparingly, the latter forms a large part of what he has to say about prayer.

The image of a beggar appears explicitly only once, but is surely implicit in the following representative statements: "It is . . . by the benefit of prayer that we reach those riches which are laid up for us"; "So true is it that we dig up by prayer the treasures that were pointed out by the Lord's gospel," and, "[S]o He will cause us to possess abundance in poverty."[55] Explicitly it appears in the following.

> [I]t follows that only sincere worshippers of God pray aright and are heard. Let each one, therefore, as he prepares to pray be displeased with his own evil deeds, and (something that cannot happen without repentance) *let him take* the person and disposition of a beggar.[56]

The image is a conventional one, of course—Calvin uses it elsewhere,[57] as does Zwingli, for example.[58] But it is noticeable here that the reformer

---

54. Kelsay, "Prayer," 173.

55. *Inst* III.xx.2, III.xx.52, respectively. He speaks of "the weight of our poverty," *Inst* III.xx.28. See also, *Inst* III.xx.44.

56. Ibid., xx.7, (emphasis added).

57. See, for instance, Calvin's sermon on Galatians 1:6–8 where he says that "We should approach God as miserable beggars, if we would be justified in the name of our Lord Jesus Christ," *Sermons*, 37.

58. Zwingli, *True and False Religion*, 3.281, "Our praying to God is nothing else than a begging for aid."

speaks of what appears to be a self-conscious decision, the believer has to "*take* the person and disposition of a beggar" before God. This is the active, self-conscious, self-chosen position of faith. It is an acknowledgment of one's own poverty, together with recognition of divine riches that are found only in Christ.

Wherein lies the poverty? Calvin seems to distinguish three areas of weakness or poverty. First, external to the believer, are the circumstances in which they find themselves. He speaks of "the weight of our present ills," the "troubles, discomforts, fears and trials," the "dangers [that] at every moment threaten."[59] He mentions the resultant misery[60] and, particularly, the anxiety[61] associated with these tribulations[62]—these indicate the fallen-ness of the world in which we dwell, they impinge upon the believer's well-being and certainly ought to drive them to prayer. Not surprisingly, he speaks, too, of Satan in all of this.[63]

Second, the reformer speaks of our nature—he understands weakness to be inherent in fallen humanity. Throughout his lengthy exposition on prayer Calvin characteristically accumulates a list of the faults: we are feeble, blind, stupid, inert and dull, insufficient, lazy, hypocritical, proud, unclean, guilty, ignorant, doubting, ungrateful, unworthy, presumptuous, impudent, and so on. His conclusion appears to be that we are "destitute and devoid of all good things," for only what is corrupt comes forth from us.[64] So, naturally, we approach God in "great shame."[65]

Third, he is conscious that believers are still sinners—he knows the poverty of our behavior and depicts us as "miserably burdened with sins"[66] and "oppressed by [our] evil deeds."[67] But in warm pastoral application, Calvin urges his readers to be assured that "prayers poured out

---

59. See *Inst* III.xx.11, III.xx.7, respectively.
60. Ibid., xx.3, III.xx.12, III.xx.15, III.xx.47.
61. Ibid., xx.4, II.xx.5, III.xx.11, III.xx.34.
62. Ibid., xx.11, III.xx.28. He recognizes in these some who are "unjustly afflicted" and others "wrongly oppressed," *Inst* III.xx.15.
63. Ibid., xx.46.
64. Ibid., xx.1.
65. Ibid., xx.41.
66. *Inst* III.xx.2. See also, *Inst* III.xx.7, III.xx.37.
67. Ibid., xx.11.

by the godly do not depend upon their worthiness."⁶⁸ What are believers to depend on?

*"If he seeks resources . . . he must go outside himself."*⁶⁹

As we have already seen, other reformers affirm that prayer is a means of acknowledging our dependence upon God. Melanchthon particularly stresses our weakness and the weakness of our situation as context for faithful prayer. However, it seems to me that Calvin, while quite clearly continuing the tradition, brings this relationship together in what we might call a more theologically explicit manner at the opening of his lengthy chapter on prayer in the *Institutes*. Affirming how destitute and abject man [sic] is, he comments, "Therefore, if he seeks resources to succor him in his need, *he must go outside himself* and get them elsewhere." He continues,

> For in Christ [the Lord] offers all happiness in place of our misery, all wealth in place of our neediness; in him he opens to us the heavenly treasures . . . [W]hatever we need and whatever we lack is in God, and in our Lord Jesus Christ . . . [I]t remains for us to seek in him, and *in prayers to ask him*, what we have learned to be in him.⁷⁰

These comments imply several things. They are reflective of the fact that Calvin's theological thought and his teaching on prayer, in particular, is essentially grounded in the complex matrix of the divine–human relationship.⁷¹ In Marijn de Kroon's words,

> [P]recisely in this connection [of prayer] the bipolarity of God and man will assume a vivid form. Prayer is the mutual orientation of God and man in practical experience. Existential communion between God and man finds its expression in prayer. . . . It is a back-and-forth movement . . . of the mutuality of God and man.⁷²

---

68. Ibid., xx.7. Stevenson, *Lord's Prayer*, 165, speaks of Calvin's writing on prayer lacking Luther's pastoral zeal. That is certainly not evident in this chapter.

69. Ibid., xx.1.

70. *Inst* III.xx.1, (emphasis added).

71. For an extended treatment of this subject, see Parsons, *Calvin's Preaching*, 27–94.

72. De Kroon, *Honour of God*, 122, 123. Later, he defines prayer as "dialogue with God, the space in which the bipolarity of God and man is experienced," 125. Similarly, Moeller, *Calvin's Doxology*, 130, speaks of prayer as "the fundamental dialogical relationship between us and God". "Prayer," she says, "functions as a microcosm of the dialogue of relationship," 132.

They also imply the radical difference that the Reformer posits between God and humanity, together with the relationship that exists, formed by the gracious initiative of God. Men and women have nothing *in and of themselves* to sustain life and faith—we are utterly devoid of such things, but God is not.

It is Calvin's anthropological understanding that human beings by nature are *dependent beings*.[73] That is so, simply because we are contingent creatures; but this fact itself has been underlined by the presence of sin since the Fall. Yet, says Calvin, God has given us all we need in his Son, Jesus Christ. Therefore, we need to *go outside ourselves*; not in any secondary, random direction, for creatures cannot supply our needs, but solely in the direction of the God who *offers* "all happiness in place of our misery," and *offers* "all wealth in place of our neediness."[74] That is, for Calvin, the strength of our weak praying is not so much God strengthening *us*; but the strength we look for is in God himself, or (more exactly) God in Jesus Christ. The reformer does not posit a simple linear model: we are weak; we need God to strengthen us. For the reformer, it is somehow more complex than that: it is inherent in a faithful relationship with the Lord that we acknowledge *our* weakness and find *his* strength in Christ. Notice, in this context, the following words from Calvin's conclusion on prayer.

> By this ["for thy name's sake"] the saints not only express the end of their prayers but confess themselves unworthy to obtain it unless God seeks the reason *from himself*, and that their confidence of being heard stems *solely from God's nature*.[75]

We might say that prayer "works" because God is God, because the dynamic and logic of prayer is somehow inherent in the nature of the triune God, not in the first instance in the human–divine relationship itself. It is, therefore, the picture not so much of a father holding the child's hand as hesitatingly he learns to walk, but of the father lifting and carrying the child off the ground. The former would imply some ability in us; the latter indicates where Calvin believes strength really to be. Having put

---

73. Bouwsma, "Spirituality," 322–23, speaks of "total dependence". Stevenson, *Lord's Prayer*, 165, speaks of "an Augustinian sense of dependence on God."

74. Later, Calvin speaks of God giving hope to "the utterly miserable," *Inst* III.xx.14, and says that "he will cause us to possess abundance in poverty, and comfort in affliction," *Inst* III.xx.52.

75. Ibid., xx.47, (emphasis added).

it in this way, however, we need to be cautious. Calvin does not entirely deny the believer's own effort that springs from faith and hope. Indeed, he insists that in prayer "all the devotion of the heart should be completely engaged."[76] Nevertheless, even a cursory reading of Calvin suggests that it is the Holy Spirit who prompts this effort or engagement.

"To embrace God's generosity"[77]

Ultimately, of course, Calvin's theology is theocentric,[78] but he paints God as a Father who interacts with and accommodates to his children because his desire is to bless them from his inexhaustible riches. Jon Balserak rightly insists that Calvin affirms "God's willingness to lower himself to the simplicity of his children" and speaks of his "lavish love" and even of his indulgence.[79] As we have already noted, whatever in our poverty we lack is to be found "in God, and in our Lord Jesus Christ."[80] Elsewhere, for instance, the reformer links prayer and the divine fatherhood in the following manner, "We should have no doubt but that God has a mind to welcome us kindly, is prepared to hear our prayers, and is readily inclined to help us."[81]

It is Calvin's teaching that the divine riches are "laid up for us with the Heavenly Father"[82] and by this he is able to personalize the riches (they are put aside *for us*), to recognize them as gift and to associate them fully with our adoption by God. Indeed, that the Lord speaks of himself as Father and allows us to address him as such is indicative of tremendous love, "since no greater feeling of love can be found elsewhere than in the Father."[83] Though we are unworthy of such a father,[84] he shows his kindness, grace, mercy, and abundant goodness to us in the context of prayer. He promises to help his children and urges them to call, anticipating their

---

76. *Inst* III.xx.50.
77. Ibid., xx.14—'*Dei liberalitatem*'.
78. See Bolonesi, "L'Héritage", 121–29, particularly 125.
79. Balserak, "God of Love," 185, 186, 194, respectively.
80. *Inst* III.xx.1.
81. *Comm. Mt.* 6:9, *CNTC* 1.206.
82. *Inst* III.xx.2.
83. *Inst* III.xx.36.
84. Ibid., xx.37.

coming.⁸⁵ More than that, though, he works in them by the Holy Spirit stirring them up to pray, by attracting them,⁸⁶ by prompting, empowering, and even by composing prayer.⁸⁷

But there is yet more to it, and it is here that we come to the crux of Calvin's understanding of prayer. Notice how the following centralizes Christ himself in the midst of our poverty and need.

> Since no man is worthy to present himself to God and come into his sight, the Heavenly Father himself, to free us at once from shame and fear...has given us his Son, Jesus Christ our Lord, to be our advocate... [W]e can confidently come to him, and with such an intercessor, trusting nothing we ask in his name will be denied us, as nothing can be denied to him by the Father.⁸⁸

Later, he speaks of Christ, "by whose intercession the Father is for us rendered gracious and easily entreated."⁸⁹ No wonder that he affirms the divine compassion to be "incomparable."⁹⁰ Not only are the riches that we plead and experience to be found *in* Christ, but also they will not be denied to us because, as Calvin remarks, the Father *cannot* deny the Son.⁹¹

According to Calvin, it is solely because of Christ that God looks favorably upon us as his children. Indeed, it is because of his relationship with his own Son that he "tolerates even our stammering and pardons our ignorance;...as indeed without this mercy there would be no freedom to pray."⁹² He is generous to us, even indulgent.

> For he warns and urges us to seek him in *our every need*, as children are wont to take refuge in the protection of the parents whenever they are *troubled* with any *anxiety*. Besides this, since he saw that we did not even sufficiently perceive how straitened our *poverty* was, what it was fair to request, and what was profitable for us, he also provided for this *ignorance* of ours; and what we had been

---

85. Ibid., xx.13.
86. Ibid., xx.14.
87. Ibid., xx.5.
88. Ibid., xx.17.
89. Ibid., xx.19.
90. Ibid., xx.12.
91. This assertion stems from what the reformer calls "the presumption of faith," *Inst* III.xx.12. See also, *Inst* III.xx.9, III.xx.11.
92. Ibid., xx.16.

lacking to our capacity he himself supplied and made sufficient from his own.[93]

Notice here the italicized words, indicating our poverty and need, and the image emphasizing the Lord's sovereign ability and willingness to help us in our difficulties.

REFLECTIONS

There is a great deal more to say on Calvin's understanding of prayer, of course—his chapter on the subject covers 70 pages of the Battles' English translation. Yet enough has been said to indicate the following brief reflections in line with the intention of this present volume.

First, it is clear that, together with the other leading reformers, Calvin sees humanity in desperate need. Whether we agree in detail with his somewhat negative thesis or not is not really the point. But it is worth reflecting on the fact that men and women demonstrate dependence and a lack in the face of personal and universal problems that face them. Though this makes us vulnerable, we recognize and acknowledge our weakness and poverty.

Second, Calvin is very clear that only by prayer to a God who has already proven himself in Christ to be faithful and capable can we truly seek to have any strength and influence. However, he is also insistent that we draw near to a Father who longs to give, from his riches in Jesus Christ.

According to Calvin, then, our task is first to recognize the truth that it is *only* in Christ that we find our strength—and *never* in ourselves. We are poor, yet he is rich. We are bankrupt, though his treasures are abundant. The reformer says, "[I]t remains for us to seek in him, and *in prayers to ask him*, what we have learned to be in him."[94] That last phrase is so significant. Calvin insists that we have already learned through experience that this is the nature of the relationship we have with our generous God. Calvin's pastoral encouragement concludes with this thought,

> And so [God] will cause us to possess abundance in poverty, and comfort in affliction. For though all things fail us, yet God will never forsake us, who *cannot* disappoint the expectation and patience of his people.[95]

---

93. *Inst* III.xx.34, (emphasis added). See also, *Inst* III.xx.36.
94. Ibid., xx.1, (emphasis added).
95. *Inst* III.xx.52, (emphasis added).

9

In the power of the Lamb—and of the Lion

Power and weakness in the early theology of Karl Barth

Michael O'Neil

INTRODUCTION

Assessing Karl Barth's understanding of strength, power, and weakness is not a simple undertaking—not only because he wrote so much, but also because strength, power, and weakness as such are not themes he directly addressed. Rather, his treatment of these particular matters arises in his work in the context of reflection about more substantial theological topics. To say this, however, is not to suggest that Barth's somewhat ad hoc reflections and comments on the issues and problems of power and weakness are of no value. Indeed, we can learn that from early in his career Barth had quite firm ideas about these issues (which remained more or less consistent over the course of his career), and that his theological reflections on these matters were primarily oriented toward shaping the practice of the Christian community in its engagement with the wider society. As such, Barth's reflections remain valuable for anyone engaged in the conduct of Christian ministry. Certainly this has been the case in my own ministry as a pastor of a local congregation, where Barth's reflections have contributed significantly to the way in which we practice our ministry—more about this later.

The essay begins by examining how Barth understood the concept and reality of power in the period 1915–1920. These are the immediate years after Barth's initial break with the liberal heritage during which the fundamental outlines of his theology were being laid. Following this overview, I consider how the implications of Barth's understanding of power find expression in his understanding of ecclesial practice, before concluding with a brief reflection on the particular nature of Barth's thought regarding these matters.

THE YOUNG BARTH'S UNDERSTANDING OF POWER

Examination of Barth's early works indicates that his thought about power involved several primary categories. First, Barth is concerned that God's power is correctly understood. Second, he insists that over against God's power there stand other alien powers that remain hostile and in opposition to the power, kingdom, and purpose of God. Third, Barth is also insistent that humanity cannot, in and of its own power, establish the kingdom of God that is peculiarly God's concern. This does not mean, however, that people can and should do nothing with regard to the kingdom, for finally, Barth can speak of the empowering of God's people in such a way that the kingdom of God comes to expression among them and advances historically toward the consummation that God is preparing for his creation.

Understanding the power of God

The theological crisis endured by Barth in mid-1914 as a result of the *Kriegstheologie* ("war theology") of his theological mentors and their support of the war policies of Kaiser Wilhelm is well known. If the theology ultimately deriving from Schleiermacher and grounded in human experience could be used in support of a war, which for Barth, was so alien to the being and purposes of God, it must be seen for what it is—theologically and ethically bankrupt. As George Hunsinger has noted, it was intolerable for Barth that the sovereign God and his Word should be misused by the contemporary church to support the political and social horror of World War I.[1]

In fact, for Barth it had become evident that the god of nineteenth century theological idealism was not really *God* at all.[2] Rather than the

---

1. Hunsinger, "Conclusion," 200–201.
2. A great part of Barth's theological career was directed toward overturning the idealistic notion that God is a human projection, a "grand idea" that brings meaning and

In the power of the Lamb—and of the Lion

transcendent God of the New Testament who stands for the ultimate transformation of all things, many of Barth's contemporaries had chosen to believe that God

> is that which binds man with necessity to his nature and to the general laws of nature, which throws him into the struggle for existence.... Faith then means the courageous taking up of the struggle for existence under the given conditions *and* incidentally the sad attempt to find meaning in the nonsense of life that arises from this.[3]

Under the impulse of this theology there arose a "religious veneration for nature and modern culture."[4] Barth asks,

> *Why not*? God speaks everywhere. But without ... noticing it, everything that existed began to be surrounded with a peculiar halo of religion—the State and the Hohenzollerns and the Prussian military, the German citizen with his incomparable "efficiency," capitalism, trade, enterprise, in short, the whole Germany of Kaiser Wilhelm.[5]

Against this idealistic conception of God, Barth found in the "strange new world of the Bible" that *God is God*. Drawing on the lives and experiences of Johann and Christoph Blumhardt, Barth began to develop a distinctive theology grounded in the sovereign aseity or independence of God.[6] From the Blumhardts Barth learned that the whole of existence

---

unity to human life, a postulate needed to secure some form of ultimate moral authority and so on. Rather, Barth argued that God is not some idea—whatever form that may take as we seek to co-opt the concept of God for our own purposes—but God is who he has revealed himself to be in the person and activity of Jesus Christ. It is *there* that the living God may be truly known, and it is illegitimate to seek to conceive of God in some other fashion than he has revealed himself in Christ.

3. Barth, "Past," 37, (original emphasis).

4. Ibid.

5. Ibid., 37–38, (original emphasis).

6. According to Timothy Gorringe, Christoph Blumhardt was Barth's most important theological teacher, despite the fact that he was not a theologian! Gorringe-"Eschatology," 93. Gorringe also says of their influence: "[T]hey lived the affirmation 'God is God' which was at the heart of Barth's early theology, and they did so in the midst of society without ever giving politics priority over faith." (See Gorringe, *Karl Barth*, 34.) James Smart, *Divided Mind*, 61, agrees: "The Blumhardts in Bad Boll had recaptured in actual life the eschatological dimension of the New Testament faith." For a brief overview of the Blumhardts' lives and ministries see Newell, "Blumhardt," 76–77. For a more extensive account of the Blumhardts, including a collection of 19 sermons from Christoph Blumhardt, see Lejeune, *Christoph Blumhardt*. For Barth's own account of their lives,

occurs within the great circle of divine sovereignty. This sovereignty is not understood as raw power, however, because God is gracious, "always the life-bringing, wonderful God who touches us also so that we have hope for our own life."[7] Further, God's kingdom does not come in destructive power or punitive judgment as though God's intent is the damnation of the world and humanity, but in the "unutterable compassion" of God's triumphant grace revealed in the saving events of the gospel.[8] Thus, even in this early period of his career, Barth understands the power of God in Christological terms. It is the power demonstrated in the life and ministry of Jesus, taking the form of Isaiah's Servant and dwelling in lowliness.

The "powers"

Second, over against the power of God are other powers and forces hostile to God. These powers have their genesis in the independence of the human will as it asserts itself against the sovereign reign of God. It was and is this human quest for autonomy in relation to God that sets in motion the destructive powers of sin and death.[9] In his first commentary on Romans, Barth refers to the reign of sin and death as a

> perverted, retrogressive, centrifugal, disintegrating movement . . . a power of disorganisation [which] deranges, makes unhealthy, undermines and disintegrates the organisms in their vitality, functions, and finally in their existence.[10]

Death is an alien power that drives everything away from its centre in God.[11] In his famous Tambach lecture of September 1919 Barth insists that "society is now really ruled by its own logos; say rather by a whole

---

thought and significance see Barth, *Protestant Theology*, 629–39.

7. Barth, "Action," 25–26. Note that the citation is Christoph Blumhardt's.

8. Lejeune, *Christoph Blumhardt*, 161. Cf. Torrance, *Karl Barth*, 36.

9. This is the perspective of Barth in his first commentary on Romans (see, for example, Barth, *Der Römerbrief*, 177–78. In his review of Blumhardt, however, Barth cites Blumhardt apparently with approval: "The present war has been instigated by such forces hostile to God and men. The Bible calls all these things together *Satan*." See Barth, "Action," 30.

10. Barth, *Romans I*, 176.

11. Henry, *Early Development*, 128.

In the power of the Lamb—and of the Lion

pantheon of its own hypostases and powers,"¹² so that God's people "are engaged in Life's revolt against the powers of death that inclose it."¹³

When Barth makes reference to such powers he has in mind the primary powers of sin and death, but these also find expression as social ideologies such as monarchy, liberalism, capitalism, patriotism, and militarism, and as social problems such as alcoholism, poverty, class strife and the like.¹⁴ Barth's great criticism of the contemporary church was that it had been co-opted by the secular powers to legitimize national ideologies and serve agendas and priorities that were fundamentally alien to its proper being, and that led inexorably to the devastating capitulation of the church to Kaiser Wilhelm's war agenda in 1914. The inability of the modern church to stand apart from and against German nationalism was, for Barth, an indication of its theological weakness and thus its cultural assimilation to the dominant cultural powers. At the root of the terrible weakness of the church in the face of these alien powers was *theological* weakness, which it tried to compensate for by striving after secular power. Ironically, the church that sought social, cultural, and political relevance, affirmation and power became a plaything in the hands of the secular powers and was rendered powerless against the powers of death, which so devastated early twentieth century Europe. Barth provides a description of the role church and religion had come to play vis-a[set grave over a]-vis these powers.

> Consider . . . the religion of Bismarck, which provides the most magnificent example of the way the world pleases itself and wins the applause of the representatives of religion. Therefore Bismarck is the best-known advocate of the indispensability of religion for all earthly effectiveness. He had religion simply in order to keep his hands free for secular work. . . . His religion was erected on the basis of his self-esteem. Moreover, it was something which he had reduced to the size of a personal plaything and which he could lay aside at any time. But the fact that he could play with it and occasionally had a Christian notion was sufficient in the eyes of the modern advocates of Christianity to make him a Christian, even a model Christian . . . Thus Christianity has now been handed over

---

12. Barth, *Word*, 279–80.
13. Ibid., 291.
14. See, for example, Barth, *Word*, 19–20; cf. 272 and Barth, *Romans I*, 509.

to every holder of power. So cheap is today's canonization in the Christian heaven.[15]

Human powerlessness

In face of the conflict that exists between the kingdom of God and powers of death at work in the world, Barth insists God's people cannot and must not attempt to establish the kingdom of God in their own power. The dawning kingdom is not a human possibility, nor a development within existing life possibilities, but the in-breaking of divine power creating a new possibility of life.[16] Because this is so, the kingdom of God cannot be identified with any human movement, including especially the church, but also other groups and movements such as idealism, morality, pacifism, or social democracy.[17]

In a reference to the early days of his own pastoral career, Barth recalls the triumphal attitude of the church and religion in 1909–12 which had become an "immensely prominent power." He alludes to the publication of the influential *Die Religion in Geschichte und Gegenwart* (*Religion in the Past and the Present*), the student movement of John Mott, the World Missions Conference in Edinburgh in 1910, and the International Socialist Congress in Basle in 1912.[18] Although each of these proclaimed the strength of the church, Barth's complaint was that God was expected to crown the valiant efforts of humanity with his blessing. The problem, however, was that

> Everything was always settled without God.... The fear of the Lord did not stand objectively at the beginning of our wisdom.... From God's standpoint that is more of a hindrance than a help, since it continues to delude people about the need for the coming of his kingdom. Our "movements" then stand directly in the way of God's movement; our "causes" hinder his cause, the richness of our "life" hinders the tranquil growth of the divine life in the world.... The collapse of our cause must demonstrate for once that God's cause is exclusively his own. That is where we stand today.[19]

---

15. Barth, *Theology*, 67–68.
16. Busch, *Karl Barth*, 100.
17. Barth, *Romans I*, 42.
18. Ibid., 400–1.
19. Ibid., 401–402, original emphasis.

Barth rejected, therefore, the ecclesial triumphalism of the pre-war era, and with it, all forms of hero worship. He railed incessantly against the triumphant posture of the modern church that sought to possess the divine and bring it under its own management.[20] Barth considered it axiomatic that humanity could not in and of its own power establish the kingdom of God—this was peculiarly God's own concern. This lack of power was not considered a curse by Barth, however, but rather a blessing, for humanity was also freed from the impossible responsibility of having to establish the kingdom. For this reason he insisted that

> religion's blind and vicious habit of asserting eternally that it possesses something, feasts upon it, and distributes it, must sometime cease, if we are ever to have an honest, a fierce, seeking, asking, and knocking.[21]

Empowered by God

That humanity stands powerless against the powers, and is likewise powerless to establish the kingdom, was not an occasion of despair for Barth. On the contrary, Barth insists that his message is one of hope, grounded in the sovereign purpose of God revealed in Christ.[22] In this period of his career Barth followed Blumhardt and J. T. Beck to construct a theological ontology in which the coming of Jesus introduced a change into history, a movement of his presence and reign that will not cease until all is fulfilled. "With Jesus," says Barth, "the good actually began already, the good to which mankind and nature alike are called, which towers right into our own time also and goes forward toward a revelation and a consummation."[23]

In Christ, then, God has initiated a *movement*, one in which *God* himself is in eschatological procession. That is, God himself is advancing in history towards the ultimate consummation of all things. Barth conceives of this procession in terms of actualistic breakthroughs, so that while it is ever pressing toward the realization of the kingdom of God, its appearance in the historical world is often in hiddenness, and hence it is not "a state of affairs, nor an actuality, not a stable 'reality!' . . . it is a

---

20. See, for example, Barth's devastating critique of Friedrich Naumann in Barth, "Past," 35–40.
21. Barth, *Word*, 86–87.
22. Ibid., 275.
23. Barth, "Action," 32.

matter of a course, a movement, a struggling and a triumphing."[24] Such a procession leaves traces in the ongoing march of history, but which cannot be identified with any institution or cultural development within history, including the organized churches. It is composed of those who are gathered by the power of the resurrection when they obey the gospel—"an international people of God."[25] This company already stands in the movement of God.

> No longer under judgement, but under grace, no longer in sin but in righteousness, no longer in death, but in life. That is the course of salvation which the power of God wills to take and will take, now with us and someday with the whole world. Now with us![26]

Barth's "now with us" indicates his belief that even now, during which time the divine eschatological procession goes forth predominantly in hiddenness, the community of faith serves as a proleptic witness and paradigm of God's intent for the world at large. In this community the righteousness of God will come into visibility, albeit in an actualistic form. "On earth as in heaven," Barth says, "God's work has begun to come to pass. In the midst of the world of flesh, an enclave of God's world has arisen."[27] For those who are in Christ, the possibility of doing the good has become a "genuine reality" on account of the "power of God which appeared in the life of Christ" appearing once more "in us as the members of his body."[28]

It is clear, then, that there remains a possibility of a life empowered by God, but this is a divine rather than a human possibility. Genuine Christian existence is being caught up, grasped and led by the Spirit in the eschatological movement and procession of God. It is not something a person "possesses," nor is it something grounded in the Christian themselves. Rather, when we respond in faith to the revelation that lays hold of us, our lives are inserted into a new order, an altered world-context.[29] In Christ, believers have been placed under "the creative power of the good,"

---

24. Barth, *Romans I*, 189–90.
25. Ibid., 21.
26. Ibid., 20.
27. Ibid., 303.
28. Ibid., 303–4.
29. Ibid., 206–7.

and as they "abide in the 'body of Christ'... the power of the resurrection inaugurated in him" comes to expression in them.[30]

THE WEAKNESS AND STRENGTH OF THE CHURCH

These four categories of thought regarding the concept of power have important implications for the way in which Barth considered the being and activity of the church during this period of his career. Again, although he did not develop his thought explicitly in terms of strength and weakness, his theology is not without some important developments in these directions. The first and most important of these implications concerns the notion of "waiting and hastening" (*warten und eilen*), which Barth developed in his interaction with Christoph Blumhardt. The second is his understanding of the way in which the church was to represent God in the world.

Waiting and hastening

In September 1916 Barth penned "Auf das Reich Gottes warten," a review of devotional materials that had recently been published by Blumhardt.[31] In the article Barth refers to Blumhardt's work as an "important and beautiful book," and says of it, "for me it is the most direct and penetrating Word from God into the need of the world that the war years have produced so far."[32] In a statement that reveals an important shift in his own thought, Barth confessed appreciation for Blumhardt's book saying that "our cause, our hope, is at the moment served better with prayers than with treatises. Our dialectics have come to a dead end."[33]

The cause Barth speaks of is religious socialism. He had originally written the article for inclusion in a paper published by Leonhard Ragaz, a leading figure in the Swiss religious socialist movement. Ragaz rejected the article on account of its "quietist" position. In light of the devastation—war, turmoil, and the movement towards revolution—that had befallen Europe, the response of Ragaz to Barth's article is perhaps understandable. Nevertheless, although Barth portrays the church in terms

---

30. Barth, *Romans I*, 263–64.

31. In *Der Freie Schweizer Arbeiter*, 15th and 22nd September, 1916. The translation used here is from Barth, "Action".

32. Barth, "Action," 19.

33. Ibid., 22.

that speak of "weakness," this weakness is only apparent and the position outlined is actually one of strength.

The brief article outlines the major contours of Barth's new theological understanding, including the sovereign independence of God, the prominent eschatological horizon, and the divine procession toward the eschaton that began with the coming of Jesus and his resurrection from the dead. While the actual fulfillment of the divine purpose belongs to God alone, his people may pray, and in praying may become participants in the new creation. According to Barth, with Blumhardt's emphasis on prayer "we are face to face with the innermost of his thought. . . . *[T]his living waiting on God for the world* . . . constitutes the nerve center of this book."[34] It is this "living waiting on God for the world" that Barth wants to commend to his readers:

> pleading unceasingly and unwaveringly before God and to God "Thy Kingdom come!" and waiting and hastening with men toward this coming. *Is that not the highest and most promising thing a man can do at this moment?*[35]

For Barth, this waiting signifies not inactivity, but is, rather, "in its essence, revolutionary."[36] First, and most significantly, waiting means invocation—calling on God.[37] The reason we call upon God is simply that the establishing of the kingdom is pre-eminently *his* concern. To cry out to God is to seek the divine establishing of his kingdom in the entire world. Prayer that cries for the action of God, however, finds itself caught up in a divine movement that instigates responsive human action. Prayer, then, is neither the cessation, nor the end of, human action, but its beginning and proper foundation. Thus Barth says, "When we 'hasten and wait' toward God like this, the consummation is prepared, coming from God himself." Waiting for the kingdom of God, then, "means just the opposite of sitting comfortably and going along with the old order of things."[38]

Second, this waiting is revolutionary because it functions to liberate a person "from the powers of this world, from the trust in its strength and

---

34. Barth, "Action," 34, (emphasis added).
35. Ibid. 23, (emphasis added).
36. Ibid., 40.
37. Ibid., 34.
38. Ibid., 40.

from the fear of its forces."[39] Although this notion of the freedom and independence of the church will find its sharpest expression as a critical tool during the Barmen period, it appears likely that Barth is already moving in this direction.[40] His emphasis on waiting in this article functions to direct the Christian community to God as the primary focus of its activity, so that all other activity in which it engages may be a faithful expression of its own integrity and identity. In this way, the church is freed from its debilitating enculturation to become a genuinely prophetic voice of an alternative way and an alternative world. Thus, the apparent weakness of the church—its refusal to be co-opted by other movements and powers which promise a new and better world, its prioritizing of prayer and waiting over the urgency of activity—is actually its strength.

Representing God in the world

Barth also found in Blumhardt one who could do what most others could not: namely "represent God's cause in the world yet not wage war on the world, love the world and yet be completely faithful to God."[41] One aspect of Barth's theology in this period of his career is the prominent critique he levels against the bourgeois nature of contemporary Christianity, particularly its individualism, and any form of privatized, interior or wholly eschatological understandings of God's identity and purpose in salvation. While it is true that the Bible teaches that those turning to God will inherit a kingdom of blessedness in the next life, and may experience even in this world, inner comfort and peace, Barth asks,

---

39. Lejeune, *Christoph Blumhardt*, 78.

40. See Holloway, *Barth*, 5–8, for a copy of the Barmen declaration. Although the entire declaration is a theological assertion of the church's freedom and independence, certain statements stand out—the first thesis, "Jesus Christ, as he is attested for us in Holy Scripture, is the one Word of God which we have to hear and which we have to trust and obey in life and in death;" thesis two, "Jesus Christ . . . is God's mighty claim upon our whole life. Through him befalls us a joyful deliverance from the godless fetters of this world for a free, grateful service to his creatures. We reject the false doctrine, as though there were areas of our life in which we would not belong to Jesus Christ, but to other lords;" the third thesis, "The Christian Church is the congregation of the brethren in which Jesus Christ acts presently as the Lord . . . [I]t has to testify that . . . it is solely his property, and that it lives and wants to live solely from his comfort and from his direction in the expectation of his appearance."

41. Barth, "Action," 22.

> Is *that* all of God and his new world, of the meaning of the Bible? . . . that here and there specimens of men like you and me might be "converted," find inner "peace," and by a redeeming death go someday to "heaven." Is *that* all? . . . Is not God—greater than that?[42]

When Barth turns to the question "Who is God?" he utilizes the trinitarian formula to provide a positive statement of the divine identity. Nevertheless, he develops his statement in such a way as to repudiate dualistic and privatized forms of Christian thought and existence. Thus,

> Who is God? The heavenly Father! But the heavenly Father even upon *earth*, and upon earth really the *heavenly* Father. He will not allow life to be split into a "here" and "beyond". . . . He purposes naught but the establishment of a new *world*.[43]

In a similar manner, God is the Son, not merely as "mediator for my soul," but as the redeemer and mediator of the whole world. The events narrated in Scripture about him are the "glorious beginning of a new *world*."[44] Finally, God also is "the Spirit in his believers."[45] By means of a hymn-citation Barth affirms that it is the Spirit by whom "we own the Son" and that "through quiet hearts forever flows." But once more he is unwilling to allow this to be the limit or extent of the divine activity. Thus he also affirms that

> God is also that spirit (that is to say, that love and good will) which will and must break forth from quiet hearts into the world outside, that it may be manifest, visible, comprehensible: behold the tabernacle of God is with men! The Holy Spirit makes a new heaven and a new earth, and, therefore, new men, new families, new relationships, new politics. . . . The Holy Spirit establishes the righteousness of heaven in the midst of the unrighteousness of earth and will not stop nor stay until all that is dead has been brought to life and a new *world* has come into being. This is within the Bible. It is within the Bible for us. For it we were baptized. Oh, that we dared in faith to take what grace can offer us![46]

---

42. Barth, *Word*, 47, (original emphasis).
43. Ibid., 48–49, (original emphasis).
44. Ibid., 49, (original emphasis).
45. Ibid.
46. Ibid., 49–50.

In the power of the Lamb—and of the Lion

In this brief and potent conclusion to his lecture on the strange world in the Bible, Barth makes clear that the purpose of the Father is nothing less than the establishment of a new *world*. As such, the coming of Jesus must be understood as nothing less than the commencement of the new *world*, while the activity of the Spirit is nothing less than the making visible of the new *world* purposed by the Father and inaugurated in the Son, precisely through his regenerating activity in the old world.

Barth's emphasis on the "worldliness" of the triune God in this section reiterates his contention against forms of dualistic Christianity that would separate faith from life, the inner from the outer, the heavenly from the earthly, and the future from the present. God's love is directed toward the *world*, not the soul or even the church—his purpose is all-encompassing. Indeed, in face of the devastating realities of life in this world, God does not bless us "with the power of the church but with the power of life and resurrection."[47] Barth, therefore, will brook no theology, ideology or spirituality that would deny, despise or forsake the world. But it is equally clear that Barth does *not* dismiss the church, as such. What he rejects are bloodless or anemic forms of Christian existence, or a church grounded in its own life and power. The Christian community is an essential aspect in the coming of the new world. "For [this] we were baptized," says Barth. It is the harbinger of the new world, not as responsible for its emergence, but in the sense that it announces and indicates the approach of the new world in and through its being and life. Through the Spirit's activity in its midst, it makes visible and comprehensible the new world in the midst of the old. The "new men, new families, new relationships, new politics," which are indicative of the new world, are to be found and seen here first of all.

Barth believes that the people of God are to "represent" God and his goodness in this world, sowing justice, and crying out against sin and death, opposing self-will, greed, and all evil.[48]

> [The people of God] gather round Christ not for their own blessedness *but for the redemption of the world*, comparable to the servant of God in Deutero-Isaiah. They are to represent God's cause in a

---

47. Barth, *Word*, 49.

48. Barth, "Action," 27, 36, 44. For further evidence that Barth thought the church ought to maintain a "prophetic" stance towards the world deriving from life in accordance with "the norms of the world of the gospel," see his letter to Thurnysen (October 5, 1915) in Smart, *Revolutionary Theology*, 33–35.

special way and in doing this they are encompassed by God's love in a special way too.[49]

Importantly, this shows that for Barth, Christian life, far from being an idealistic or amorphous entity, has a definite shape and tendency. He utilizes the image of the Isaianic Servant to indicate the "special way" in which the church is to "represent God's cause." The church's existence is not for itself, but it is *in* the world, *for* the world. The posture of the church toward the world is that of the Servant.

In his first commentary on Romans, Barth insists that the life of God's people must reflect the movement of divine grace, which is a movement *from below*. For Barth, there can be no neutrality in this.

> You belong under all circumstances to the common folk.... God is certainly a God of the Jews *and* the heathen, but not a God of the powerful *and* the lowly, but rather, one-sidedly, a God of the lowly; not a God of the great *and* the small, but rather recklessly, a God of the small.... The movement of the Kingdom of God within social and cultural conflicts is ... fundamentally and one-sidedly a movement from below. Those who participate in it must ... be willing to stand below where everything depends on God. I can certainly become a Jew to the Jews and a Greek to the Greeks, but not a lord to the lords.... Where idols are erected, I may not be present. Over against everything that wants to be great I must take the standpoint of the small people, with whom God begins.[50]

The nature, therefore, of Christian action that reflects the being and activity of God will show itself as such by its echoing of the divine preference for the lowly, over against the mighty. For Barth, the only legitimate dependency is dependence upon God, which is the foundation of true liberty. Against the backdrop of revolutionary movements in his own milieu, Barth proclaims the revolution of Christ: "What Christ brings in fact is revolution, the dissolution of all dependencies. For the dependency into which Christ transfers us is precisely freedom in God."[51]

---

49. Barth, "Action in Waiting," 37, (emphasis added).
50. Ibid., 490, (original emphasis).
51. Ibid., 196.

In the power of the Lamb—and of the Lion

A Strength Revealed in Weakness

From the foregoing discussion, it is evident that Barth has a dialectical approach to issues of power and weakness during this phase of his career, in the sense that he does not reject either power or weakness in themselves—but is able to affirm both. Certainly Barth deplored the manner in which the church of his early career had become co-opted by the prevailing powers of the time, and by the manner in which it sought to *be* a power among the other powers of the culture. Against the organized liberal and pietist churches Barth sought to encourage the emergence of a *living* church, a concrete fellowship of believers gathered around the resurrected Lord Jesus Christ waiting for and hastening toward the coming of the kingdom of God by their obedience to "the command of the moment,"[52] in preference to the maintenance or growth of the institutional or hierarchical church. Christian existence is necessarily corporate, a fellowship of faith, love and freedom that stands in dependence upon God and in solidarity with the poor and oppressed.

Yet it is also evident that although Barth also deplores the notion of "power-in-itself," and the idea of a church grounded in its own power, he does not eschew the concept and reality of power altogether and so adopt an ideology of weakness. Although the church is to adopt the posture of the Isaianic Servant and so to enter into solidarity with the poorer, weaker and more vulnerable of society over against the mighty, it is not thereby rendered *weak*. Indeed, though real, its weakness is yet only apparent because in its human, institutional and cultural weakness, the church that is grounded in and oriented toward God alone is sustained and borne along in the triumphant eschatological divine procession toward the dawning new world. Because the power of the resurrection comes to expression in and through the people of God, the community becomes the harbinger of the new world, a cruciform witness, which yet reveals glimpses of the new age of the resurrection. Thus the weakness of the church as it seeks its dependence upon God alone is its strength, a strength revealed in weakness.

In bringing this chapter to a close, it is profitable to note that Barth's early reflections on these matters continue throughout his career. For the entirety of his career Barth will insist that the notion of power-in-itself is a demonic notion, that alien powers exert their will and influence in the

---

52. For Barth's early discussion of the divine command see, Barth, *Romans I*, 484–86, 524–25.

world generally, and that God's people are called to resist these powers by binding themselves solely to the one Lord who is their creator and redeemer. He ever refutes the possibility that the church or the believer can be self-grounded, while certainly acknowledging that they may be empowered. He will continue to emphasize the centrality of prayer, and of the primacy and immediacy of the divine command for ethical existence. His theology will continue to exhibit an orientation towards socialist praxis and the solidarity of the church with the weaker and poorer members of society. Yet in all this he will not capitulate towards an ideology of weakness. In his most sustained reflections on the theme of power as it pertains to humanity, Barth rather boldly affirms the will for life as "the will for power." He goes on to describe his meaning:

> We mean by this man's determination to make use of his capacity, to come to grips with the advancements and hindrances of life which impinge upon him from without, exploiting the former and resisting or at least enduring the latter. . . . As God calls man to life, as and so long as He addresses him as a living person, He wills that man should not neglect this capacity, the power, strength and force which he has been given, but affirm, will and accept it.[53]

In typical fashion, however, Barth is careful to delineate how this power may be recognized and distinguished from that power which is "from below." It is the power that can only be received as a gift and as such exercised in humility and with gratitude. It is power that serves, elevates, and liberates those around us and that enables us to be faithful and obedient in our own place.[54] Finally, it is power that is Christologically determined for

> The power of God Himself, reflected in the power which He gives to man, is the power of Jesus Christ, and therefore the power of the Lamb as well as the Lion, of the cross as well as the resurrection, of humiliation as well as exaltation, of death as well as life. . . . For some it will almost always be only the one, for others only the other, but usually it will be both for all of us in rapid alternation. . . . Either way it is grace. . . . It will not be a rigid but a fluid or flexible will, not merely in the direction in which we normally look when we speak of the will for power, but also in the other direction in which strength is made perfect in weakness.[55]

53. Barth, *Church Dogmatics* III/4, 390.
54. Ibid., 392–96.
55. Ibid., 397.

In the power of the Lamb—and of the Lion

REFLECTIONS

Finally, how relevant are Barth's reflections on power, strength, and weakness for the practice of church and ministry in the contemporary context? Perhaps the first aspect to consider is his implicit warning against seeking to *become* a power in the secular arena, particularly in light of the devastating capitulation of the church to the cultural powers in Barth's own time. As election campaigns in Western countries escalate it is evident, as in Australia as I write, that politicians from both major parties court those sectors of the church they believe will return them increased votes. In such an environment it is imperative that the church not be seduced with the prospect of increased influence, access and power. Barth would steadfastly remind us that we are to be bound to one Lord and are to find our hope and strength in him alone.

A second implication of Barth's reflections is that it is not the role of the church to establish the kingdom, build the kingdom, "win our city for God" or any of the many other rhetorical exhortations that are often heard, especially in evangelical churches. The establishing of the kingdom belongs to God, the role of the church being to witness to God's kingdom and its presence in our midst, a witness that will often take the form of the Isaianic Servant. It is appropriate, therefore, to resist a triumphalist demeanor on the one hand, and a passive or defeatist attitude on the other, in the knowledge that the advance of the kingdom is *God's* mission before it is our mission. In this we may be hopeful, trusting that God is *already* active in our midst and our community, if we but have eyes to see. His kingdom is *already* advancing in and among the people of our community. He is *already* at work and invites and leads his church to participate with him in the work of the harvest. A corollary of this, of course, is the requirement that we do follow God into an active interaction and engagement with the world, refusing to settle for any form of privatized religion or cultural isolation.

This leads to a third implication of Barth's reflections—his insistence that corporate prayer, worship, and discernment lie at the heart of all genuine Christian mission. This is the meaning of his emphasis on "waiting and hastening." We are to wait prayerfully on God, seeking to discern the directions and moments of his appearing and movement in the arena of our service, and then hasten with all the might he gives us toward it, following his movement as Israel followed the pillar of cloud through the wilderness. This is the true strength of the church in its ministry toward the surrounding world. In this way we may become participants in his eschatological procession. In this way we may be led by the Spirit who makes

> a new heaven and a new earth, and, therefore, new men, new families, new relationships, new politics.... The Holy Spirit establishes the righteousness of heaven in the midst of the unrighteousness of earth and will not stop nor stay until all that is dead has been brought to life and a new world has come into being. This is within the Bible. It is within the Bible for us. For it we were baptized. Oh, that we dared in faith to take what grace can offer us![56]

---

56. Barth, *Word of God*, 49–50.

10

God's vulnerable strength

Omnipotence as love

Clark Pinnock

INTRODUCTION

MY CONTRIBUTION TO THE theme, strength in weakness in relation to ministry, is to correct a widespread error wherein the almightiness of God is exaggerated and the weakness of God is overlooked with harmful results. Strength in weakness is not a riddle over which to puzzle, it is God's truth about the world. Because the universe is a project of love, weakness and vulnerability are unavoidable in it. Love is a delicate thing and requires the omnipotence of love to nourish it, and strength in weakness to sustain it, as the cross of Jesus so clearly shows. The reason we speak here about the ministries of strength in weakness is because God in his ministries toward us adopts this very pattern.[1]

DIVINE SELF-LIMITATION

The Apostle's Creed begins with the phrase, "I believe in God, the Father Almighty, maker of heaven and earth." The language is familiar and the words rattle off our tongues smoothly, but one should not be surprised when I say that calling God the Father "almighty" without qualification is

---

1. Scholarship over the last century has placed strong emphasis on divine transcendence with less concern about divine immanence. See Fretheim, *God*, 22. I penned an earlier version of this paper as "Constrained by Love."

not the most apt expression to use when God so often "retreats," if that is the right word, in order to give humans room to flourish. So often in the Bible God deploys his power in ways that make him appear vulnerable. No doubt God could win when challenged by overpowering the rebellious partner but God does not seem to want to "win" that way. God does not seem to want that kind of "victory." His is not raw power, the power that makes everything else surrender. It is greater than that. God's power can call the world into being but also sustain delicate relationships. Not total control glorifies God, but shared sovereignty is what draws us to him. His power is not greater in proportion to what it controls and makes dependent but in proportion to how it loves.

The definitive image of God surrendering his power is the man hanging on a cross. God's Son did not come to be served but to serve and give his life as a ransom for many (Mk 10:42). What an unheard-of criterion for measuring divine power! In the Son, the Father found "glory" in his suffering not by smashing his foes to dust (Jn 12:28). The God of Jesus seems to have chosen not to overcome human rebellion by compelling obedience, as if that would accomplish anything useful. It would only demolish the integrity of the creatures to whom he had granted freedom. No, our God has chosen a harder path to salvation, the path of winning sinners over through the experience of the pain that they were heaping upon him. God has decided to deploy his power as love and to suffer for and with the creation, all because he wants freely chosen loving relationships. For this God made himself weak and powerless in the world.

What a paradox this is. God the Almighty "self-limits" for our sakes! He shows himself to be "great enough" to allow himself be constrained by love. How very different from the self-centered deities of this world that can think of nothing but themselves and cannot enter into relationships lest their perfection be diminished! Professor Thomas F. Torrance (on the other hand) writes of "the openness of God for the world that he made." He exults in the God revealed in Jesus Christ who shares our lot and makes himself poor to make us rich. We have an "almighty" God willing to restrict his power and risk the pain of rejection and loss. This is a God who one can really love.[2]

The notion of a voluntary divine restraint is a category that arises from the nature of the divine project. In a world where loving relations

---

2. Berkhof, *Christian Faith*, chapter 21. On the self-limitation of God, consult Olson, *Mosaic*, 129–32; Torrance, *Space*, 74–75.

are central, God is "required" (in a certain sense) to exercise it. It will be necessary for God to self-restrain, self-constrain, self-limit, if this kind of world is to exist. Otherwise it would be crushed. This insight has been neglected in classical theology where God's transcendence (his being very far from us) tends to eclipse God's condescendence (his being very close to us). In a one-sided emphasis, the attributes of transcendence have been over-noticed while the attributes of condescendence have been understudied.[3] This has resulted in the image of an omnipotent God and an impotent humanity omitting the "strength in weakness" dimension that one sees in the cross of Jesus Christ. Unlimited power fosters subservience, not fellowship, and that is not what God wants. God is unwilling (as it were) to be almighty without us. God wants covenant partners, not slaves. He has decided to be with us in faithful ways and to be involved in historical passage at cost to himself.[4]

This action could be called a "kenotic" act of self-restraint. It is voluntary on God's part and does not reflect any limitation in God or any ontological diminishment. God surrenders power because he does not want to squelch the creature. God is moved by love to restrain the divine power, temporarily and voluntarily, out of respect for the integrity of creatures, even creatures whose activities fall far short of God's purposes. Because God wants to be involved in creation and give the creature some "say so" in the flow of history, he restricts (to take the most familiar example) the full exercise of his power. This is not (as I have said) a renunciation of ontological powers but a way of exercising these very powers in love. Not wanting to compel love, which would hardly be worth having, God seeks, mostly by persuasion, to draw us to himself. God thus restrains himself in accordance with the way he has chosen to relate to the world. In light of the divine project, we must speak of certain restraints that God accepts for the sake of relationships with humans. Personal relationships require, if love is to be mutual, that God not force himself upon us, thereby subverting the precarious and vulnerable nature of love. E. Frank Tupper writes,

---

3. Wolfhart Pannenberg reviews the problem of hellenistic influences in the early traditions in "Appropriation," 119–83. To avoid misunderstanding, open theologians must take care not to exaggerate the negative and minimise the positive side of these influences.

4. Polkinghorne, *Work*, is very informative. His own chapter in the book touches on four areas of divine self-restraint, employing the metaphor of self emptying (kenosis): a kenosis of omnipotence, a kenosis of simple eternity, a kenosis of omniscience and a kenosis of causal status.

> The (continuing) self-limitation of God coincides with the act of creation and the movement of history, a self-limitation that God the Creator has established for the sake of a measure of independence of the world, as well as the possibility of genuine human freedom in the world.[5]

This is possible because of the freedom of God, which makes it possible for him to undergo changes in his modes of existence. He can restrain (for example) the exercise of certain of his properties and decide in his wisdom when and how to act and/or not to act. God is "sovereign" even over his sovereignty. While remaining blissful, God can risk the pain of rejection. God can share the human condition and feel the suffering of every creature as well as (one should add) the joys of our happiness. I believe that there are gains and losses for God in this. It is not just a matter of giving up assets for others but also a matter of adding valuable experiences to God's own life, experiences perhaps not gained in any other way. What God gives up in pure happiness, he regains in having those experiences that can only be had in this way. What God loses in giving up complete control (for example), he gets back in gaining community. God restrains his divine properties in order that a universe of finite free agents might exist and, in so doing, he realizes new aspects of his own nature as he enters into relationships of love with creatures. Keith Ward writes,

> If we can speak of a kenosis in God, a renunciation of his absolute and unmixed perfection, we must also speak of a *pleroma* or fulfilment in God by which new forms of perfection are added by creatures to the divine life.[6]

---

5. Tupper, *Scandalous Providence*, 327.

6. Ward in Polkinghorne ed., *Work of Love*, 160. See also, Sanders, "Concept," 224–28. The idea of God experiencing certain restraints on his freedom is not a new one. We are used to thinking, in terms of his nature, that God can be restrained. For example, God cannot cease to exist or change his nature and God cannot commit a moral evil or break a promise. There are things God cannot do. We are also used to thinking, in relation to creation, that any world that God created would become a new factor in God's experience—as something that was not there before. Just choosing to have a creation at all would constitute a self-limitation of God because he would have to deal with it. God cannot both create and not create at the same time and the selection of any action limits him to that action and not to another. Free will theists would say that God cannot both give libertarian freedom and practice meticulous sovereignty at the same time. God's power is limited by the existence of finite beings, however weak, because they enjoy some level of capacity to oppose him. God's knowledge is limited by the freedom of creatures to actualize new states of affairs and his happiness is affected by the suffering involved in

God's vulnerable strength

It seems to be proper to say that God experiences certain restraints that are appropriate in different circumstances. Aquinas was right to insist (for example) that God cannot do the logically impossible and that God cannot both do and not do some particular action at the same time. This does not make God finite because the latter (finiteness) would require there to be a rival deity or an irrational given that God could not control, even if he wanted to. What I am talking about are *voluntary* self-restraints, taken on for the sake of the project God has put in place.

AREAS OF DIVINE SELF-LIMITATION

In relation to creating

One could posit that creation itself came about as a free act of self-limitation on God's part. God decided not to be alone and was determined to be the creator of a non-divine world, which would require restraint. Out of many possibilities, God chose this world and not another one, a world that he did not want to see crushed by divine reality or be absorbed into it, a realm that is not divine but not just "nothing" either. God made a created reality outside of himself and other than himself to stand before him and relate to him. Only God could decide to do such a thing and, having decided to do it, needed to "withdraw" in order to make "space."

The world might be thought of as existing, thanks to a kind of contraction in God, thanks to an act of self-emptying on God's part, which would lead ultimately to the divine descent into history and the divine self-surrender on the cross. The story of our world is the story of the self-emptying and self-limiting of God who respects the integrity of human beings. The beloved receives "space" in which to grow as lovers. Who other than the "almighty" could do such a thing? Who could pull back and create space for the creature, in order to make it relatively independent and capable of loving? In the divine act of self-restraint, paradoxically, we recognize an act of true omnipotence. God, in his freedom creates non-divine beings coexisting with his own being and capable of affecting him.[7]

In traditional theology, one hears much more about the self-emptying of Christ than the self-emptying of God. We are familiar with the idea that, in order to be incarnate, the Son had to curtail the independent

---

creaturely existence.

7. Moltmann, *Trinity*, 108–11 and "Is the creation?" 144–48.

exercise of certain properties, properties that were retained by the Father and the Spirit. Only an act of self-restraint made it possible for him to become fully human without contradiction. Thus we have learned to think of the Word giving up the use of those attributes which would have conflicted with his human nature.[8] But when the Lord immersed himself in history, there were also changes experienced by God. The incarnation, for example, made it possible for God to experience suffering contrary to the Platonic concept. It challenged the idea that the timelessness is superior to the temporal and the changeless to the changing. Rather than God being timeless and changeless, we should think of him as free, creative, and relational. In classical thinking, God is a completely self-contained perfection which, if it were to change in any way, would suffer diminution. Therefore, nothing outside God can be thought to affect him. But now we are free to think that God's perfection includes real relationships with created realities that do affect him. To speak boldly, God is a little different than he would have been had there been no such creatures and no such relationships. In a relational view, it would be less than perfect if God did not know what creatures experience affectively, than if he did know them. This is a self-emptying that (paradoxically) spells gain, as well as loss, enrichment as well as diminution for God.

God did not create the universe and humanity on the basis of some insufficiency in himself but out of the overflowing joy of life that burns within him. God did not have to create because, in the pre-creation situation, God lacked something. In the Trinity there exists from all eternity a relationship of love and communion between the persons of the godhead that is wholly satisfactory. No world need therefore exist for God to be love. A richness of divine life existed apart from creation and has always been there. Nevertheless, by restraining himself, God enriched himself in new ways and, by creating the world he realized possibilities that are eternally present in the divine being and experienced new forms of value that otherwise would not have been actualized. This capacity for self-enrichment in God is (I think) limitless.[9]

---

8. Erickson, *Word*, chapter 22.
9. Edwards, *Breath*, 107–10.

God's vulnerable strength

In relation to the use of divine power

God is omnipotent and has more power than any other being could possibly have. But God is also free in the exercise of his power. He can grant creatures their own autonomy and integrity. If he creates free agents, then he reins in his power. What gets "limited" in this case is not the fact, but the use of his power, which is voluntarily restrained. The qualification of God's power is the most widely recognized and accepted aspect of the divine limitation.[10]

When you think of it, self-limitation is implicit in the promises God makes. By making a promise, God limits his options. In Noah's time, for example, God said that such a flood would not recur. In saying this, God limits his options, he would be unfaithful, if he did not honor the promises he made. Here God has set a limit on the exercise of his power. When his people sin, God is self-limited and cannot be present with them as he might wish. A personal relationship also involves a limiting of power. A creature may be weak but it is not impotent. As so often in Israel's history, God was not able to accomplish all that he wanted because of the failure of creatures who did not use their power properly. What is possible for God may be conditioned upon the nature of the situation. God has chosen to be dependent on human beings in carrying out his work in the world, but what he has to work with in terms of the human resources is often not the best. God has to accept what people do with the power they have and the results can be very mixed. Creatures have power to reject God and make him appear to be helpless, although not permanently. The point is this: God self-limits his power in accordance with the way he has chosen to be related to the world.[11]

God reveals himself as one who gives us room to move, even when we are rebellious. God wants to be humanity's partner even when we choose to be his competitor. God withdraws and give us room and, like the father in the parable, gives the inheritance even to the rebellious son,

---

10. Open theists think of the self-limitation of God to be voluntary but process theists believe it should not be viewed in this way. For them, retaining almightiness is not something God can do or would want to do. They take God to be metaphysically and necessarily limited and not only voluntarily. As for the model of open theism, see Pinnock, *Most Moved Mover*, and for a process critique of it see Griffin, *Evil Revisited*, 14–22.

11. Fretheim, *Suffering*, 71–78. "The Old Testament understands God's power as limited in some ways in order for God to be consistent with the way in which God has chosen to be related to the world" (77).

so respectful was he of the boy's freedom. Paradoxically, weakness can be an expression of God's greatness because there is always the hope that love will melt the resistance away. God is prepared to take a risk in obtaining it and accepts the real possibility that he may not get all that he wants. This is not taking risks for risk's sake; it is taking risks for the sake of the project.[12]

In relation to the world

God also self-limits in relation to the world. Traditional theologians tend to be anxious about any idea that the world could impact God and affect him. Aquinas (for example) taught that God, being outside of the order of creation, could not be affected by creatures, though he could affect them. This meant that God is essentially nonrelational and uninvolved with the world. The picture is one of an indifferent metaphysical iceberg or solitary deity who suffers from his own completeness. It would mean, among other things, that God would be unable to suffer—even in a divine way—with a suffering creation.

Against such traditions, we take the relationship of God with creation to be real, on the side of God as well as on the side of creatures. God is really involved in creaturely life. The relations are mutual and reciprocal and involve each side impacting the other side. In such a situation, not only is creation dependent on its creator but God is also (in a way) dependent on creation. God is affected by the world. One could say that God is transcendent over, but does not dwell in, isolation from the world. God has chosen to be bound up in history and accepts the limitations that this implies. God does not change with respect to his steadfast love but he does change in light of what happens in the interactions between himself and the world. With respect to space, we could say that God made a realm in which to be active. For example, he created space and inhabits it as his abode. Heaven and earth are his dwelling place and creation is his living space. He stretched them out like a tent to dwell in (Ps 104:1–3). He is not absent from, but very present in the world. He has no need to work from outside the world when he is present inside it. Though ontologically Other than the world, God immerses himself in the world. He is in residence, so to speak. As Paul says, "In him we live and move and have our

---

12. On divine risk taking, see Sanders, *God Who Risks*.

being" (Acts 17:28). God penetrates the whole universe and can say, "Do I not fill heaven and earth?" (Jer 23:24).[13]

In relation to time, God created cosmic time and relates to it as a temporal agent. God is at home with temporality and has a life (at least for now) that is temporally ordered. God's temporality is strongly taught in Scripture. For example, God makes plans and carries them out. God speaks of past, present, and future. God anticipates and plans for the future, he remembers things that are past, and he addresses his people in the present. He is not thought of as timeless in spite of most traditional theology. The divine life has been temporally ordered, at least from the creation. Thus God is not above the flow of time and history looking down on the earth but enters the historical flow. If God did not have temporal experiences, reciprocal relations would be impossible. If God did not have temporal experiences, he would not have a history and the Bible story would be unintelligible. He could never change his mind or experience the joy of discovering something new. History would be a boring drawing out of what has already been determined. The personal dimension of the divine life would be unintelligible. By bringing into existence a temporal creation whose nature could be realised in its unfolding history, God has given great significance to time. God has also revealed self-limitation in his willingness to function as a temporal agent out of love for us.

In relation to divine knowledge

Open theists, unlike other free will theists, believe that there is a self-limitation in terms of what can also be known by God. John Polkinghorne writes,

> The metaphysical picture with which we are working is that of a world of true becoming, open to a future that is brought about by intertwined causal principles, such as natural law, human agency, and special providence. Such a world is radically temporal. The future does not yet exist, which leads us to the belief that even God does not yet know it. In other words, creation involves a kenosis of divine omniscience. We can say that God knows all that can be known and possesses a present omniscience but divine engagement with the time implies that God does not yet know all that will

---

13. Fretheim, *Suffering*, chapter 3. Compare Clayton and Peacocke, *In Whom We Live*.

eventually be known and does not possess absolute, exhaustive, and definite omniscience.[14]

Creating a significant universe had an effect on God in the realm of knowledge. It confronted him with a degree of uncertainty respecting the future. In scripture we hear God saying things like these: "Perhaps they will listen" and "If they will amend their ways" (Jer 26:3) Or, we hear God wanting to consult with Abraham or Moses, concerning what to do next. He seeks their advice on hard decisions (Gen 18:7; Exod 32:7). Sometimes, God asks a question like, "What am I going to do with you?" (Hos 6:4) or "How can I pardon you?" (Jer 5:7). In such texts, God shares the decision-making process with those whose very future is at stake. Even for God there are things about the future that are not yet settled. There is a genuine openness to it.[15]

This is not a self-limitation, at least not in the sense that God could have an exhaustive definite foreknowledge but keeps it locked up. But (yes) in the sense that in making a genuinely temporal order, God knew he would face a future partly unsettled, as having a genuinely temporal world would imply. So it is not as if God actually limits his knowledge, but that God created a universe with real temporality and true becoming, one feature of which would be that the future could not be definitely and exhaustively foreknown. It is not the case that "God limits his knowledge" exactly. It is more like God creates a project that has room for the unexpected and where things are left open, making space for contributions to be made to the creative project.[16]

In relation to sin

God certainly self-limits when it comes to creatures rebelling. Having created a significant universe, moral evil has become a problem and places limits on God. He has given humans significant freedom so that they might opt for a relationship of love with their maker and with each other. This was a worthy goal but (at the same time) a risky project, given the fact that we are free to say, "Yes" or "No" to God. In the case of humanity, there was a fall into sin, a historical event (I believe) that predates record

---

14. Polkinghorne, *Work*, 103–4.
15. Beilby and Eddy, *Divine Foreknowledge*. Fretheim, *Suffering*, chapter 4 and *God*.
16. It was a little misleading to have entitled my chapter, "God Limits his Knowledge" in the book edited by Basinger, *Predestination*.

keeping, but which set in motion a corrupt process.[17] Something has gone badly wrong, introducing a situation of conflict between God and creatures now at cross-purposes with the divine plan. History has become a cycle of cumulative degeneration with disastrous historical consequences and it threatens to thwart the good purposes of God.

Even worse—something has gone wrong in the realm of what the apostle Paul calls the principalities and powers. Paul identifies the problem,

> Our struggle (and God's struggle) is not against enemies of flesh and blood but against the rulers, against the authorities, against the cosmic powers of this present darkness, against the spiritual forces of evil in the heavenly places (Eph 6:12).[18]

Here is another dimension of rebelliousness that characterizes life in this world, something beyond the human sphere, something more mysterious and sinister even than the Fall. Supra-human powers that God does not entirely control mount resistance to God's will, posing a threat and a menace.

We know all too little about the nature of this opposition but we know about its harmful effects. We meet it in Genesis 1:2 which states, "In the beginning, when God created the heavens and the earth, the earth was a formless void and darkness covered the face of the deep, while a wind from God swept over the face of the waters." Verse two (it would seem) is a circumstantial clause describing the conditions existing at the time of the principal action, indicated in verse one. According to this creation story, God faced a negative state of affairs not attributable to his own actions. A dark power was strangely present—something that is not good and that God did not will. There was something wrong with creation at the outset. In creating the world, God has to deal with what is called "formlessness and emptiness." This language does not suggest just a disordered situation. The words are associated with divine judgment (Jer 4:23). This is not something that God made or would make (Isa 45:18). However this situation came to be there, it was a desolation contrary to God's will and introduced without any explanation. It was something contrary to God's will and displayed the fragility and vulnerability of the creation itself. It tells us that God established a life sustaining order in the teeth of a threat,

---

17. As to its historicity, I cannot understand the historical record, filled as it is with such hatred and violence without believing in the Fall or in something very like it.

18. See Boyd, *God* and *Satan*.

which Barth calls *das Nichtige* or nothingness. God can keep it at bay but it still poses a threat.

In creating, God had to work with something already in existence, something that he could circumscribe but not (at least for now) annihilate. This means that God was not the only power in existence when he created in Genesis 1. Thus God's effort was not uncontested. It posed a challenge to *shalom*. God can keep it at bay but it can arise again to do harm, especially when humanity embraces the rebellion and the destructive power reawakens. Having delegated freedom to creatures, human and angelic, God finds himself with a fight on his hands from foes whose power is not inconsiderable. We do not know much about these dark forces and whence they came but we know that they occupy "space," enjoy "say so," and are disregarded at our peril. It would appear that they exist because God made them and that they opted for evil not for good. An important implication is that the creation of Genesis 1 was not itself "a creation out of nothing" and is not (therefore) just compliant putty in God's hands that could be blown away without much of a fuss.[19]

In relation to the Incarnation

The Incarnation constitutes an ultimate in divine self-limitation. Although a New Testament (even, Johannine concept) its roots are found in the Old Testament. It is important to recognize that incarnation is not alien to the kind of thing the God of Israel does. On the contrary, in the Old Testament, God often appears to Israel in human form, long before the new covenant dawns. We call them "theophanies" and Hagar reported having seen God like that and lived to tell the tale (Gen 16:13). Such experiences were not unusual. One has the impression that God prefers to approach his people wrapped in a body rather than in a bodyless and vague way. Even if veiled in fire or cloud, God comes to humanity as human in the fire and cloud, indicating that human form is not foreign to him. He chooses to take on this form and to "incarnate" himself in weak flesh, and to be present among us. I think that he does it because he wishes to communicate in as personal way as possible. Revealing himself in a thunderstorm is one

---

19. I agree with May, *Creation* and Levenson, *Creation*, that Gen 1 does not teach "creation out of nothing." I was unconvinced by Copan and Craig, *Creation* to the contrary. However, I would add that there are other creation texts in the Old and New Testaments that may teach it or come closer to teaching it, in which case, I suppose, Gen 1 describes a restoration or recreation, not the original creation.

thing but appearing as a man is something more. Storms overwhelm us and shut us down but God embodied in frail flesh, why that is something even better. Even the God of Israel wants to be known as "incarnate" (and vulnerable) not as "un-incarnate" (and invulnerable) and it provides a glimpse of his heart.[20]

The theme of God's own experience of strength in weakness is clear when we see God opening himself up to the sufferings of his people. When they are bent on turning away, God feels it but cannot give them up (Isa 1:2–3). His heart is broken but he does not execute wrath on them (Hos 11:7–9). God is affected by what they do—it moves him deeply and he mourns on account of them. He cannot remain cool and collected. God is wounded by the broken relationship. Even for Moab, a non-Israelite nation, God's heart cries out (Isa 15:5). He wonders how long this rebellion will last but he cannot let them go. He will remain gracious, yesterday, today, and forever. God is still prepared to work with his faithless people, allowing them opportunity to participate in shaping their own future. God even suffers for them. Bearing the brunt of Israel's rejection, God cries out like a woman in travail—he gasps and pants (Isa 42:14). It is as if God has to go through labor pains in order to birth a new creation. He makes himself vulnerable in attempting to save them. Human sin is not without cost to God. It requires assuming a burden that God alone can bear. Sin necessitates the suffering of God, as if redemption can only come in this way.

The divine self-limitation comes to expression best in the Christian gospel where it is claimed that the Son of God became incarnated. This was an act of divine self-restraint by the Word of God assuming our nature and participating in human life and death. God stoops to take our flesh and become an actor on the stage of history. Paul writes, "Though he was in the form of God, he emptied himself taking the form of a slave" (Phil 2:7–8). In becoming a man, the Word gave up the use of certain of the divine attributes for a season for the sake of becoming fully human. God entered fully into the human situation and came to understand it from the inside. Jesus did not give up the qualities of God but the privilege of exercising them. Perhaps he even gave up the consciousness that he had such capabilities that he had exercised with the Father and the Spirit prior to incarnation.[21] This is not a kenosis only of the humanity of Christ,

---

20. Fretheim, *Suffering*, Chapter 6.
21. Erickson, *Word*, 248–50.

but a kenosis of the divinity as well. Jesus belongs to the divine identity but is also the revelation of God who suffers. We need to be willing now to include suffering and death in the identity of God. For this is the heart of the good news.[22] Moltmann writes,

> What is true of the self-limitation of omnipotence in God's love for those he created can also be said about the other metaphysical attributes of his divinity: omnipresence, omniscience, inviolability, and self-sufficiency. God does not know everything in advance because he does not will to know everything in advance. He waits for the response of those he has created and lets their future come. God is not incapable of suffering. He opens himself for the suffering of his people and in the incarnation for the sufferings of a love which will redeem the world. In a certain way, God becomes dependant on the response of his beloved creatures. In Christian theology one would not go as far as to declare God as in need of redemption together with his people Israel but nevertheless God has laid the sanctification of his name and the doing of his will in the hands of human beings and thus in a way the coming of his kingdom. It must be viewed as part of God's self-humiliation that God does not desire to be without those he has created and loved and therefore waits for them to repent and turn back, leaving them time so that he may come to his kingdom together with them.[23]

The incarnation of Jesus constitutes the definitive disclosure of God and gives assurance to us of the goal of creation, which is the coming of the kingdom of God. Our understanding of God in his self-limitation distinguishes a genuinely personal model of God's relationship to the world from an unqualified monarchical model with its implicit historical determinism, as well as from various existential and process models that minimize God's purposeful participation in and direction of the history of creation en route to eschatological fulfillment.[24]

---

22. Hallman, *Descent*.

23. Moltmann in Polkinghorne ed., *Work of Love*, 148. There needs to be a re-thinking of the attributes of God in the light of the biblical testimony. How can God be apathetic if he so loves the world? How can he be immutable if he is the living God? How can God be irresistible power if his Son is weak on the cross? Above all, how can God be love without being vulnerable and a risk taker? Let God be the one who he has revealed himself to be.

24. Compare Tupper, *Scandalous Providence*, 63–64.

CONCLUSION

God in freedom and love, desiring communion with finite creatures, adopts the posture of kenotic grace with the attendant risks of constraint and restraint, without which mutual love is not possible in the world. We picture divine self-restraint at the beginning and pleroma at the end of history. We imagine God permitting creaturely unfaithfulness and then introducing a plan whereby these same creatures would share in the bliss of the triune God. I see cosmic movement from the divine self-emptying and restraint to creaturely fulfillment in God. We are in the middle of a sacred history in which a vulnerable God redeems all that went wrong and in which the new creation is being birthed. Listen to Keith Ward:

> There is a definite cosmic vision implicit in a Christian view of creation as a kenotic and *pleromal* process and as the beginning of creation involves kenosis so the consummation of creation will be *theosis*. God shares in the pain and permits the wayward freedom of creatures in order that, finally, they should share in the bliss of God.

It is that cosmic movement from divine self-emptying to creaturely fulfillment in God that is the sacred history of the cosmos, and it seems to me to be the deepest meaning of the Christian gospel for this planet in the midst of its journey.

11

David and Foucault

Extreme violence and innocent suffering in a post-September 11 world

Brian Holliday

INTRODUCTION

Twisted rubble, burnt-out cars and deep crimson stains where shattered bodies bled and died are all too familiar scenes today. In a dangerous world where violence often carries a religious message, the proclamation of the Christian gospel can sound like the neo-colonial rhetoric of an agenda backed by coalitions of the West.[1] While aggressive actions of religious groups around the world seem increasingly confronting in this age of terrorism, what is common to all people across the globe is the universal experience of suffering. How can the church in the West speak to those who are suffering, and how can it proclaim a Christian gospel from the place of its own suffering? In a post-September 11 world, has the perception of strength and weakness changed?

In this essay, it will be proposed that the narrative of David's life, especially his encounter with Goliath and his adultery with Bathsheba,

---

1. The term "the West" is problematic, especially in a post-Cold War, post-September 11 world, but in this essay the phrases "the West" and "the Christian West" mean the countries of Western Europe, North America, Australia and New Zealand. It is recognized that the ideas, theologies and divisions within this grouping are many, but their overarching ideology is taken to be liberal democratic within a postmodern era.

David and Foucault

can be used as a frame to examine the re-emergence of extreme violence in the West and the unease it creates in the church in the West.[2] It will be argued that Simone Weil's concepts of suffering and affliction are helpful constructions of "strength in weakness," which can be used to call the church in the West to a renewed sense of postmodern awareness about itself, its message, and the world.[3] The starting frame for this argument is the biblical narrative of David and Goliath.

DAVID AND VIOLENCE

The biblical portrait

The story of David and Goliath is traditionally told as a tale of strength being routed by weakness—the triumph of the underdog.[4] However, an alternative reading of the narrative, which foregrounds the violence, can raise disturbing insights for the Western reader. In this frame, David was not a demure, guileless, and effeminate youth, for he had already killed a lion and a bear with his shepherd's staff and bare hands. David, a zealot for God, believed in the rightness of his cause and ran to meet the giant with the supreme confidence of a religious fighter. The smooth river stone that floored Goliath did not kill him, so David took the giant's sword, hacking off his head and holding it aloft for all to see the gory sight of victory in the name of God. Later in the day, when David met with the king, he was still carrying the giant's severed head.

Subsequently, Saul offered David his younger daughter, Michal, in marriage on the condition he collect a bridal dowry of one hundred Philistine foreskins. David, in his enthusiasm, collected not one but two

---

2. For a fuller discussion on framing, its inevitability, complexity and limitations, see MacLachlan and Reid, *Framing*.

3. It is important to keep in mind that postmodernism invites diversity, and this essay focuses on the re-emergence of extreme violence and innocent suffering, which are only one facet in the life and proclamation of the Church in the West. What will be argued is the need for the Church in the West to seriously engage with a theology of suffering to complement, rather than replace, existing emphases.

4. Among biblical scholars, there are many who think that David did not kill Goliath, but that feat was accomplished by Elhanan of Bethlehem (2 Sam 21:19; 23:24). Further arguments have been raised about the text of 1 Samuel 17 in terms of the sequence of events, additions added later and other inconsistencies. "In short," Birch ("First and Second Books," 1109) comments, "the textual history of this chapter is complex". However, what informs this essay is not the textual issue, but the theme and the readings and interpretations that surround it.

hundred foreskins and presented them to Saul.[5] By the standards of any era, to slaughter one or two hundred Philistines and sever their foreskins is an incredibly inhumane incident.

But such events continued in the life of David. He ordered the man who brought him the news of Saul's death to be unceremoniously struck down in the camp (2 Sam 1:15). A similar fate, at the orders of David, awaited the Benjamites who killed Ish-Bosheth, the surviving son of Saul, for they were killed, their hands were cut off, and their bodies hung by the pool in Hebron.[6]

By Western standards, David was a most brutal and bloody man. His actions appear to be similar to the terrorist killings, beheadings, and massacres that recently have revolted viewers of the evening news. This Old Testament champion, this founder of the dynasty through which Christ came, this metaphorical figure of art masterpieces across the centuries, was a callous and violent killer. This conclusion is acknowledged in the Scriptures, in that God did not allow David to build a permanent temple for him in Jerusalem because of his violent and bloody life.[7]

Violence in the artworks of David

Similar to the scriptural narrative's apparent ease with violence, many of the artworks of David from earlier centuries intentionally include the severed head of Goliath in their work. Gardner's volume, *Art Through the Ages*, for example, in comparing Verrocchio's statue with Donatello's, comments,

> As in Donatello's version, Goliath's head lies at David's feet. He poses like a hunter with his kill . . . [and it] shows how closely Verrocchio read the biblical text and how clearly he knew the psychology of brash and confident young men.[8]

Art and God-vindicated violence from the Bible cohabit in seamless harmony in the fifteenth century sculptural works regarding David. Similarly, a large number of the paintings of David feature the severed head of

---

5. Birch, "First and Second Books," notes that the Septuagint and some subsequent translations do not increase the number of foreskins (see also 2 Sam 3:14), but suggests David doubled the number because he was "so enthusiastic to become the son-in-law Saul does not want" (1122).

6. See 2 Sam 4.

7. See 1 Chron 22:8.

8. Kleiner, *Gardner's Art*, 594.

Goliath, confronting the viewer with a range of visual and violent graphics. These works include

- Andrea del Castagno's "The Youthful David" (circa 1450)—David with a sling standing over the severed head of Goliath;
- Cima da Conegliano's "David and Jonathon" (circa 1505-10)—David holding Goliath's severed head while walking and talking to Jonathon;
- Raphael's "David's Triumph" (circa 1519)—David returning in a parade with Goliath's head and torso held high on spears;
- Titian's "David and Goliath" (1540s)—Goliath's severed head and headless torso;
- Caravaggio's two separate paintings entitled "David with the Head of Goliath" (the first circa 1601-02)—David twisting the hair of Goliath's severed head around his hand to get a good grip on it; (the second circa 1610)—David gazing at Goliath's severed head, which he holds it up by its long hair;
- Rembrandt's "David Presenting the Head of Goliath to King Saul" (1627)—David kneeling before Saul and presenting him with Goliath's severed head);
- Nicolas Poussin's "The Triumph of David" (circa 1630)—David gazing at the dark, severed head of Goliath hanging on his shield leaning against a wall.

In contrast to Western sensitivities, these masterpieces of the Renaissance, the age of the Reformation and the Baroque period were not bloodthirsty aberrations, but significant works communicating a gruesome and violent theme, which understood David as a man similar to men in their own times.

The West, both secular and Christian, has rightly rejected such overt violence, and has championed the cause of the oppressed. The West does not condone physical violence against others let alone triumph in gory public displays of mutilated bodies. For many years, the human rights agenda of the West has been linked to trade, and it has seen itself as the champion of those suffering political oppression. The church in the West has also preached against violence and stood with the victims of aggression. It has seen suffering as a failure, a weakness, which needs to be confronted, alleviated, and overcome.

Much of the Western church's Christian witness to the world is based around the strength of bringing health and economic aid to those who are suffering and in desperate need.[9] In fact, much of life in the West is built around a positive rejection of suffering, for the vast majority of people have no experience of war and violence, and life holds an increased expectation of affluence, comfort, health, and improved life expectancy. Suffering is hidden in sanitized hospitals, aged care facilities, prisons, and other institutions. But on September 11, 2001, pictures of the disintegrating twin towers of the World Trade Center were beamed live around the world, and the West was suddenly confronted with public images of extreme violence and innocent suffering—violence and suffering being inflicted on people just like us at the very heart of Western society.

FOUCAULT AND VIOLENCE

The West's gradual, progressive sanitization of suffering and violence into institutions is described by Michel Foucault in *Discipline and Punish*.[10] Foucault uses the 1757 public torture and execution of Damiens for regicide to show how the physical marking of the body through the mechanism of the public spectacle served a particular and important function in pre-modern societies.[11] During the classical period examined in Foucault's book the spectacle was the scaffold. In the Davidic period, and through the time of Israel's monarchy, the public spectacle included beheadings, hanging bodies, and decapitated heads on city walls, and the dispersion of dismembered body parts to all corners of the kingdom.[12] These acts, abhorrent to Western people today, have been common in many periods of history and served a very specific purpose. Foucault asserts,

---

9. The meeting of Christian and political aspirations in this Western ideal is seen in the recent phenomenon of incumbent Australian political leaders visiting mega churches, which hold to what Amanda Lohrey calls the 'Prosperity Gospel'. See Lohrey, "Voting."

10. Foucault's interest is in suffering and violence related to crime and punishment, and the birth of the modern prison, but his descriptions also inform our broader examination of the West's perceptions towards violence and suffering.

11. Damiens attacked the unpopular Louis XV of France, but only succeeded in slightly wounding him. Louis forgave Damiens, handing him over to the Parliament. Bernier, in *Louis the Beloved*, claims that, "in this case, Christian charity was singularly misplaced" (188). The Parliament had Damiens brutally tortured and quartered before a huge Parisian crowd, and when the spectacle went wrong it revolted the crowd who blamed the king. So the king of the greatest kingdom in Europe, became even more weak and unpopular.

12. See 1 Sam 31:8–13; 2 Sam 4; 21:1–14 for examples in David's lifetime.

> An offence, according to the law of the classical age, quite apart from the damage it may produce, apart even from the rule that it breaks ... attacks the sovereign; it attacks him personally, since the law represents the will of the sovereign; it attacks him physically, since the force of the law is the force of the prince.[13]

A king maintained discipline and reinforced his power by violence to the criminal who broke the law, or the enemy who challenged the power embodied in the king.

Furthermore, the public severity and brutality of the justice was intentionally far in excess of the weight of the crime. The aim of the ritual of public executions in the seventeenth century, explains Foucault, was not primarily to discipline the society by creating an extreme example, but had at its core a more stark and simple purpose. It imposed "a policy of terror: to make everyone aware, through the body of the criminal, of the unrestrained presence of the sovereign. The public execution did not re-establish justice; it reactivated power."[14] David's brutal and emphatic victory over Goliath, then, was not just a victory for God but was a reinforcement of the authority of the king. This is seen in Saul's reaction to the women who were singing of the triumph of David, while the triumph of the king was of a lesser order. Reinforcing the rule of the sovereign, centered and performed around "a whole ceremony of triumph,"[15] is clearly illustrated in the frames of many of the artworks of David and Goliath mentioned above, for they display all the trappings and features of a European court.

VULNERABILITY IN VIOLENCE

But, while this spectacle is present in much of the art work about David and Goliath, a deeper awareness of weakness and vulnerability is also evident. In the work of the artists, David was a conqueror yet remained vulnerable; he was caught in bloodguilt yet innocent; he was lauded, yet out of place; he was fair and light of skin, but a dark and troubled background threatened; and he was victoriously strong, yet youthfully weak. The vulnerability of David throws into sharp relief the surprising twist, which makes the narrative of David and Goliath such a powerful metaphor in

---

13. Foucault, *Discipline*, 47.
14. Ibid., 49.
15. Ibid., 51.

many contexts. In the enactment of this public spectacle, the suffering and violence is inflicted on the stronger party by the apparently weaker, less experienced and more defenseless party. It is a tale of triumph over enormous odds—a tale of divine intervention. It is a turning point in the story of the monarchy of Israel, for it is the moment in which Davidic power first captures the minds and hearts of a kingdom. It is a story that will be told and retold, taking its place in national mythology.

It is almost unthinkable, then, that David himself could become a Goliath figure, but he did. In a covert incident, as a powerful, mature king, he committed adultery with Bathsheba and had her husband, who was a loyal soldier of honorable principles, sent intentionally to his death (see 2 Sam 17–18). God did not intervene on behalf of the weaker parties until Uriah was dead and David had taken Bathsheba as one of his wives. Nathan's parable, which so angered David, exposed the hero king to be a Goliath who destroyed his neighbor to satisfy his own lust. Where was God for the innocent, loyal Uriah? How long did Bathsheba grieve her husband? David repented, but how many Uriahs and Bathshebas lived in Israel, the land God freed from Goliath by the hand of the youthful David? It is this violent, less celebrated story of the strong and powerful inflicting suffering on the innocent and weak that is the more common experience of violence in human history.

Like David, the West and the church in the West have a hidden violent side they struggle to acknowledge and engage. While the West is to be commended that it does not condone physical violence against others, it is often unaware of the fiscal and environmental violence it perpetrates in order to maintain its comfortable lifestyle. While it is praiseworthy that the West does not permit violent punishment in the form of public spectacle, it indulges in the violence of public character assassination through its popular tabloids and magazines. Similarly, the church in the West destroys people and their faith through holy gossip in church communities, and it has too readily covered its ugly shadow side, hiding its sexual abuse of women and children, its political abuse of leaders, and its spiritual abuse of communicants. Most significantly, in protecting its own right to comfort, the church in the West has yet seriously to engage with the aspects of its theological heritage that find in extreme violence, and the suffering of the innocent, a means of spiritual growth and relevant witness. This heritage is particularly germane to a postmodern age.

The call for the West to re-engage suffering in a more complex way has especially come with the events of September 11, 2001, and its aftermath. No longer can the West and Western Christians live in benevolent isolation from the violence, suffering, and poverty of a divided world. But the church in the West had received an earlier wake-up call. World War II, which engulfed Christian Europe, had raised questions that were not easily answered by the triumphal paradigms of a Christianity that had circled the world beside European colonial expansion. The questions raised were similar to those of Job. As Richard Rohr suggests in his discussion on Job, "Job's questions could be our own: Is God for us or against us? Is God loving? Is it an indifferent universe? A benevolent universe? Or a toxic and dangerous one?"[16] It was out of the extreme suffering of war that a spirituality began to emerge in response to the difficult questions. It was a postmodern spirituality, based in a theology of suffering.

A THEOLOGY OF SUFFERING IN A VIOLENT WORLD

Ann Astell, in *Divine Representations: Postmodernism and Spirituality*, claims that World War II, and in particular the symbol of Auschwitz, mark the historical shift from a modern to a postmodern spirituality.[17] In this context, Astell suggests, "[W]e may rightly look to the saints of the World War II era as prophets of a new, postmodern spirituality."[18] To develop the characteristics of a postmodern theology in this context, Astell draws on the writing of Dietrich Bonhoeffer and Simone Weil who both died during World War II, and on the writings of Joseph Kentenich and Chiara Lubich who, having survived the war, both went on to found new Christian communities.

The common themes in these writings include a recognition of the divine incarnation in all relationships in life (no separation of secular and sacred), a profound faith in God's unconditional love no matter what the circumstances, "including the cruellest of experiences and the monstrous

---

16. Rohr, *Job and the Mystery of Suffering*, 84.

17. In a postmodern instance of deferment and repetition, Astell takes this symbol of Auschwitz from Lyotard who took it from Theodor Andorno. Lyotard saw Auschwitz as marking the end of modernism and its ideals. He states in "Defining the Postmodern," "Following Theodor Andorno, I use the name Auschwitz to point out the irrelevance of empirical matter, the stuff of recent past history, in terms of the modern claim to help mankind to emancipate itself" (172).

18. Astell, *Divine Representations*, 3.

deeds of history," which leads to "the unconditional acceptance of God's will and entrustment of one's self to his mercy," and to the cross as "the most fundamental ground of vertical and horizontal mediation."[19] As Astell states,

> In all four postmodern spiritualities under discussion here, the idea of divine and human abandonment answers to the much-discussed experiential "absence" of God in our secularised world. Instead of confusing an experimental with a metaphysical absence (as the Death of God theologians did in the sixties), they find in it another form of God's mysterious presence and activity.[20]

This sense of the mystery and presence of God in his absence is not a new thought. Saints from the time of Job till the present have spoken of it.[21] But the theologians and Christian thinkers whose ideas were formed in and around the cauldron of World War II challenge the church in the West today about its need to integrate the suffering of the innocent and the "absence of God" with the lived experience of postmodern life.

Simone Weil and suffering

Simone Weil's work on suffering and the "absence of God" is, in many respects, less well-known and less orthodox than other Christian thought of her time.[22] Dying at a young age during World War II, much of her writings have been collected from notes and letters. Weil's style is lucid and intense. The focus of her theology of suffering can be summed up in her words in *Gravity and Grace*, where she writes, "The extreme greatness of Christianity lies in the fact that it does not seek a supernatural remedy for suffering but a supernatural use for it."[23] This supernatural use of suffering is what Weil, with her French-Jewish heritage, explores during the years of the Third Reich. She sees that suffering's usefulness is made

---

19. Astell, *Divine Representations*, 6–9.
20. Ibid., 9.
21. See Johnston, *The Mystical Way*.
22. Nevin, *Simone Weil*, 260, sees Weil's faith as eclectic and states that in his opinion, "There is a tendency to regard Weil as some sort of Christian, manqué or otherwise, because she is often inclined to express her thoughts in the language of Christian faith. This tendency must be resisted." While it is helpful to keep Nevin's comment in mind, it does not change the value of Weil's thought to a process of rethinking a theology of suffering in a postmodern, Christian context. Weil's writings are a useful frame with a postmodern edge.
23. Weil, *Gravity*, 73.

possible by the impartiality of God to the processes of life, whether those processes be good or evil.

Weil's reasoning for God's attitude of impartiality to good and evil in "the mechanism of the world" is that nothing is ever wholly good or entirely evil. She argues that all positive and negative attributes carry within themselves their opposite attribute. She calls this "contradiction".

> All good carries with it conditions which are contradictory and as a consequence is impossible. He who keeps his attention really fixed on this impossibility and acts will do what is good. In the same way all truth contains a contradiction.[24]

Weil further clarifies contradiction when she states, "Evil is the shadow of good. All real good, possessing solidity and thickness, projects evil. Only imaginary good does not project it."[25] All good carries in it the silhouette of evil, so that doing good, for example, may turn into oppression—unless one keeps one's attention on this impossible situation. Being comfortable carries its own propensity to suffering, so that the drive for comfort may result in isolation and break down in relationships. Strength has its own inbuilt weakness, so that removing any opposition may lead to egocentrism and insensitivity. Weakness, in turn, has its innate strength which allows it the power of unrecognized, gentle subversion.

To Weil, the union of contradictions creates balance in the world, and the awareness of them, together with the loosening of one's attention from them, brings detachment. But, in a postmodern paradox Weil assets, "The union of contradictories involves a wrenching apart. It is impossible without extreme suffering."[26] In the union of good and evil, we are called to focus on the good within the contradiction and absorb into ourselves the suffering of the evil. What is important when suffering evil is innocence. Weil describes it as

> Blood on snow. Innocence and evil. Evil itself must be pure. It can only be pure in the form of the suffering of someone innocent. An innocent being who suffers sheds the light of salvation upon evil. Such a one is the visible image of the innocent God. That is why a God who loves man and a man who loves God have to suffer.[27]

---

24. Weil, *Gravity*, 89.
25. Ibid., 93.
26. Ibid., 92.
27. Weil, *Gravity*, 83.

Thus the suffering of the innocent bears testimony to the love of God in Christ.

Martyrdom and mission

Suffering of the innocent as a testimony for Christ was a strong component in the early church's mission. It is also a part of the re-evaluation of Christian mission in a post-September 11 world. Norman Thomas, reflecting on "the new forms of violence" post-September 11, sees the rise in religious persecution as an important contributor to a new approach to Christian mission.[28] Thomas cites Barrett and Johnson's worldwide research as estimating that 167,000 Christian martyrs lost their lives in 2004, while they predict that the number of Christian martyrs will have risen to 210,000 by 2025. In an equally arresting claim, Barrett and Johnson consider martyrdom now to be "the most significant and far-reaching of all the modes and methodologies of evangelisation."[29] This dramatic shift is already being felt in the two-thirds world, and will increasingly challenge notions of Christian life in the West.

September 11 brought the harsh reality of the daily suffering of many around the world into the very heart of Western civilization. The shock of this experience of suffering still reverberates ominously in the soul of the West. However, for the Christian, states Thomas, "The symbol of God's own martyrdom restores and gathers together those who suffer and have been driven apart in violence and conflict."[30] This global shift in a postmodern era does not mean that Christians in the West will need to face martyrdom, but it does mean they cannot ignore the presence of increased suffering in a pluralistic, violent world. They need to understand that embracing and explaining suffering in a dissonant world will be a key role for the church in the West and will bring people face-to-face with the suffering God in Christ.

A current Christian writer who seeks to understand and explain both suffering and martyrdom is Rowan Williams. In an echo of Foucault who saw public spectacle as a reactivation of power, Williams states that the issues in martyrdom surround who you are, where allegiance lies, and there-

---

28. Thomas, "Radical Mission," 2.
29. Ibid., 2.
30. Ibid., 3.

David and Foucault

fore "where *power* is recognised, and what kind of power."[31] In the context of Jesus' trial, Williams argues, martyrdom is not about heroism and drama, but about "freedom from the imperatives of violence" and being "fully at home in creation."[32] Williams explains his understanding, that

> Martyrdom is the ultimate statement of belonging in and to the world as God made it, not to a particular order of earthly authority . . . it means being at home in the world, and this is what threatens the world's systems of power, because it gives no legitimacy to the defensive violence and fear of the other that marks these systems.[33]

For Western Christians, Williams suggests, the question "to ask is how is this freedom to be realised when the test, the trial, is the undramatic context of daily life . . . [or] how a life which may never have to face violent challenge may yet express the *truth* that violence is overcome and silenced in Christ."[34] In fact, for Williams, our willingness to be silent, to let Christ's silence work on us, and to sense Christ's gaze on us is central to a Christian's response to suffering and martyrdom.[35] Similarly, this movement into silence is also the spontaneous response of the sufferer to what Weil calls affliction.

Weil and affliction

For Weil, there is a suffering which goes beyond martyrdom and the normal call to suffer. This intense suffering she calls "affliction." All affliction is suffering, but not all suffering is affliction. Weil states, in *Waiting on God*,

> Those who are persecuted for their faith and are aware of the fact are not afflicted, although they have to suffer. They only fall into a state of affliction if suffering or fear fills the soul to the point of making it forget the cause of the persecution. The martyrs who enter the arena, singing as they went to face the wild beasts, were not afflicted. Christ was afflicted. He did not die like a martyr. He

---

31. Williams, *Christ*, 99. In some cases martyrdom has overtones of Foucault's public spectacle and the reactivation of disproportionate power—a policy of terror.
32. Williams, *Christ*, 107.
33. Ibid., 111.
34. Ibid., 107.
35. Ibid., 139.

died like a common criminal, confused with thieves, only a little more ridiculous. For affliction is ridiculous.[36]

Affliction, as Weil defines it, is the agonizing pain of intimate lovers torn apart by the greatest distance. This tearing love describes the Triune God who is love. It is God torn from God. Weil elucidates,

> There is a love which is intimate and close, found in union like the Trinity, and there is love which is faithful and fulsome, found in the separation of God from his Son on the cross. . . . One can only accept the existence of affliction by considering it as a distance. . . . God . . . created beings capable of love from all possible distances. Because no other could do it, he himself went to the greatest possible distance, the infinite distance. This infinite distance between God and God, this supreme tearing apart, this agony beyond all others, this marvel of love, is the crucifixion. Nothing can be further from God than that which has been made accused. . . . This tearing apart over which supreme love places the bond of supreme union, echoes perpetually across the universe in the midst of silence, like notes, separate yet melting into one, like pure and heart-rending harmony.[37]

It is in this affliction of God that the afflicted of the earth find themselves immersed. This is a true expression of incarnation. Thus, for Weil, a deep harmony of the human and the divine meets in the inner person of the afflicted. In affliction, she states,

> We are the furthest from God, situated at the extreme limit from which it is not absolutely impossible to come back to him. In our being, God is torn. We are the crucifixion of God. The love of God for us is a passion. How could that which is good love that which is evil without suffering? And that which is evil suffers too in loving that which is good. The mutual love of God and man is suffering.[38]

In language reminiscent of St John of the Cross Weil depicts the anguished soul as moving through a dark thickness, feeling tentatively, "in search of him it loves."[39] In this place prayer and questions are met by impenetrable silence, but the soul clings to the hope of the deep loving of a God who seems in every respect absent.

36. Weil, *Waiting on God*, 69.
37. Ibid., 68.
38. Ibid., 81.
39. Weil, *Gravity and Grace*, 80.

In this state of affliction, those who are so wounded no longer have the capacity to reach out to others. They cannot be missional in the traditional sense of active proclamation, but like Job, can only respond through the fog and darkness of affliction to those who seek to comfort them. They do not choose their affliction, but in their faithful love for Christ they provide a powerful, though passive, proclamation.

Furthermore, as in World War II, affliction can be spawned by great evil, involving excessive violence, brutality, and public humiliation. Weil uses the theology of Christ's presence in the bread and wine to describe the redemptive work of Christ in affliction generated by such evil. "As God is present through the consecration of the Eucharist in what the senses perceive as a morsel of bread, so he is present in extreme evil through redemptive suffering through the cross."[40] Here, in silence, enfleshed within violent and profane circumstances, the redemptive life of Christ works in unrecognized and unheralded ways.

This redemptive work in affliction is also recognizable in communities and churches as well as individuals. Where suffering so profoundly impacts a church that they can no longer reach out, nor fully understand the cause of their pain, they can demonstrate in their silent witness to the world the contradiction of the deep loving of the God who seems absent. Sometimes affliction in churches is caused by great evil that tears individuals, families, and church communities apart. The ability to stay in the place where God should be present, but seems absent, is a testimony to the world of the affliction of Christ. To absorb evil in the contradiction of what is gives a silent answer to the questions of the soul who searches for the one it loves. This is a difficult, unfortunately common, and necessary witness. It is as essential to the church in the West's message in a post-September 11 world as are the traditional and popular messages of church growth and evangelistic proclamation. The acceptance, and caring integration, of the silent witness of church communities, and individuals, in pain, affliction and even death will make the church in the West far more relevant to the many who suffer in a postmodern age.

CONCLUSION

The frame of the story of David, especially his encounters with Goliath and Bathsheba, illuminates a number of issues for the church in the West in a

---

40. Ibid., 82.

post-September 11 world. It reveals that the time for the rhetoric of superiority and assumed strength is past. In a world where great evil, extreme violence, and the suffering of the innocent is becoming more common place, the church in the West needs to engage with suffering, not just as a weakness to be overcome and alleviated, but as a strength to be absorbed and understood as a true expression of the incarnation. The call, then, is for a re-invigoration of a "theology of suffering". However, in a postmodern world of variety and multiplicity, any theology of suffering needs to complement rather than replace other emphases of the church in the West.

Furthermore, a theology of suffering may also include, or be juxtaposed with, a "theology of silence," which would explore both the silence of God and the silent witness of the Christian church to the God who seems absent. A silent testimony that absorbs evil and focuses on the good may still be an active witness, like yeast in bread dough. The church in the West needs to value the role of innocence in the absorption of evil in a complex world of contradiction. It needs to live with the recognition that all is not black and white, but that evil is in good and good is in evil. But moving beyond the active witness, the call is for an acceptance of "passive proclamation," which affirms the value and message of those in affliction, who are unable to reach out to others, but who also provide another relevant and effective witness to the gospel.

Moreover, explaining affliction through a theology of silence is the ultimate theology of strength in weakness. The church in the West must recognize its own afflicted parts, and begin to accept, comfort, and learn from them. It needs to be a true comforter of the afflicted, because it recognizes the impartiality of God and that affliction can be understood as embracing the heart of the loving God who seems absent. This would deepen the church in the West's engagement with, and ability to journey in, the dark regions of life, of painful relationships with others, and of the deep recesses of its own pain and the pain of the wider world.

But, finally, remembering that all things in this world will pass, including the age of terrorism and postmodernism, the church in the West must not take itself too seriously, but embrace all that it means to live and be at home in God's world, enjoying the richness of postmodern variety and living free from "the imperatives of violence," challenging it with the silence of Christ.

12

Turning Teflon™ into Velcro™

Making words stick in an image-based culture

Stephen McAlpine

INTRODUCTION: SENTENCED TO DEATH

"Words matter. Words convey moral clarity."[1] So writes US journalist Steven Vincent concerning the battle for definition rights to the Iraq conflict. Vincent's words highlight the semantic fog obfuscating a struggle within a struggle. At an immediate level he laments the Left's preference for descriptions such as "the resistance" over the "death squads" it previously favored when describing Latin American killers. But there is more at stake—an Orwellian struggle no less, to define "moral clarity and lucid thought." He rejects the "distortions of our language" that allow evil to flourish under the panoply of verbiage. At least he used to. Vincent was murdered in Iraq shortly after, leaving others to squabble over the culprits' nomenclature.

Yet despite Vincent's words it is *images* that primarily shape our view of Iraq.[2] The mediaeval mindset of the resistance/death squads is proving thoroughly postmodern, employing every image-producing and reproducing means available in conveying its own brand of moral clarity. Beheadings, frightened hostages, and digital footage of rocket attacks are posted on web sites and beamed around the world. Note too the sack-

---

1. Vincent, http://occhronicle.blogspot.com/2005/08/steven-vincent.rip.hotmail.
2. Edwards, "Power," 31–32.

ing of a US military contractor who released photographs of flag-draped military coffins coming home from Iraq.³

The fear is that with the advent of cyber-communications, and the subsequent and exponential increase of images, words are being out-muscled, and bullied into submission by a stronger opponent, and an increasingly stronger one at that. The result, as David Lyon observes, is not moral clarity, but a blur: "Today's hyper-real world dissolves distinctions between objects and their representations, leaving only simulacra, which refer to nothing by themselves."⁴

But lest we simply accuse image of bullying word into submission, word has been weakened by self-abuse. Hence we witness the steady erosion of word's authority, both through *misuse* and *mistrust*. Don Watson, speechwriter to former Australian Prime Minister Paul Keating, laments misuse stating,

> In the information age the public language is coming down to an ugly, sub-literate universal form with a fraction of the richness that living English has. . . . [I]t struggles to express the human. Buzz words abound in it. Platitudes iron it flat. The language is hostile to communion, which is the purpose of language.⁵

Word, which was once powerful and beautiful, has withered and wizened like a prize fighter whose only role now is to sit wistfully ringside and watch image deliver the knock-out blow.

Meanwhile Kevin Donnelly highlights how ideological mistrust of "word" is penetrating the English syllabus in Australia so that; "novels, plays, poems and short stories that say something lasting and profound about the human experience"⁶ are being replaced by so-called "multi-model texts which also make use of visual, auditory and digital features".⁷ The result is that

---

3. Bernten and Rivera, http://settletimes.nwsource.com/htm/localnews/2001909527_coffin22m.html.

4. Lyon, *Jesus*, 65.

5. Watson, *Death Sentence*, 12.

6. Donnelly, "Hasta la vista," 19. There has been an ongoing debate in *The Australian* newspaper in 2005 over the use of radical reader-response theory being employed to "politicise" the high school English syllabus.

7. Donnelly, "Hasta la vista," 19. This is a quote from the Victorian State Syllabus. The wording is a good example of Watson's point!

> The dialogue from an Arnie Schwarzenegger movie has the same value as a Shakespearean sonnet and students can spend their time watching films and giving oral reports instead of reading sustained works of fiction and having to write an essay in response.[8]

Note the words "the same value." Donnelly's primary concern is the deconstructionist push to flatten all texts, whether written or visual, and invest Schwarzenegger with the same "moral clarity" as Shakespeare.

This concept of values—whether moral, spiritual, philosophical, ethical or social—indicates that the struggle between the word and image has theological roots, even though many appear blithely ignorant of this. It is the contention of this essay that word and image are engaged in a struggle that will only be resolved when we take seriously God's intention that word and image should complement each other, rather than one try to dominate the other. To commence we will briefly examine the contemporary ecclesiological scene along with a number of theological perspectives on the strength of image in our culture, before exploring, also briefly, ways in which the Scriptures speak of word and image.

IMAGE AND THEOLOGY

Because mainstream sociological trends percolate societal substrata the church is not exempt from the word versus image battle. Churches have witnessed a general increase in image use, and a corresponding increasing of the "buzz words" and "platitudes" of Watson's description. If such language is indeed "hostile to communion," is the ecclesia—*the gathering*—the last place we should find it? Consider the following from the pastor of one of Australia's newest and fastest growing churches:

> "You're the best-looking congregation on the Gold Coast," he told the mostly young worshippers yesterday. "You come in here and God gives you a makeover! Remember, we're the cheeky church!"[9]

Is this a playful comment, simply a bit of fun? Or is there more to it, a deeper philosophical assumption about what is important?

The response of the church to the increase in images ranges between breezy optimism and abject pessimism. At one extreme a technical Q&A article on church technology advises:

---

8. Donnelly, "Hasta la vista," 19.
9. Fraser, "God's flock," 3.

> Broadcast ministries are an effective means of spreading the gospel and should be pursued whenever possible with an eye toward excellence as well as stewardship, since the *image* quality must equal that of any neighboring program on television in order to provide a basis for viewer interest.[10]

This highlights an uncritical acceptance of image's presence, with the emphasis placed firmly on maintaining "viewer interest" in the face of competing images.

On the other hand, Jacques Ellul berates image in church stating, "A person pays closer attention to the means of communication than to a worship service."[11] Ellul, and his contemporaries such as Carl Henry[12] and Malcolm Muggeridge, who like him speak from an earlier modernist perspective, hold a high degree of suspicion towards image, with television the primary culprit.[13] Yet barring a technological implosion images will increase exponentially. In the decades since Ellul, Henry, and Muggeridge we have progressed from video to the digital age: clearer, more dramatic, and more convincing images are here to stay.[14]

Are images "genetically" designed to overpower and subvert words? Or are they value-neutral; simple tools at the beck and call of a communicative act? It appears that, in general, most of the thinking is being done by non-practitioners. Hence we have churches that uncritically adopt whatever the culture is into at the time (and currently that is image-oriented), while others are being defined by what they are against, remaining stoically text-based only, with little interaction with image, and no admission that the way we learn things is changing.

Is there a middle ground? It is my contention that while images are not the problem per se, they are being invested with an authority not rightfully theirs and, in the process, contribute to the devaluation of words. Words are losing their ability to "grip," sliding off us like Teflon™. Images, in

---

10. Morris and Lyons, "Word," 14.

11. Ellul, *Humiliation*, 194.

12. See Henry, *God, Revelation and Authority*. At the outset Henry states, "So astonishingly clever and successful have been these media in captivating the contemporary spirit . . . that Yahweh's ancient exhortation to beware of visual idols would seem doubly pertinent today."

13. Muggeridge, *Christ and the Media*. See also, Poland "Christ," 254–74.

14. Miller, *Millennium Matrix*. Miller maps the progression in the church from liturgical to digital eras, urging us to find ways to navigate the world as it is now, while readying ourselves for further change.

true Velcro™ fashion, are sticking with us. If we are to render words "sticky" again both *redemption and reconciliation* is required. As adherents of a speaking God who reveals himself in his Word, we have a creation/salvific mandate to reconcile and redeem the current power struggle between image and word. In the following overview of the Scriptures we will see that the relationship between the two is occasionally harmonious and sometimes tempestuous.

WORD AND IMAGE IN SCRIPTURE

Much theological polemic against the rise of image is based on Scriptural prohibition of images for cultic worship, explicitly stated in Exodus 20:4–6 (c.f. Exod 34:17, Deut 5:8–10, Pss 96, 97, Isa 44–46, Jer 10:2–5), a different issue at least initially to the worship of *other* gods, but by the time of Isaiah one that was fused to apostasy.[15]

But the Decalogue is not the precedent. It is the *word* that creates everything (Gen 1:3–31, c.f. 2 Pet 3:5), yet humanity is made in God's *image* (Gen 1:26–27). Whatever God creates by word becomes visible and is described as "good." Before the Fall the correspondence between word and image is celebrated in Adam's naming of the animals (Gen 2:19–20), where Adam names what he sees and "whatever the man called the living creature, that was its name." However the Fall springs from the word that God spoke to Adam prohibiting the eating of the fruit (Gen 2:15–17)—a word passed on to Eve (Gen 3:2–3)—being disregarded when "the woman *saw* that the fruit of the tree was good for food and *pleasing to the eye*" (Gen 3:6a).

As the biblical narrative progresses, this reluctance to accept the divine word in the face of the visible image is Israel's scourge. It ranges from simple image veneration designed to encapsulate YHWH (Exod 32, 1 Kgs 12:25–33), to idolatrous worship of pagan gods (Isa 2:6–9, Jer 4:1, 2 Kgs 17:7–17, Ezek 8, Jonah 2:8), through to sophisticated alliances with pagan nations for the sake of visible security, despite prophetic exhortations to take God at his word (Isa 7, Jer 37).[16] This refusal to hear God's words is encapsulated in the final chapter of Judah's pre-exilic history:

---

15. Barton, "The Work," 63–72. Barton points out that it is the hidden nature of God in Deut 4 that is the *raison d'être* behind the prohibition, not the image's link with other gods.

16. Though, see Greenspahn, "Syncretism," 480–94. Greenspahn questions our understanding of the definitions Israel's prophets used to describe the false religious practices of their people.

> The Lord, the God of their fathers, sent word to them through his messengers again and again, because he had pity on his people and on his dwelling place. But they mocked God's messengers, despised his words and scoffed at his prophets until the wrath of the Lord was aroused against his people and there was no remedy (2 Chron 36:15–16).

The exile ends image worship and syncretism in Israel, yet the danger of refusing God's word remains. The post-exilic remnant question God's declared love for them in the face of a hostile environment.[17]

In the New Testament we are confronted with the astounding claim of John 1:14: "the Word became flesh," the very imaging of God in salvation.[18] Indeed, it is the scandal of the Incarnation that the Jewish leaders will not countenance, unable to reconcile the image of the young man standing before them with the words of Jesus; "Your father Abraham rejoiced at the thought of seeing my day; he saw it and was glad" (Jn 8:56). Hence, there is a more complex relationship between word and image in the New Testament.

Jesus's context is not so much a writing culture as a hearing culture, and he himself brings word and image together memorably in his parables (Mk 4:1–8,22–34, Lk 13:18–21). But seeing and believing are not the same, as Jesus indicates to Thomas and others in John's Gospel (Jn 20:24–31). Indeed, Jesus points out that his parables permit people to see, but not perceive (Mk 4:11-12).

While the prohibition of cultic image veneration continues in the New Testament (Rom 1:18–23; Acts 17: 16, 29; 1 Cor 10:14; 1 Jn 4:21), Paul subverts the Roman Emperor cult, stating explicitly that Jesus "is the image of the invisible God" (Col 1:15), " ... in a poem composed with the goal of providing alternative images for a subversive imagination."[19]

---

17. Malachi deals with this issue at length.

18. Interestingly, Ellul, *Humiliation*, 48, uses this passage to highlight the speaking nature of God against the image and states, "it goes without saying that when we read that God speaks, it does not mean at all that he pronounces words, and that he has a vocabulary, and syntactical rules." This is curious given (a) the Incarnation comes into a specific linguistic culture, and (b) the subsequent words of 1 John 1:1–3 and 2 Peter 1:16 where sight and sound are presented as mutually endorsing. By contrast Miller, *Millennium Matrix*, 22, ties Jesus's words tightly to the created order: "His words were so connected to the composition of the universe that they calmed raging seas, gave sight to the blind and raised the dead."

19. Walsh and Keesmaat, *Colossians*, 84.

Peter bases apostolic authority on the basis of being "eyewitnesses of his majesty" (2 Pet 1:16b), while John states that not only was the "Word of life" heard, it was something that "we have seen with our eyes, which we have looked at, and our hands have touched" (1 Jn 1:1). Finally, John's Revelation is an unveiling of what could not previously be seen *in order* to strengthen faith, constantly employing the refrain "then I saw" (e.g., Rev 1:12, 5:1, 6, 7:1, 8:2, 10:1, 13:1).

Hebrews has a more mixed response. The introduction highlights the Son—God's ultimate mode of speaking—is "the radiance of God's glory and the exact representation of his being" (Heb 1:3), yet is also adamant that true realities are unseen (Heb 8:3–5, 9:23–25, 10:1), culminating with chapter eleven's faith passage. Indeed, Jesus himself sustains the universe "by his powerful word" (Heb 1:3). It is the refusal to listen to God's words that proved the downfall of the desert generation (Heb 3:7–4:7), and could endanger the writer's contemporaries (3:12, 4:1–3). Chapter 4 climaxes with the affirmation "For the word of God is living and active. Sharper than any double-edge sword" (Heb 4:12–14).[20]

WORD AND IMAGE IN CHURCH HISTORY

Leaving aside Christianity's flirtation with Platonic distrust of the image, historically our evangelical DNA links us with the iconoclasts of the Reformation. Those, such as Ellul and Henry, who decry the rise of image, appear to base their foundations on the Old Testament, building on the theology and ideology of reformers like Calvin. According to Oakes,

> the iconoclasm of Western Puritanism was born out of Calvin's reliance on Old Testament Law. When Calvin re-established the validity of Old Testament Law, he inevitably made the ban on *images* a living commandment once again.[21]

The Reformers, as Edwards posits, understood that images were highly influential spiritually, something we, as their descendents have forgotten:

> Protestants are inclined to underestimate the power of *images* in religion. Yet at the founding of Protestantism and in its early

---

20. In this passage the word's sword-like qualities are a pointer to the "falling by the sword" in Numbers 15. Those who rebelled, refusing to take God at his word and enter the Promised Land, furthered their rebellion, in spite of God's subsequent prohibition, by trying to enter it and being slaughtered by the inhabitants.

21. Oakes, "Icons," 37–44.

decades its leaders were very much aware of the power of religious *images* and did all they could either to remove the *images* entirely—the iconoclasts' solution—or to recast them in a way that exalted word over *image*.²²

Certainly Luther, who would be no friend of idolatrous icons, was aware of this power when conferring upon the Eucharist the status of being a visible gospel for those who, weak in their faith, are still not convinced by what they hear.

Luther aside, Edwards' comment highlights a lack of any third way in the present among those who, rather than seek redemption and reconciliation between word and image, would do away with image altogether, or contest that word and image are so opposed that reconciliation and redemption are impossible. In critiquing Ellul's deep suspicion, and his insistence that *only* in the Incarnation did word and image come together truthfully William Dyrness asks:

> Why can't we forge a new alliance between word and image that will help us meet the challenge of this generation? Why did this union of word and image necessarily happen only once, in the Incarnation? Does Scripture contain no support for thinking that this event furthered God's purposes with the visual creation, by adding to it "the Word made flesh."²³

In other words, if Pandora's box is open, and the powerful image has been unleashed, is the weaker word's *humiliation* a logical necessity? Ellul's language is often that of an abusive relationship. Dyrness does not claim to be a cultural optimist in the vein of a Mitchell Stephens—who sees the advance of the image over the word as secular salvation in the current cultural upheaval. But he questions why we would want to return to the supposed image-less past given "that Christ continues to be Lord of history, that he is working out his purposes in and through human history, and that he calls us to a glorious future kingdom."²⁴

This desire to engage rather than decry image highlights the cultural and philosophical chasm between modernist and postmodernist theological thinking, itself an echo of the secular setting. Hence, for every Kevin Donnelly worried about the fall in literacy standards in Australia, there is

---

22. Edwards, "Power," 31–32.
23. Dyrness, http://www.cornerstonemag.com/page/show_page.asp?442.
24. Ibid. See also, Stephens, *Rise of the Image*.

an academic saying, "Relax!"²⁵ However, as we shall now see, it is not as simple as taking sides with either image or word. As we observed earlier, the controlling issue is theological, not cultural. It is not the rise of image and the devaluation of word that is the chief concern, but rather the more foundational issue of the loss of a controlling meta-narrative.

THE CRITICAL LOSS OF META-NARRATIVE

It is my contention that Ellul and Dyrness have far more in common with each other than either has with his secular counterpart. Both have a controlling biblical meta-narrative and an eschatology based on the resurrection of Christ. Where they differ is that Ellul permits sight to be redeemed only in the eschaton.²⁶ But, as Dyrness' statement above indicates, there are many Christians whose eschatology is more "realized," permitting redemption between image and word in the present age, not simply promising it as a treat in the age to come. The visual age has caught up with us in the present and the question is, can it be redeemed *in the present?* Even the most distrustful implicitly admit this possibility, given their constant plea to Christians to be employed in the visual media.²⁷ The problem we are contending with today is the *unfettered* use of imagery to create reality rather than to reflect reality.²⁸ Image has been loosed from the control of an overarching meta-narrative, and is subsequently free and, due to its intrinsic plausibility, able to create its own eschatology, a future of its own design.

Advertising is the supreme example. A luxury car cruises a windswept coastal highway replete with hunk and babe eyeing each other

---

25. University of Queensland English Professor, Gillian Whitlock, http//www.theaustralian.com.au, states in defence of the curriculum changes: "[T]he idea that great books are inherently civilising, and produce enlightened and virtuous individuals through a kind of osmosis, is a false promise.... New media, mass media and the literary tradition; reading and writing and speaking the language; the work of interpretation through emotion and reason: all are in the mix of contemporary Australian English ... [and] are the texts and skills essential to a literate everyday life."

26. Ellul, *Humiliation*. In the final section, "Reconciliation," Ellul's concern is that the "audio-visual venture is identical to that of the mystics," meaning that in the same way the mystics desired to see something *now* that was permitted only in the eschaton, so too our age is grasping at only defining ultimate truth by what it can perceive visually.

27. Both Poland, "Christ," and Muggeridge, *Christ*, call for a deeper engagement in the media.

28. I say this in the sense not that reality can be fully known, but that it can be partly, but accurately known.

off. Immediately we fill in the blanks. They are going on a cozy romantic weekend getaway for good food, great wine, and even better sex. This ultimate reality could all be yours should you purchase the car. Of course, no such romantic weekend exists. There is no food, no wine, no sex: just two actors, a car, and a team of stylists, consultants, and camera crew. Being media-savvy we know it, yet we do not *feel* it. An ultimate reality—an eschaton—has been created to fill the void for those with no other eschaton. Even the industry admits that this is how it works when it tricks us with advertising campaigns that present the desirable image, only to memorably pull the rug out from under us with a humorous, unexpected, or shocking twist.[29]

The real battle for people such as Kevin Donnelly is the loss of a meta-narrative implicit in many of the classics: one based in Enlightenment principles of liberal humanism. The wax of image has not only coincided with the wane of word, but also with the dismantling of meta-narratives. Even in pop culture alarm bells are ringing. Generation X-er Alissa Quart laments the manner in which teen movies no longer present "moments of veracity, or have responsible, liberal reflexes to guide them."[30] By contrast, today's teen movies are littered with characters that are "empty vessels, slathered with beauty products."[31]

What Donnelly, Quart, and their ilk vainly search for in this visual age is a sense of transcendence, a compass to provide meaning and direction. Yet the loss of meta-narrative is not a direct result of the visual age replacing the word-era, but an unfortunate coincident. There is no necessary corollary between loss of meaning and rise of image.

This brings us back to Dyrness's question: "Why can't we forge a new alliance between word and image that will help us meet the challenge

---

29. A recent Toohey's beer advertising campaign features a woman undressing to sensuous music before slipping into a spa surrounded by candles. The mood is broken by her laddish boyfriend doing a "bombie" into the spa, soaking her, the candles and all of the towels, before offering a mystified "What?" and downing a bottle of Tooheys.

30. Quart, *Branded*, 102 She presents 1985's *The Breakfast Club* as the type of teen movie that has gone missing, in which characters, though flawed and nerdy from start to finish, learn a lesson that makes them better. Today's movie heroes, by contrast, are the jocks and home-coming queens who remain bullies and vacuous bimbos. A recent exception was the cult hit *Napoleon Dynamite* which grossed 100 times its production costs in the US. There is still a yearning for such redemptive stories!

31. Quart, *Branded*, 125.

of this generation?"[32] Only the transcendent can break the circuit and offer redemption and reconciliation between the two, and for that we must turn to the only transcendent text available to us—the Word of God. We will examine how the Bible communicates to us through both word and image, highlighting the thinking of Kevin Vanhoozer, whose search for hermeneutical integrity occurs at literary criticism's coal-face. We will then see how, when guided by a controlling meta-narrative, word and image work in tandem to communicate God's message in and through the church.

LIVING THE TEXT: THE ENACTED IMAGE

That evangelicals must remain biblical in the face of a society replete with suspicion of the text is part of what it means to be evangelical. Kevin Vanhoozer asks "Why be biblical?" before providing the answer:

> Because the Bible communicates the gospel of Jesus Christ—the account of what God has said and done as sovereign Lord and as suffering servant for our salvation. "Evangelical" designates theology that seeks to know the "God of the gospel."[33]

He then makes this important point:

> Theology done in accord with the *euangelion* highlights two divine initiatives that together make up God's good news about God. First, God acting: There is only news if something has been done. Second, God speaking: There is only news if someone reports what has been done. Evangelicals accept these divine initiatives—the divine acts and their inspired events—as the two givens with which theology begins.[34]

Vanhoozer's work on biblical hermeneutics recognizes that there is no going back—that a new hermeneutic is needed in the visual age in which literary criticism reigns. Speaking (along with its subsequent reportage) and acting are a platform upon which to build the alliance Dyrness seeks. As receivers of "the Word" (albeit not the original receivers) we are called not simply to hear the words, but to do them—to act them out (Matt 7:24–27). Such acting offers a redemptive and reconciliatory process between word and image, for acting itself is foundationally a kinetic and

---

32. Dyrness, "A Turn to the Visual."
33. Vanhoozer, "Voice," 63.
34. Ibid.

corporeal imaging of what has been said or written. Vanhoozer adapts Austin and Searle's work on speech act philosophy, incorporating a transcendent author; hence we have "God's mighty speech acts."[35] Austin and Searle, in opposition to the likes of Jacques Derrida, assert that the *speech act* rather than the *word* is the "basic unit of meaning."[36] Vanhoozer transfers this to our interpretation and enactment—or imaging—of Scripture. Only this, he believes,

> overcomes the ruinous dichotomy between historical-actualist and verbal-conceptualist models of revelation, that is, the dualism between God-saying and God-doing. Scripture is neither simply the recital of the acts of God nor merely a book of inert propositions. Scripture is rather composed of divine-human speech acts that, through what they say, accomplish several authoritative cognitive, spiritual and social functions."[37]

That Vanhoozer takes what he believes is a necessary step further than Austin and Searle in asserting a theistic framework is vital. He proffers "Christian Doctrine" as the only satisfactory alternative to "Derrida's Doubt."[38] Hence he states, "We can formulate the following thesis: *the design plan of language is to serve as the medium of covenantal relations with God, with others, with the world.*"[39] This places the battle for meaning within a moral context, and denies the apparent neutrality of Derrida, who Vanhoozer labels a "countertheologian" for asserting that words are playthings with no determinate referents.[40] Meaning is a communicative action, involving the doing and the deed. It incorporates several stages; the propositional content; the illocutionary force (the energy and trajectory effected by the propositions); and the perlocutionary effect (the teleology or final purpose—the "thing" that happens as a result).[41]

---

35. Vanhoozer, *First Theology*, 127–58.
36. Vanhoozer, *Is There a Meaning?* 209.
37. Vanhoozer, *First Theology*, 131.
38. Vanhoozer, *Is There a Meaning?* 213. "Deconstruction may be the death of God written into language, and Searle may ultimately be no better off in substituting society for God. Without a properly theological moment, it may be that speech act philosophy cannot restore trust in language and authority to the author."
39. Vanhoozer, *Is There a Meaning?* 206 (italics original).
40. Vanhoozer, *First Theology*, 211.
41. Vanhoozer, *Is There a Meaning?* 218.

Turning Teflon™ into Velcro™

That unsupervised play, as espoused by Derrida, can lead to violence of the playmate (in this instance, the text), should come as no surprise to those of us who have children, or who have played a competitive team sport without an umpire or referee. Indeed when interpretation is only "from below," or to put it in more familiar terms, from "the reader," the results may not be as joyful and pleasant as those such as Derrida would have us believe. So, while we offer the church as the enactment/imaging of the written text that determines meaning, we must caution against finding the natural reading only ever within the interpretive community. To do so would be to ignore the text's supernatural ability to speak from above, and to fall into the violence trap. As Vanhoozer notes,

> The theological diversity within the Scriptures is nowhere near as pronounced as the theological diversity of the believing community.... In which community do we best see God's inspiring presence? Should we include the German Christians who supported Hitler? ... Even a casual reading of the Old Testament and New Testament discloses communities that are primarily *unbelieving* for much of their histories.[42]

At the very least, this should tell us that even the church of God is not immune from breaking the link between the meaning of the spoken/written word and the enactment/imaging of it by the people of God. If this is the case even with those who, outwardly at least, adhere to a stated meta-narrative then it is no surprise when it is so among those for whom image is completely unfettered from text.

Elsewhere Vanhoozer states that "drama reminds us that the action is itself a form of interpretation, with genuine performance serving as the goal.... [T]he actor is to embody the meaning behind the words—the subtext."[43] The governing, and guarding framework that ensures such acting does not descend into mere free-play, impromptu ad-libbing taking away meaning rather than sustaining it, is again the biblical meta-narrative.[44]

---

42. Vanhoozer, *Is There a Meaning?* 149.
43. Vanhoozer, *Voice*, 95.
44. Vanhoozer "Trials," 131, says that "the imagination, formed and guided by the canon, may be an organ of truth."

LOSING THE PLOT IN CHURCH: IMAGE UNLEASHED

Unfortunately, the level of biblical illiteracy within the Christian community is growing to the point that many are losing the "big story." The dramatic act has ground to a halt in many churches and denominations because the biblical eschaton has first been enervated by, then replaced with, the pseudo-eschatons of the car and white goods commercials. That these all-powerful eschatons are conjured up by *disembodied* images, ones that are not grounded in reality and are simply nonexistent, makes matters worse. It is this loss of meta-narrative that results in the words of that Gold Coast pastor about his church having "the best-looking congregation" and being "the cheeky church!" This highlights the obvious connection between "images" and "image." Images—especially television advertising—promote and project social currency, offering the chance to present the right *image*, which today includes "best-looking" and "cheeky." If your church can get that mix right it is on to a winner, and will attract a certain buyer who believes this is the product for them.

However one cannot imagine the apostle Paul making such a statement to the Corinthian church. Indeed, it was largely to correct such misconceptions that he wrote to them in the first place. The Corinthians had bought into the myths of the image-makers in their own culture, myths that established this age's wisdom and outward impressiveness as the canon. By contrast, Paul presents a different image altogether, "[B]ut we preach Christ crucified: a stumbling block to Jews and foolishness to Gentiles." This sordid image of a weak Messiah crucified cannot and will not make sense, and hence cannot be enacted by the community, unless that community is steeped in a biblical eschatology. That is why 1 Corinthians 15 is so important. Only the resurrection of Christ, and then by consequence, of believers in the age to come, allows the chapter's final imperatives:

> Therefore, my beloved, be steadfast, immovable, always excelling in the work of the Lord, because you know that in the Lord your labor is not in vain (1 Cor 15:58).

In the face of myriad *disembodied* eschatons, we hope in an *embodied* one.

The task of the theologian in today's image-saturated world, therefore, is to take the same biblical template, replete with meta-narrative, and let it re-form the imaginations of today's hearers of the Word. Unless it does so, the powerful stories that value "best-looking" and "cheeky" will subdue "Christ crucified" every time. Brian Walsh and Sylvia Keesmaat highlight this subversive reimaging of the world in Colossians. In Colossians 1:15 Paul quotes a poem about the one who is "the image of the invisible God, the firstborn over all creation." Walsh and Keesmaat observe,

> Images of the emperor were as ubiquitous in the first century as corporate logos are in the twenty-first century. The image of Caesar and other symbols of Roman power were literally everywhere ... the sovereign rule of Caesar was simply assumed to be the divine plan for the peace and order of the cosmos.[45]

Given we are "confronted every day by somewhere between five and twelve thousand corporate messages, all geared to shaping a consumer imagination,"[46] Walsh and Keesmaat call for a "Christian imagination" to be rekindled across culture, in the arts, local politics, environmental protection, and business.[47] But this will not simply happen. It can only occur through a reimaging that permits "the discourse of Scripture to become our first language, our normative discourse."[48]

N. T. Wright does something similar with his concept of "the fifth act." He likens the biblical story to a newly discovered Shakespearean play of which acts one to four are intact, but the fifth has been lost. Each generation of actors (God's people) is given the freedom to "play out" a fifth act in its own context, keeping in mind that it must remain interpretatively faithful to the previous four acts, the first being universe-creation, through to the fourth; ecclesiological-creation. Wright says that "The church would then live under the "authority" of the extant story, being required to offer something between an improvisation and an actual performance of the final act."[49] The "authority of the extant story" reminds us that the reading is not from below, and that faithful fifth-act imaging is dependent on faithful first-to-fourth-act interpretation. This keeps the fifth act fresh;

---

45. Walsh and Keesmaat, *Colossians*, 83.

46. Ibid., 84.

47. Ibid., 85.

48. Ibid. Walsh and Keesmaat offer a radical upgrade of the Colossians 1:15ff poem with the following: "In an image-saturated world, a world of ubiquitous corporate logos permeating your consciousness: a world of dehydrated and captive imaginations in which we are too numbed, satiated and co-opted to be able to dream of life otherwise: a world in which the empire of global economic affluence has achieved the monopoly of our imaginations: in this world, Christ is the image of the invisible God, in this world, driven by images with a vengeance, Christ is the image par excellence."

49. Wright, "How Can The Bible Be Authoritative?" 7–32.

stops it from ossifying; and ensures intergenerational continuity with the "big story" into which we have been drawn.

In the same, Australian youth worker Andrew Stewart highlights the need for a new way to read the text for those born into the image age, as opposed to those who straddle it. Stewart worries that we are losing young people to the Bible because we persist with modern metaphors of engagement such as "rule-book" and "foundation." He offers alternate postmodern metaphors that reflect "the non-linear inter-connectivity of the Scriptures such as "Lonely Planet for the Spiritual Pilgrim" and "God's homepage."[50]

These and similar attempts have a common goal, they all desire to "thicken up" theology: to make it "look like" something, not simply "sound like" or "read like" something. It is hermeneutics where the battle is being fought. Word and image must come together in meaningful congruity. We leave the last word on this subject to Vanhoozer: "Meaning has less to do with the play of linguistic elements in an impersonal sign system than with the responsibility of communicative agents in inter-subjective social systems."[51]

The choice is clear. Society has two options: life within a culture driven by powerful, yet ultimately meaningless disembodied images, or life within an oft-scorned and seemingly weak, yet embodied community journeying towards ultimate meaning grounded in God's big story. This means that the time has come to put some flesh on the bones. As the embodied community living in an era of disembodied images, how are we to stage our "fifth act" *faithfully* for the sake of God's glory in the church, and *fruitfully*, for the sake of God's mission in the world? Hence we conclude with an examination of ways in which we can do both of these things, a call to keep on exploring ways to faithfully enact the drama wherever the culture takes us.

THE FAITHFUL FIFTH ACT: GOD'S GLORY IN THE CHURCH

In what he refers to as "the digital age," Rex Miller signals a number of spiritual "hungers" that cry out to be filled, including the crucial three of "authenticity, mystery, and depth."[52] Given Jesus' statement that "whoever

---

50. Stewart, "Simpsons," 6–10.
51. Vanhoozer, *Is There a Meaning?* 203.
52. Miller, *Millennium Matrix*, 127–32.

comes to me will never go hungry" (Jn 6:35), the church's challenge is to *faithfully* embody the gospel in such a way that deep-seated, spiritually-charged hungers such as these are sated.

Unfortunately, many attempts to "do church" in the image age fail to fill these hungers because the images presented are often inauthentic, lacking in mystery and, ultimately, shallow. The root problem is the neglect of our meta-narrative and our eschatology. Consequently, what church sounds like is often divorced from what it looks like. Walsh and Keesmat put their finger on the issue:

> What does a community renewed in knowledge according to the image of the Creator look like? It looks like the Creator. It *images* this God. By embodying in its communal life the virtues that are formed by this God's story.[53]

In Colossians 3 Paul describes the virtues of such a community: compassion, kindness, humility, forgiveness, peace, love, and unity. These are fine words to read, but impotent unless imaged by the people of God (c.f. Jas 2:14–17, 1 Jn 2:9). Celebrity, hero-worship, and images that present "cool" as the highest currency pervade the church, especially among those born into the image age. Not that this is simply a problem in our day, as James's admonition of the favoritism shown by those who "believe in our glorious Lord Jesus Christ" towards the wealthy demonstrates.[54]

Emergent church people take note! This malaise comes in many guises. Scott Bader-Saye notes about the rediscovery of historical practices in the alt-worship scene:

> Despite the undeniable power of these retrieved practices, one must wonder if the incense, candles, labyrinths and all the rest are being retrieved simply because they've become cool. Tangible, multi-sensory worship has a currency among younger generations, and this is all to the good. But if this recovery is linked only to generation and style, what will happen when styles change? . . .

---

53. Walsh and Keesmaat, *Colossians*, 174.

54. Jas 2:1–4, "My brothers and sisters, do you with your acts of favoritism really believe in our glorious Lord Jesus Christ?[1] For if a person with gold rings and in fine clothes comes into your assembly, and if a poor person in dirty clothes also comes in,[2] and if you take notice of the one wearing the fine clothes and say, 'Have a seat here, please,' while to the one who is poor you say, 'Stand there,' or, 'Sit at my feet,'[3] have you not made distinctions among yourselves, and become judges with evil thoughts?"[4]

> One test for the emerging church will be whether ancient practices are retrieved as practices or simply as preferences.[55]

This tendency to default to consumptive employment of imagery is why our controlling image must be the subversive image of the cross and all of its weakness. The fact that the despised, rejected one is the glorious Christ, who in dying brings eternal life, is ironically what redeems and restores the relationship between word and image, and lays to rest the constant desire to reflect the values of the image devoid of the biblical meta-narrative. Pilate's charge-sheet above Jesus's head, "The King of the Jews," was designed to draw attention to the ludicrous gap—strong words nailed about a weak dying image of a man; Rome's mocking reassertion of its power. Yet here is Jesus's kingship at its most victorious!

While Rome has fallen, the powers and values that upheld it have not. There is a strikingly contemporary feel to the famous third century Roman graffito that depicts a man saluting a crucified human figure with a donkey's head. The Greek caption reads, "Anaxamenos worships his god." The dissonance between the church's position in Christ, and its place in the world, has always hinged on whether one considers the crucified Christ to be an object of worship, or an object of scorn.

What the cross does, however, is permit us to engage in subversive acts. It encourages us to present images that expose as fraudulent the dominant social, cultural and economic images of the day, to show them as ultimately *powerless* despite their protestations to the contrary. Subversive actions will remain as long as this overlapping age remains. Although by the Spirit we taste God's future *now*, a future in which image and word will realign completely, it has *not yet* fully come. Attempts to completely close the gap *now* will fail. That is why much *overt* Christian imagery appears over-earnest and twee, easily hijacked by popular culture and rendered kitsch. Phillip Yancey notes that T. S. Eliot's subversive poetry retains its spiritual vitality, while his obviously Christian sermons and tracts appear dated and quaint. His poetry gets under the skin in a way that his sermons do not because the former strikes at the unprotected cultural assumptions.[56]

Christianity subverts the power play between image and word, speaking ludicrous strength into what is seemingly weak: "Blessed are the poor

---

55. Bader-Saye, "Emergent Matrix," 20–26.
56. Yancey, *I Was Just Wondering*, 128–34.

in spirit, for theirs is the kingdom of heaven" (Matt 5:3). Meek inherit, tax-collectors are justified, Samaritans are good, prostitutes and sinners are socialized with, poor widows give more than rich men. Word and image appear dissonant, but only if we forget that the cross is the great cosmic reversal of strength and weakness, a truth subsequently tattooed onto the apostles' imagination post-resurrection. Peter says, "When you suffer you are blessed." John says, "When he appears we will be like him, for we shall see him as he is." James asks, "Has not God chosen those who are poor in the eyes of the world to be rich in faith and to inherit the kingdom?" Paul declares, "For the message of the cross is foolishness to those who are perishing, but to us who are being saved it is the power of God."

If the congregation is the hermeneutic of the gospel, as Newbigin puts it, how do we perform a subversive, yet faithful, fifth act in this image-oriented age?[57] By proclaiming eternity to a "get it now" society, celebrating misfits in a culture of cool, being thoughtful practitioners not mindless consumers, demonstrating contentedness in an era of superseded models, maintaining spiritual and relational fidelity in a smorgasbord of options, saying "Enough thank you!" instead of "Super-size me!" practicing costly community not easy individualism, and offering unified sanctuary in the fractured face of racial, religious and economic hostility. Simply put, we play out the irony uncovered in the contrast between the cross's weak appearance and the cross's powerful achievements. As the Hyundai™ slogan says, we are "Future Driven." Our future is one in which "those who are last will be first, and those who are first will be last."[58]

THE FAITHFUL FIFTH ACT: GOD'S MISSION IN THE WORLD

While recognizing that Newbigin's hermeneutic concept is also mission-oriented, twenty-first century nonbelievers have little or no contact with a gospel congregation. Increasingly, the fifth act is a dress rehearsal, played out only to ourselves. While this is no bad thing, our role as hermeneutic of the gospel *to those outside* is being lost.

---

57. Newbigin, *Gospel*.

58. Luke 13:22–30. Jesus contrasts the end-time fortunes of those who belong to the children of Israel and therefore view themselves on an "inside track" with God, with those far away who will come from "east and west and north and south and will take their places at the feast in the kingdom of God."

One popular response has been to offer an experience of church more recognizable to outsiders; one with greater links to the way they already live. This attractional model seems to be fruitful, if some of the mega-churches are any indication. Yet fruitfulness rests within the call to faithfulness. While it is important to be contextual in mission, it is equally important not to be syncretistic. Because syncretism is more obvious in a non-Western context, it is more dangerous in a Western one. What happens when an image-saturated and image-driven culture sets the church's agenda for fruitfulness? The divine-drama is reduced to the divine-variety show—a format familiar to people soaked in an image-oriented culture. The corresponding replacement of the biblical-meta-narrative with talk-show host style sound-bite theology, rather than redeeming the relationship between word and image, actually maintains the dysfunction and violence. The subversive element has been lost. This is particularly clear among church youth culture, where the search is on for "cool" Christian alternatives to secular popular culture. The problem is that "cool" becomes the defining paradigm—those who were misfits and outcasts in the outside world remain so within the church's walls, as the cult of celebrity takes over.[59]

Ironically, our attempts to ape cool are futile anyway, because the gatekeepers of popular culture stay one step ahead. *The Simpsons*™, a show that devotes much of its time to religion, takes great pleasure in mocking Christianity's attempts to "get with it."[60] Another iconic animation, *King of the Hill*™, puts it succinctly in a scene in which Hank's son Bobby is enamored with a self-consciously pierced and tattooed Christian rock-band at a summer-camp he attends. Hank laments: "Can't you see you're not making Christianity better, you're just making rock n' roll worse?"

While the sins of youth go before it, the sins of middle age are more subtle. Cool is replaced by credible. What the church offers must, if it is to be taken up, make sense to those immersed in the economic, individualistic Western lifestyle. How church "looks"—its worship and sermons; its activities and projects—all too often seek to sanctify and control the rush towards busy lifestyles, spiraling debt and accumulation of white goods. There is no time to dramatize the subversive fifth act because the limelight has been stolen by a renegade troupe maintaining the status quo.

---

59. The winner of the 2003 *Australian Idol*® competition, Guy Sebastian, who is a Christian, was being touted by many as a solution to the church's falling attendances among young people.

60. Pinsky, *Gospel*.

Turning Teflon™ into Velcro™

Lest this appear simply to be a rant against modern media culture, we return again to Dyrness's question: "Why can't we forge a new alliance between word and image that will help us meet the challenge of this generation?" The way forward is through the subversion of the cross. Just as God took the cross's degrading familiarity and subverted it for his glory, we can do the same. Rather than missioning by creating a "sounds like/looks like" imitation of the culture in the hope that nonbelievers will come along and be taken in before they realize the difference, why not simply be subversive with the images they already know?

This is the premise behind Robert Johnson's book *Reel Spirituality*, which explores the biblical themes of morality, sin, salvation, restoration, death, love, and so on, that pervade Hollywood movies.[61] He notes how Phillip Yancey says it took movies such as *Jesus Christ Superstar* (1973), and *The Last Temptation of Christ* (1998), for him to realize how truly *human* Jesus is.[62] What comparable "sacred" film dares come as close in depicting how desirable and noble a temptation such as love, sex, and marriage must have been to Jesus; one so strong it could get in the way of the cross and fidelity to his Father? It is the same with less overtly "religious" movies, such as the invitation in 1999's *American Beauty* to "look closer," beyond the beautiful suburban facade to the empty centre. What a secular indictment of the culture at a time when, ironically, the prosperity gospel was in full swing.

This is just the tip of the iceberg. The challenge is to search out the cultural "itches," and discover ways to redeem them through the enacted drama of the biblical story. Currently, images are the most obvious, but something will inevitably replace them in the future. Whatever does, only the biblical meta-narrative, steeped in a resurrection eschatology, can by the all-powerful Spirit of God create an embodied community that will enact God's divine-drama in such a way that all images, save that of the one who is the very "image of God," will pale into insignificance.

---

61. Johnson. *Reel Spirituality*.

62. Ibid., 80. Ironically *The Last Temptation of Christ* was the subject of a boycott by major Christian groups around the world.

13

Preaching in weakness

Reflections on the self in preaching

Brian S. Harris

INTRODUCTION

Let me start with two stories, the relevance of which should become clearer as this essay unfolds. I had just finished preaching at a church I was visiting for the first time. A woman came up and thanked me, informing me that I reminded her of her favorite preacher, whom she then spoke about at great length. Knowing her preaching idol, and not sharing her views on his giftedness, I politely concealed my irritation at the unflattering comparison. As she went on and on, I noticed another woman with a teenage daughter politely waiting in line to speak with me. The current occupant of my attention was not one to be easily interrupted and it took a fair while and some less than subtle prompting to get her to move along.

Personally, I was surprised that anyone would have waited so long to comment on a sermon of mine, but the woman and her daughter were still there. Her message was simple. Her husband had died that week. During the sermon I had made some comments about the resurrection that had touched her deeply and led to her having a God-encounter. She thanked me for having been the conduit of strength for the impossible week that lay ahead. As she spoke, my irritation at the previous encounter faded, and

I was humbly grateful for the remarkable things that sometimes happen through preaching.

That reminded me of another conversation. A woman came and saw me to thank me for a comment I had made while a guest preacher at her church about a year previously. Apparently, I had said something about the importance of embracing what is, rather than what is not. She quoted me: "Rather than lament time past, embrace the time ahead—even if only a little remains." The comment came after she had spent some months living with the verdict that she was suffering from a terminal disease. Until then, she said, each day was filled with resentment and bitterness at what was not going to be. Since then, her focus had shifted. She had seized each day and lived it as fully as she was able. She had recently heard that her cancer had progressed to the next stage of its relentless and unwavering journey. She wanted to thank me for a comment that had made the final stages triumphant rather than sour.

When she left, I sat back in confused amazement. I had no recollection of the sermon, let alone the comment—just another of the throwaway statements that may or may not take root in someone's life and journey. Death did indeed come to her a few weeks later. How remarkable to think that an unremembered comment from a forgotten sermon had helped to ensure it came in the guise of friend, not foe.

I rather like those two accounts. They move so comfortably in the right direction. The strong, all together preacher, speaking words of comfort and challenge that help strugglers to face their dilemmas with courage and good cheer. Except . . . Except that it's never simply like that. True, through the mysterious working of the Spirit the preached word often impacts people in ways beyond our imagining. But the all together preacher . . . well, hardly!

IMAGES OF THE SELF IN PREACHING

While each preacher has a cluster of glorious stories to tell, what is a more realistic view of the "self" of the preacher? In this essay I explore five paradoxical images of the self in preaching. They are as follows:

- The authentic but boundaried self.
- The believing but doubting self.
- The idiosyncratic but communal self.
- The despairing but hopeful self.
- The finite self and the infinite God.

The authentic but boundaried self

Preaching is not primarily mouth to ear, but heart to heart. Two truisms spring to the fore when thinking of the self and preaching. First, each preacher has to find his or her preaching voice, and second, this voice should never be *less* than an authentic voice.

While axiomatic, each aspect becomes more complex when interrogated more closely. Do you find your voice, or does your voice find you? Alternatively put, are we creators of or created by our voice? Is the voice our voice, or the voice of the congregation, or the voice of Scripture, or the voice of society, or a combination of the above with some added extras? Is there freedom for the voice to change over time? As regards authenticity, whose authenticity? For whom should we be authentic? What level of authenticity is appropriate? What about those who are revealed (exposed?) via our self-revealing?

In his excellent book, *Preaching to a Postmodern World*, Graham Johnston notes that,

> What preachers perceive to be an issue of belief may well end up being an issue of trust. Before people ask, 'What have you to say?' they may ask, 'Why should I even listen to you?'[1]

A large part of the answer is likely to be intuitive. I have chatted with enough people about why they did or did not respond to a sermon to realize that, for large numbers of people, the answer has little to do with the sermon's content and a great deal to do with whether they did or did not relate to the preacher.

The relational windows are often small. It can be the way the preacher speaks about her family (or the absence of any mention of family); depending on cultural context, a story told in a self-promoting way in one setting may need to be told in a self-effacing manner in another.[2] Sermons that take no relational risks and that lack self-disclosure are perceived to disclose a preacher unwilling to be vulnerable or known. At the same time, too much confession and the pendulum swings in the opposite direction. I remember the less than charitable comments made of a preacher after he spoke of his almost-but-not-quite adultery. For that congregation, the

---

1. Johnston, *Preaching*, 78.
2. Woe to the confident, self-assertive preacher in the Australasian context, for example. See Harris, *Of Tall Poppies*.

Preaching in weakness

self-revelation had been a bridge too far. With another congregation, the response might have been quite different.

Finding strength in weakness involves a journey of discovery of the authentic self, and an awareness of which aspects are vulnerable and might need to be boundaried, and those that are more robust and able to be open to public scrutiny.

In the broader theological discussion, there has been a move from thinking of truth as a boundaried set to truth as a centered set.[3] Truth and authenticity are related to the center. They flow from our deepest commitments, hopes, disappointments, and longings. They are formed through pain, joy, love, shame, hope, courage, frustration, excitement, and despair. They are also deeply relational. To be *imago Dei* is to be, like the triune God whose image we are called to reflect, in relationship.[4] The idealized image of the autonomous self, forging its own path, has been shown to be a myth of modernity—and an undesirable myth at that.[5]

For the Christian preacher, the centre of relationship lies in relationship with Christ. Personal identity cannot be severed from this identity-conferring relationship. This is then placed within a broader web of relationship, life within the community of the church. The ecclesial self of the preacher is centered in relationship with the triune God and the community of faith who worship and serve the triune God. The Pauline insight that "for me to live is Christ, to die is gain" flows from an awareness of this strong center.[6]

However, the journey towards embracing the self who is centered in Christ and his people also incorporates the journey of embracing the fragmented and sometimes shattered self. The integration of these contributing streams of the self is complex and never fully attained in this penultimate era.[7] Part of maturing self-insight involves recognizing which parts of the self are struggling to find the reconciliation that flows from being centered in Christ. Rather than lament what has not yet been attained, an alternate route is to treat the fragmented self with respect

---

3. See Grenz, "Die Begrenzte Gemeinschaft"; Hiebert, *Anthropological Reflections*.

4. In this respect, see Grenz's outstanding work, *Social God*.

5. For all that, Frank Sinatra's song "I did it my way," remains popular.

6. The center of Christ ("For to me, to live is Christ to die is gain") is balanced by an awareness of the responsibilities that flow from the ecclesial self ("but it is more necessary for you that I remain in the body")—Phil 1:21, 24.

7. "For now we see in a mirror, dimly, but then we will see face to face"—1 Cor 13:12.

and gentleness. These zones where grace has not yet fully penetrated often reflect our deepest hurt, fear, and shame. Rather than proclaim what should be, we should acknowledge these areas as reflecting the perhaps-next-year or the not-now-but-maybe challenge of growth and maturing. Until then, they may be boundaried areas, areas from which we politely but firmly exclude others.

Excluded areas are not only related to the self. They may be related to the self of others. Not every family story should be used as a sermon illustration and every decision to self-disclose needs to be cleared with those who may be impacted. A personal quest for openness and transparency should not be pursued at the expense of those not yet ready to embark on the journey.

While authenticity and transparency in preaching is desirable, it needs to be appropriate and responsive. Jesus' statement that we should not cast pearls before swine is relevant (see Matt 7:6). Preachers should be risk takers, but not reckless risk takers. As in other human relationships, disclosure is filtered on the basis of the response of the recipients. While no congregation should be patronized or fed on half-truths or trite escapism, the ecclesially responsible preacher aims to use self-disclosure not for personal catharsis, but to lead the congregation to deeper levels of faith, trust and insight. That involves a willingness to start from where the congregation is, rather than where the preacher is.

The believing but doubting self

A second paradox of the self, uncovered through preaching, is that most preachers are simultaneously doubters and believers. Part of having something to offer through preaching comes from paying attention to the deep restlessness within the self. The reflective self is usually aware of the longing for something more. Whether this desire is linked to our sinfulness (as in Eden's garden where the forbidden fruit had greatest appeal), or an awareness that being *imago Dei* opens the possibility of a loftier terrain than the one we are travelling, the longing needs to be explored.

Part of the dilemma is that the preacher's journey has to be concurrently public and private. The preacher who too often confides what he does not believe, is likely to find that the shrinking remnants of the congregation reply that they would rather hear of what can be believed, than what cannot. While optimism in the pulpit can be overdone, its absence is usually met by a corresponding absence from the pews.

This sometimes leads some to find escape into cynicism. As a pastor and preacher starting, out I remember being horrified at the gap between what I heard my preaching heroes say in the privacy of ministers' meetings, and what I heard them say in the pulpit. For a while it led me to doubt the "Church Inc." enterprise. As I matured, I realized that the gap often flowed from unresolved hurt or unacknowledged disappointment. Though they faithfully followed the seven foolproof steps to a thriving church, no megachurch had resulted. Who to blame at such times? The accusing finger sways between the self, and God, and the church and society, and anyone else who happens to be in the way. How then does the preacher acknowledge and accompany the doubting self, while at the same time feed and nurture the believing self?

Step one—though the journey is not linear—is to embrace doubt as the friend who might well lead to a deeper level of trust. It is *doubt denied* rather than doubt itself that is the opposite of trust. Doubt denied adopts its ostrich-like position out of fear of what might be discovered. Anxious that unwelcome answers might flow from hard questions, the path of least resistance is the denial of the existence of such questions. In my own journey, a moment of liberation came when I realized that I believed in the goodness of God too much to accept some silly answers that I was then being fed. Finding the freedom to say, "But that I can't believe" released me to discover how much I do believe. Now, more than ever, I believe that when or if answers to the unresolved questions are found, they will lead to my affirming even more loudly, "God's love is greater. God's love is greater." Divine love is greater than my incomprehension, greater than my confusion, greater than my incredulity.

Another source of liberation is the realization that being a preacher does not mean that one has to defend every action that the church takes. Loyalty to Christ's church does not require blindness to her faults. Indeed, a major turning point in the journey comes when we recognize that we should love the church too much to accept a pale caricature of her. While the preaching task begins in the particularity of the local context, it passionately points to what could be. It is shaped by the eschatological ecclesial vision. What the people of God will be becomes the guiding star for present practice.

Lofty though the previous sentiment is, it can be difficult to translate when the question becomes, "So what does that mean when you're the preacher at the Smith St Church, membership 43, average age 71, average spiritual maturity—huh?" Discussions of whether the church should be attractional or incarnational become impossibly theoretical. Too often we are neither. Preaching itself is also sometimes a springboard for doubt. Is the lone voice of the preacher the appropriate communication tool for the third millennium? Many rush to the insights of Brian McLaren and Robert Webber to see if a new kind of church can be birthed.[8] Their insights are helpful, albeit that they are a tad elitist at times.[9]

The conversation with the preacher's doubting believing self should not be aimed at finding answers. Complexity is better acknowledged than solved. Paradox is best when embraced. The collision of truths could see the creative birthing of something new—a world without easy answers, a world where we are comfortable with paradox, a world rather like the real one.

The idiosyncratic but communal self

The late Stanley Grenz proposed that the integrating motif for theology should be community.[10] The Bible's message revolves around the creation of a reconciled community: humanity reconciled with God, with creation and with one another.

None of us exists in isolation. Social constructionists convincingly argue that rather than living in a set and given world, we live in a social-cultural world of our own construction, but whose construction and interpretation is dependent upon the tools and interpretive framework we imbibe from the society in which we participate.[11] John Donne put is somewhat more simply and poetically back in 1624 when he wrote, "No man is an island entire of itself."[12]

The preacher is not exempt from the struggle between the communal and idiosyncratic self. Sermons cannot take any shape or form.

---

8. See e.g., McLaren, *Generous Orthodoxy*; Webber, *Ancient-Future Faith*.

9. An astonishing number of people would prefer *not* to draw a picture or write a poem about their personal *angst* and trauma; and candles rapidly become passé.

10. See e.g., Grenz, *Revisioning*; idem. *Theology*; Grenz and Franke, *Beyond Foundationalism*.

11. See e.g., Berger, *Sacred Canopy*, 3–13.

12. Donne, J. http://www.enotes.com/famous-quotes/no-man-is-an-island-entire-of-itself-every-man-is.

The content needs to be in accord with the teaching of Scripture and the tradition of the church. At the same time, they need to be sensitive to the cultural context of their recipients. This is not problematic when the idiosyncratic and communal self are in accord. Much more difficult are those occasions when the biblical text requires us to go in a direction we would rather avoid.

The tension can be resolved in a variety of ways. Some simply avoid large portions of scripture. Topical preaching enables us to be in charge of what we will preach on and what biblical passages will be allowed a voice. However, topical preaching often lapses into idiosyncratic preaching. One senses the glazed stupor that settles over a congregation as the preacher announces that yet again her favorite topic will be the focus for the week. Topical preaching and poor exegesis are also often synonymous. One has to find a way to fit the text into one's theme. The result is often that one does justice to neither the topic nor the biblical passages selected.

More demanding is the discipline of expository preaching. As a particular Bible book is worked through over a number of weeks, the text rather than the preacher sets the agenda for the sermon. Yet even avid expository preachers spend much time deciding which biblical book to preach from. Few would be happy to preach on the basis of drawing lots. After all, that could require one to preach through Leviticus!

Some have found narrative preaching to provide a doorway.[13] Spotting the homiletical plot in the narratives of scripture is an art form that all serious preachers must start to master. The marriage of scripture's voice, our own voice, and the voice of our time and setting can prove to be harmonious. It often requires listening to the heartbeat rather than the letter of a biblical passage.[14] Existential imagination is required. Such imagination presupposes a willingness to have entered into and explored the ever-perplexing question, "So what does it mean to be human?"

Sometimes the tension between the idiosyncratic and communal self does not lie at the level of the content of preaching, but between the preferences and personality of the preacher and the communal life of the congregation. As the promoter of the program of the local church, the preacher often has to enthuse over events he would rather avoid. While urging others to attend the bingo evening, he might be planning to en-

---

13. A helpful introduction to the topic is found in Standing, *Finding the Plot*.
14. For a holistic model of what he calls "the preaching swim," see Quicke, *360 Degrees*.

sure that a pressing engagement prevents his attendance. Each church community has a distinct culture. At times the preacher's persona and the church's culture are at variance. For some preachers this can lead to a sense of dislocation from the idiosyncratic self. "So who am I really?" is sometimes the lonely question asked in the sleepless early hours of the morning. Most preachers commit themselves to the preaching task for the greater good of the church. Their sense of communal obligation is strong. However, when the communal self is dislocated from the idiosyncratic self, heartache is close at hand.

Sometimes preachers have been their own worst enemy. Concerned to promote the unity of the church, they have sought solutions through focusing on that which unites. Often the resulting product is bland. It can be preferable to embrace alterity. Rather than a uniform church, the biblical portrait is of a diverse group that finds a common center in Christ. This liberates them to live creatively in diverse and changing circumstances. Ironically then, the resolution of the tension between the communal self and the idiosyncratic self is to ensure that a communal rather than a subcommunal self is embraced. Localized expressions of the church can be highly specific and strongly subcultural. The preacher who identifies too closely with such expressions is severed from the broader expression of the communion of all the saints. This community transcends both time and place. Within it, the idiosyncratic self finds the liberating truth that truly to be self is to be self with others—but others in a broad and inclusive sense. Ultimately, the idiosyncratic self is most at home in community. Within the communion of all the saints, the preacher discovers that what she may have perceived to be her own lonely story is similar to the story of many others. The narratives within the communion of all the saints can be celebrated for their idiosyncratic similarity.

The despairing but hopeful self

As preachers, we live in the penultimate age. The self is located between the "already" of new life in Christ, and the "not yet" of the coming of the eschatological kingdom. This often leads to us oscillating between the despairing and the hopeful self. The culturally embedded and located self is often despairing. There is much in society to cause disquiet. By contrast, the eschatological self lives in hope.

Preaching in weakness

German theologian Jürgen Moltmann has taught us the importance of adopting a reverse hermeneutic in theological construction. Everything needs to be understood in the light of the end, rather than the beginning. He writes, "A proper theology would therefore have to be constructed in the light of its future goal. Eschatology should not be its end, but its beginning."[15] While acknowledging "the contradiction between the word of promise and the experiential reality of suffering and death,"[16] he laments what he calls "the sin of despair"[17] where "God promises a new creation of all things in righteousness and peace, but man acts as if everything were as before and remained as before."[18]

Most preachers have been captured by a vision of the glorious future that awaits all those who are in Christ. It provides the inspiration to rise above the dreary and repetitious. The eschatological vision provides inspiration, courage, hope, and motivation. It energizes and helps one to move beyond oneself. It relativizes the problems of the present, and reframes them in the perspective of eternity. When eschatological realism shapes the agenda, the preacher is intrinsically hopeful.

Why then do we journey with the double self, the despairing hopeful self? Simply put, between the vision and the reality lies the gap. It is the gap of uncertainty ("I do believe; help me overcome my unbelief!"—Mk 9:24), the gap of delay ("How long, O Lord, how long?"—Ps 6:3), the gap of injustice ("Why do the wicked live on, growing old and increasing in power?"—Job 21:7), and the gap opened by a hundred other unanswerable questions.

The preacher faces a double dilemma. While others learn to journey with their questions, surely the role of the preacher is to provide answers? Preachers thus face questions they can answer neither for themselves, nor for the congregation. The weight of unanswered questions rests more heavily on those called to pastor and preach. At such times, self-doubt sets in. Bonhoeffer-like, we may begin the journey of unsettling introspection ("Who am I? They mock me, these lonely questions of mine"). However, if we are fortunate, we may come out at a similar place to Bonhoeffer ("Who

---

15. Moltmann, *Theology*, 16.
16. Ibid., 19.
17. Ibid., 22.
18. Ibid., 23.

am I? They mock me, these lonely questions of mine. Whoever I am, Thou knowest, O God, I am thine!")[19]

An insight from Eugene Peterson may help at this point. Peterson bemoans the introduction of the word "self" at the expense of the word "soul." He gives his reasons:

> [I]n our current culture, 'soul' has given way to 'self' as the term of choice to designate who and what we are. Self is the soul minus God. Self is what is left of soul with all the transcendence and intimacy squeezed out, the self with little or no reference to God (transcendence) or others (intimacy).[20]

While Peterson's comment is not above criticism[21] his insistence that we do not view ourselves outside of our relationship with God is important.[22] The despairing self is the self who has lost perspective of what it means to be the self who is centered in Christ and in his church. The hopeful self is the self who remembers these identity-conferring relationships ("Whoever I am, Thou knowest, O God, I am thine!").[23]

Sometimes the uneasy relationship between hope and despair takes on another face. Rather than despair arising from the pain in the world, some preachers experience despair because the world seems to offer more than enough. Often the church does not model itself on eschatological reality, but on Disneyland or pop reality. Preachers compete with TV evangelists or the pastors of megachurches. Congregations look for entertainment, not challenge. Moving down the road to another (usually larger) church is just two poor sermons away. Often the sermon (let us make that "the message"—we do not want people to feel preached at) is irrelevant. What really counts is the music. The growth of the congregation corresponds to the rising number of decibels produced by the worship band. While preachers long to address the existential *angst* of the age, an astonishing number of people do not realize they have any! Salaries are

---

19. Bonhoeffer, *Letters*, 173.

20. Peterson, *Christ*, 37.

21. The reverse can be argued: soul can sound like spiritual escapism. It can be seen as God minus the self; or the self without its earthly attachments, like muddled love and lust and greed.

22. However, Peterson rightly points out that from a biblical perspective, soul includes all these concepts. However, most people think stereotypically rather than biblically. Peterson, *Christ*, 36–39.

23. Bonhoeffer, *Letters*, 173.

soaring, job prospects are good, people are living longer, and new gadgets to entertain and amuse are produced with monotonous frequency. With PlayStation 3˚ just released, heaven can wait.

In this entertainment-saturated age, the preacher can sometimes wonder if the church is needed. Many church ministries are specifically targeted at those going through a crisis. The assumption seems to be that outside of times of trouble, God's relevance is suspect. Even images of heaven fail to inspire, largely because the portraits have nothing to do with life as we know it. For example, why have we settled for harp-playing angels floating on clouds?

Despair can thus flow from two contradictory sources: life turning sour, and life going too well. If today is too heavy, "How long O Lord" is the cry. If life goes well, why ask the God-question?

A little statement of faith begs to be made at this point. Humanity has been made *imago Dei*. While PlayStation 3˚ offers great promise, the primarily hopeful self of the preacher knows that the God-shaped vacuum in each human heart still longs to be filled. As regards the human quest, Augustine's comment is still pertinent: "You have made us for yourself, and our hearts are restless until they find their rest in you." PlayStation may last for the night, but the God quest begins in the morning.

The finite self and the infinite God

In my twenty-six years of marriage, my wife has taught me many things. One of the lessons that I have been slowest in learning has been that every problem does not have to be solved. On more than one occasion our marital bliss has been interrupted by Rosemary informing me that while my solution to the dilemma she was exploring was well intentioned, she had not been looking for an answer. Simply knowing that someone else understood the complexity of the situation was enough.

I have seen the same scenario unfold in ministry. I have often tried to solve the theodicy question. If God is all loving, all knowing, and all powerful, why do we suffer? If God was not loving there would be no problem. Likewise, if some situations escaped his attention, we could excuse the oversight. If his power were limited, we would be sympathetic—our own powerlessness helps us to understand that dilemma. But in the face of a suffering and struggling humanity we continue to proclaim the love, omniscience, and omnipotence of God. Endless sermons try to excuse the contradiction.

Yet I have noticed that often, but not always, those who should ask the theodicy question with the greatest fury, are those who appear the least concerned. In one way or another, they quietly affirm the paradox that when God seems most absent, they experience him as most present. Every problem does not have to be solved. Job-like, we sometimes find the inner tranquility to say, "The Lord gave, and the Lord has taken away; blessed be the name of the Lord" (Job 1:21).

Begging to be said is that at times the finite self is aware of being caught up in the infinite. Attempts at full explanation are futile and inherently contradictory. We can, however, attach a category of explanation. Human extremity often goes hand in hand with openness to alternate vistas. People move from requiring God to solve every problem to inviting him to be a companion for the journey. Preaching beyond solutions (with their inevitable anthropocentric focus) draws the listener in to the mystery of the nature of the revealed hidden God, in whose presence life's issues are reframed—indeed, whose presence turns out to be more than enough.

REFLECTIONS

So why is it that ordinary preachers sometimes have extraordinary feedback—feedback from the woman whose husband has died during the week, and yet finds grace to continue in the sermon, from the terminally ill cancer patient who draws inspiration to live fully each remaining day. The finite self is sometimes the vehicle for the infinite God. Attempts at explanation fail. Paul comes closest, "But we have this treasure in clay jars, so that it may be made clear that this extraordinary power belongs to God and does not come from us" (2 Cor 4:7). If this is weakness, it is a weakness to be embraced and celebrated.

Knowing this, the authentic yet boundaried preacher is able to affirm belief, in spite of doubts. He is able to celebrate his idiosyncratic self in the community of all the saints. She is able to remain intrinsically hopeful, even while acknowledging what causes despair in the present. The weak finite self of the preacher is caught up in the purposes of the infinite. Thus we affirm, in weakness is strength.

14

Strength in weakness

Developing this paradox through preaching and leading

Michael J. Quicke

INTRODUCTION

THIS CHAPTER IS SHAPED both by my recent research on preaching and leadership and also by my own life-changing experiences of God's grace through weakness. While the first influence explains my selection of issues, the second underlies my convictions about this theme's significance for Christian life and ministry, and is illustrated by some concluding reflections.

While writing *360-Degree Leadership: Preaching to Transform Congregations* I tangled with issues arising from contemporary leadership studies as they relate to preacher/leaders. I was disturbed to find how much the church's widespread use of secular leadership principles is endangering the role of biblical preaching and undermining essentials of spiritual life. Aided and abetted by western culture's preoccupation with individualism and self-fulfillment, hard-nosed business principles are displacing the delicate structures of God's grace in his church. Writing of the United States, Robert Bellah comments:

> We live in a society that encourages us to cut free from our past, to define our own selves, to choose the groups with which we wish to identify. No tradition and no community in the United States is above criticism, and the test of the criticism is usually the degree

to which the community or tradition helps the individual to find fulfillment.[1]

In a headlong desire to be successful by helping individuals find fulfillment, many churches seem to have swallowed secular leadership principles wholesale. One result is the sidelining of the paradoxes of Christian life, including "strength in weakness."

Paradoxes such as losing life to find it, becoming great by being servant of all, the meek inheriting the earth, and the apostle's claim of, "when I am weak then I am strong" (2 Cor 12:10), poorly match business practice. The last is deemed particularly inappropriate, with its assertion that "weakness" can be considered positive. This is an anathema to the human drive for organizational success. Effective leadership requires clear thinking and strong decisive action, not spiritualizing and wishful thinking. Vance Packard wryly comments, "Leadership appears to be the art of getting others to want to do something that you are convinced should be done." The notion of "strength in weakness" seems inimical to the current culture of church leadership.

Here is a clash of world views. On one hand, human leadership maximizes strength to influence outcomes; on the other hand, Scriptural principles emphasize weakness and fly in the face of common sense. But

> Life is larger than logic. Those aspects of life which cannot be caught by the camera of logic or analyzed in the dissecting room of science—those require the method of paradox for their expression. Hence Jesus made use of paradox as a means of dealing with the supra-rational elements of life. He "put to shame them that are wise" by outdistancing their worldly wisdom. Jesus did not outrage reason; he outran it . . . Jesus out-trusted the wise.[2]

So there is tension between confident secular leadership full of self-destiny and Christian trust in God's purposes. One is disdainful of "supra-rational" talk, preferring to deal with straightforward matters of fact. It claims to know how to make things work. The other offers a subversive view of reality, that "God works in mysterious ways his wonders to perform," and that he alone gives ultimate purpose.

Of course, Christian leaders do have *some* important lessons to learn from secular leadership. About some matters of fact they do need to be

---

1. Bellah, et al, *Habits of the Heart*, 154.
2. Sockman, *Paradoxes*, 45–46.

better equipped. For example, secular leadership brings realism about the necessity of change, the inevitability of conflict and the need for intentionality over implementing change process. Sadly, some preachers are naïve and woolly about the necessity and costs of such transformation. They preach "new creation" hopelessly unprepared for its consequences. Later, I shall note some positive contributions that leadership studies can make to Christian leadership.

But, as Henry and Richard Blackaby comment, "The trend among many Christian leaders has been for an almost indiscriminate and uncritical acceptance of secular leadership theory without measuring it against the timeless precepts of Scripture."[3] Churches are *not* secular organizations. They owe everything to God whose ways are not our ways; whose grace and purpose break through sin in Christ to create (as only he can) "a chosen race, a royal priesthood, a holy nation" (1 Pet 2:9). Paradoxes abound as the Savior "made himself nothing" and "God exalted him to the highest place" (Phil 2:7, 9) and calls his people to lose life to save it, to lead by serving, to find strength in weakness. At the heart of Christian faith is the mystery of incarnation, of the cross of Jesus Christ, and of his new kingdom way that upends conventional wisdom.

Those who are called to be preacher/leaders must therefore live with the tension between the common sense practices of secular leadership and the spiritual realities of Christian paradoxical living. Whenever they lean towards the former they endanger the unique nature of being God's "chosen race, a royal priesthood, a holy nation." Rather, they must heed Scripture's theme of "strength in weakness" and work through its implications for practical leadership.

"WEAKNESS" IN SCRIPTURE

Earlier chapters in this book have already examined key aspects of "strength in weakness." Against the self-confident charisma of secular leadership striding towards success, Scripture sounds out this seditious note—that "weakness" has a profound spiritual capacity. Its utter helplessness provides just the proving ground for God's power and glory. Human dependency upon God enables his strength to be expressed as nowhere else. The theme of "weakness" is developed in at least two directions—physical weakness and social/political weakness.

---

3. Blackaby and Blackaby, *Spiritual Leadership*, 10.

Most obviously, physical weakness may serve to show God's strength. Nowhere is this clearer than in the apostle's repeated plea to have his "thorn in the flesh" removed, only to hear God's promise, "'My grace is sufficient for you, for my power is made perfect in weakness.' Therefore I will boast all the more gladly about my weaknesses, so that Christ's power may rest on me" (1 Cor 12:9). Whenever physical illness or persecutions press down, exposing inadequacies, emptiness, and exhaustion, Christian believers find themselves in places of fresh gift and grace in God's strength. Because of its discomfort and disorientation at being unable to work by usual human means, genuine inadequacy opens doors and reorientates for God's unusual divine power. At such time, prayer is especially urgent yet often confused by weakness. Why does God not remove the thorn in the flesh? Yet the Holy Spirit is particularly associated with helping such prayer, "In the same way the Spirit helps us in our weakness" (Rom 8:26).

Less obvious, however, is social and political "weakness." The apostle Paul contrasts the power brokers of Corinthian society with the reality of the new Christian community: "God chose the weak things of the world to shame the strong. He chose the lowly things of the world, and the despised . . . so that no-one may boast before him" (1 Cor 1:27–29). First Corinthians 1:18—2:5 mentions power several times, but always as power through weakness. The Gospel appears utterly weak to the world because the cross lies at its center (1 Cor 1:17–25)—a negation of all that the world's "movers and shakers" emulate. The cross reverses all that constitutes human pursuit of power and dramatically subverts conventional wisdom about strength.

First, it has dislocated its hearers by calling into question their ways of knowing (1:18). Second, it has revealed God's purpose to save not through wisdom, but through the "folly of the cross itself" (1:21–25); and third, it has demonstrated God's destruction of the old world (with its valued human assets of strength, wisdom, nobility) and creation of the new world (into which he calls the weak, the ignoble, the nonexistent—1:26–31).[4]

Why did Paul describe his approach to preaching in the Corinthian context: "I came in weakness and fear and with much trembling" (1 Cor 2:3)? Some of his fear may have been due to a sense of personal inadequacy. Paul admits he was not an impressive speaker (2 Cor 10:1,10) and this was a hothouse of oratory. Critical audiences can make preachers

---

4. Brown, *Cross*, 96.

Strength in weakness

tremble. But, far more important than any personal defects, is his awareness of how profoundly unattractive is his message, *logos,* (1 Cor 2:4) to sophisticated ears. He recognizes that his logos has no acceptable "logic" to his hearers. Because the "logic" of the cross is only understandable to those who are willing to believe in God's purpose, through Jesus Christ upon the cross.

To Corinthian hearers who expect wise and persuasive words, "the wisdom of the world" (1 Cor 1:20), Paul knows he must declare this "foolish message... of Jesus Christ and him crucified" (1 Cor. 1:23). He trembles therefore not because of his human audience, but because of his divine audience. He must tell the Gospel in God's way, "not with eloquence or superior wisdom as I proclaimed to you the testimony about God" (1 Cor 2:1). He presents a radically different world view. In his important book, *Preacher and Cross*, Andre Resner Jr. argues that Paul develops a "reverse ethos" in 1 Cor 1–4 that refuses to employ rhetoric *kata sarka* ("according to the flesh") but rather *kata stauron* ("according to the cross").[5] To those who hunger after social and political power this message is totally alien.

Colin Morris, in his creative *Epistles to the Apostle,* includes imaginary letters from a leader he calls Zenas, Secretary of the Corinth Reform Party, who wants to nominate Paul to the Senate. After commending him for his obvious qualities, Zenas writes,

> There is on matter I feel I ought to report. Whilst our Party could support much of your preaching . . . there is one issue which we consider might alienate some of our Jewish and Greek voters. This is your constant emphasis upon the crucifixion of the Nazarene—a controversial issue, I'm sure you would agree. A pledge from you that this subject would be well left alone in your election addresses, etc. is all we require.[6]

Ambassadors of Christ inevitably face resistance from the world's power brokers, but their "strength" is to stay with the "foolishness of God" in the face of ridicule and rejection in order that the outcome is not manipulated by human persuasion (*kata sarka*) "but with a demonstration of the Spirit's power so that your faith might not rest on men's wisdom but on God's power" (1 Cor 2:4–5).

---

5. Resner Jr. *Preacher*, Chapter 3.
6. Morris, *Epistles*, 62.

The church's makeup should also reflect the "foolishness" and "weakness" of its message. In its cultural context the Corinthian church was undeniably weak and vulnerable, yet God chose these weak people to shame the strong (1:6–31). "Jars of clay" offers an apt metaphor—undistinguished, ordinary-looking people who can be hard pressed on every side, perplexed, persecuted, struck down, but who possess a secret. That in their apparent weakness they have "this treasure . . . to show that this all-surpassing power is from God and not from us" (2 Cor 4:7–9). Zenas writes a further letter:

> Our Party branch was very disappointed to hear your reply. If I may say so, you seem unaware that we count amongst our staunchest supporters some of the most influential and wealthy citizens of Corinth. Don't you feel you are making too much of this Cross business? . . . These eccentricities of yours are, if you will forgive me for saying so, making you look foolish in the eyes of powerful people who are in a position to further your career as a public personality with standing and respect.[7]

"Strength in weakness" calls for a totally different kind of preaching and leading. As John Stott comments on 1 Cor 1:18—2:5,

> It is not an invitation to suppress our God-given personality, to pretend we feel weak when we do not or to cultivate a fake frailty. Nor it is an exhortation to renounce arguments. . . . Here then is an honest, humble acknowledgement that human beings cannot save souls.[8]

To this we must add that human beings cannot build Christ's body or lead his people in their own strength either. Both physical weakness and social/political weakness speak of dependency on God's strength. Hudson Taylor said, "All God's giants have been weak people" but such weakness learns dependency on Christ "because apart from me you can do nothing" (Jn 15:5). It leads to deeper places of prayer and spiritual discernment about God's purposes.

SOME IMPLICATIONS FOR PREACHER/LEADERS

In my book, *360-Degree Leadership,* I argued that preachers have the primary role of church leadership. While many others also share in church

---

7. Morris, *Epistles*, 62–63.
8. Stott, *Basic Christian Leadership*, 36.

leadership, preachers are called to be on the cutting edge by delivering God's returning, changing word (Isa 55:11). You cannot deliver God's message of change with antiseptic gloves on. Those responsible for declaring God's transforming word are inevitably involved in its leadership outcomes. However, as we have already noted, many Christian leaders have seemed to adopt secular leadership theory indiscriminately and uncritically "without measuring it against the timeless precepts of Scripture." In the tension between practical common sense and Scriptural paradox, they side more with Zenas than with Paul. While secular leadership tends towards independency and self-sufficiency, "strength in weakness" calls for dependency on God.

Reflecting on my work on *360-Degree Leadership* I need to tease out some implications of "strength in weakness" for preacher/leaders. Balance is needed between independency and dependency, the plausible (and sometimes appropriate) advice of secular leadership and the implausibility (foolishness) of dependency upon God. Preacher/leaders face major challenges in at least four main areas: their character, preaching, pastoral care, and leadership skills.

Character

Secular rhetoric has long recognized the significance of a speaker's authenticity. Aristotle provided three answers to the question about how a speaker convinces listeners: *logos*, (reason), *pathos*, (emotion) and *ethos*, (ethics). He believed the last, as evidenced in the speaker's personal integrity, was the most influential.

When God calls preachers he calls whole people. He brings them into relationship with himself so that *who* they are with him is *who* they are with others. Who they are on their knees is who they are in the pulpit. Ambassadors for Christ represent Christ not only by their words but also by their character, presence, and behavior (2 Cor 5:18). I remember early advice received in seminary from an elderly visiting pastor: "Young people, be very careful in ministry. Over time your local church tends to grow like you. No member of your congregation can go to spiritually deeper places than you." This seemed gross exaggeration but I have learned since how communities *do* tend to grow like their leaders—for better or worse. Contemporary rhetoric describes this as "identity."

The challenge of "strength in weakness" requires personal practice of dependence on God. While secular leadership begins with self-confidence, listening to others, and a wealth of good ideas, spiritual leadership begins with recognition of sin and frailty, confession and listening to God, and encounter with his holiness. Unless there is dependent personal relationship in hidden places with God (Matthew 6:6–9) there is no dependent personal relationship in public places for God. Holiness must pierce complacency of sin and self-sufficiency in private or else public ministry risks hypocrisy. Oswald Chambers commented, "My worth to God in public is what I am in private."

For preacher/leaders private dependent time with God is essential. Other pathways to leadership may promise fast results by attractive activism, but Christian leadership is expressed best by those who most consistently seek God's direction through personal encounter in prayer, Bible study, and other spiritual disciplines. As the Blackabys put it: "Spiritual leaders work within a paradox, for God calls them to do something that, in fact only God can do."[9]

Preaching

Secular leadership highly prizes competent communication. "Excellence" has become a favorite word and a prime virtue acquired by skills and techniques. "Excellence" in communication assumes that right levels of training, practice, and planning guarantee optimal outcomes. When a speaker researches both audience and subject and follows rules of effective communication, success is assured. Now, as a teacher of preachers, I do not wish to drop the bar a fraction. Bill Sangster, the Methodist preacher, rightly said that "The Holy Spirit never despises hard work" and much preaching could benefit from more effort, not less. My students need more discipline to develop their preaching gift and hone their skills. However, emphasis on technique and hyped language about "excellence" can easily tip the balance away from a dependence on God's strength into pride of performance.

Competency assumptions have spilled over into the preaching sphere. The majority of books on preaching over the last twenty years have concentrated on technique and skills. Indeed, some are swathed in talk about strength and success. Titles such as *Mastering Contemporary*

---

9. Blackaby and Blackaby, *Spiritual Leadership*, 21.

Strength in weakness

Preaching, Power in the Pulpit, Preaching with Power, Best Practices from America's Best Churches give the impression that dynamic preachers with competent skills have "mastered" the art and craft of preaching. "Strength in weakness" is relegated to a footnote. Of course, many "powerful preachers" are the first to own their dependency on God and describe the vital role of the Holy Spirit and prayer. But no Christian publishing house is likely in today's culture to promote such titles as *Weakness in the pulpit*, or *Preaching out of weakness*.

The subtle impact of competence talk is evident in the way some preachers regard their task. I heard one preacher comment about his difficulty of "staying on top of his game." What a give-away expression, borrowed from the competitive world of sport that speaks volumes about his expectations. I recall another gifted preacher who was going through major personal difficulties yet appeared to be "on top of his game." "How could you keep on preaching so powerfully while you were in such personal trouble?" he was asked. "I'm a professional," he said. The ability to be excellent and to impress others with "powerful preaching" avoids any need to trust into God's strength that is given in "weakness."

What a contrast with the Apostle Paul's approach to preaching in Corinth! All preachers, especially those who have gained a reputation for their preaching, need to return to 1 Cor 2:1–5 and meditate on Paul's claim, "I came to you in weakness and fear, and with much trembling." How different is my situation? Is the *logos* of the cross still foolishness and an offence? What does this mean about my leadership? A sermon that I preached on these verses began like this:

> Everyone is interested in leadership. Leadership at the big employers down the road; leadership in the political parties; leadership in a favorite sports team; leadership in the local church. Let's hear from two leaders. 'Leadership is three things—knowing what to do next; knowing why that's important, and knowing how to bring appropriate resources to bear on the need at hand' (Bobb Biehl, *Increasing our Leadership Confidence*). 'I came to you in weakness and fear and with much trembling' (Apostle Paul, 1 Cor 2:2). . . . What? That doesn't seem the right approach! We much prefer the first leader. We want to feel confident. We want a winner. No strong leader will admit to weakness, fear and trembling. But Christian leadership works differently. Here is the contrast between how the world looks at leadership and how God does. And we had better listen to how God does.

Paul knows that many of his listeners are going to laugh at his message and reject his invitation. He *has* to preach about Jesus who died for humankind and though he knows this seems utter foolishness, he must make it central to everything else. He rams home his inadequacies by three words that you will never find on the lips of confident twenty-first century leadership: "weakness . . . fear . . . and trembling."

Pastoral Care

Aiding and abetting the focus on "excellence" in the pulpit is the phenomenon occurring in some evangelical churches where the Senior Pastor has so focused on producing powerful weekly sermon(s) that the task of pastoral care has been shifted onto others' shoulders. Though preaching and pastoral care have always existed in tension, fueled by rival demands on time, energy, and skills, many preachers seem to have opted out of pastoring. Pastoral responsibility seems to be delegated (in even the smallest church) to other staff members or laypersons. In many churches, preaching has been severed from its pastoral context. Though in the Protestant American scene "pastor" remains the preferred title, increasingly they seem rarely involved in weekly congregational pastoral issues, especially house visitation.

By "protecting" pastors from the pastoral needs of the people so that they can concentrate on better preaching, churches have actually damaged the quality of relationships out of which deeper preaching emerges. It is by engagement with the experiences of real people in their communities that preachers are earthed and rooted to speak God's word. True it costs time and effort and demands skill, but unless a shepherd knows the sheep sermons will apply to general situations rather than specific. Indeed, without pastoral contact preachers can capitulate to the mood of triumphalism that so often seems to permeate contemporary worship. By closing ears and eyes to the raw weaknesses and needs in congregational life, worship is less authentic. Sometimes worship leaders seem to expect unadulterated excitement, as though all the psalms are Psalm 100: "Shout for joy to the Lord all the earth," and none are Psalm 77: "I cried out to God to help me. . . . When I was in distress I sought the Lord. . . . I remembered you, O God, and I groaned."

The Apostle Paul's own experience of suffering and awareness of other's needs validates the claim to know God's strength in weakness. Others

Strength in weakness

have called preachers to stay strongly pastorally connected. For example, Kennon Callahan controversially suggests his "Principle of Visitation," is to spend one hour in pastoral visitation each week for every minute you preach on Sunday morning.[10] He recognizes this challenges a pastor's time management but argues convincingly for a balance between visiting those in hospital and the housebound, between those who belong within the local congregation and those outside in community. A pastor who keeps in touch with the pastoral needs of the sheep stays sensitive to the imponderables of human life, actually lived Mondays through Saturdays, and to the constant need for God's strength in weakness.

Leadership skills

While communication skills can sideline dependency on God, it is even more obvious how leadership skills, as taught by secular leadership studies, can marginalize reliance on God. Churches that view themselves as business organizations rather than as the body of Christ have leaders operating by business principles, and inevitably foster humanistic ambitions and pride. Corporate success requires marketing, and is quantified by numbers, efficiency, and achievement of goals. By means such as team building, vision and focus groups, planning strategies, and lively communication, great things *will* happen. Human action gains glory at God's expense.

On the shadow side of such expectations lie anxious, bewildered churches that sense their leadership is ineffective and misdirected. With increasing panic they view downward spiraling numbers and finances. One observer of US Protestant evangelical churches commented to me, "There is a widening gap between the haves and the have-nots. The haves glow with leadership success while the have-nots flounder in despair."

Many churches make leadership skills a key requirement in their pastoral search. For example, a recent church profile includes this statement:

> We are looking for a proven leader with God-given spiritual authority who can continue to transition us from a lay-led, staff-supported ministry organization into a more effective staff-led, lay-mobilized ministry structure. He is a team-focused leader who has significant experience in training, discipling and equipping leadership and ministry teams. He surrounds himself with other leaders whose gifts complement his own and he is willing to be

---

10. Callahan, *12 Keys*, 12.

> held accountable to them. . . . He should be a man who has the leadership ability to face and manage conflict well.

I have already noted that church leaders do have positive lessons to learn from secular leadership. This profile seeks someone with skills to lead a team and to be able to cope with conflict, and these are key aspects that benefit immensely from leadership advice.

However, preacher/leaders begin in a different place. Secular leadership puts plans into operation with no attention to the reality of sin, the need of a Savior, the power of forgiveness and miracle of God's grace that integrates believers together in "new creation" in Christ. While Christian leadership benefits from advice given from secular leadership it always begins with God's ways that are not our ways. Here the balance, to which I have referred several times in this chapter, is especially vital. Consider, for example, two areas where Christian leadership profits from secular leadership yet brings a different viewpoint. The skill to face and manage conflict well is an aspect of leadership most pastors need help with, as with the skill to make and apply evaluation. Yet both are affected by the paradox of God's strength in weakness.

Conflict management is undeniably complex requiring an understanding of the nature of conflict and its resolution. I commend my doctoral students to use exercises developed by Speed B. Leas in *Discover Your Conflict Management Style* to learn about the range of appropriate conflict-management strategies and to help each individual identify their own styles of dealing with conflict. Tests are given to score each person's "conflict inventory" helping them not only to understand themselves better, but to learn of other approaches to conflict. Leas argues that the "appropriate time to use this resource is not in the midst of a conflict—but at a time when you can contemplate and digest the information for a future use."[11]

Leas's self-help advice needs to be shaped by Scripture. How does the early church deal with conflict within the paradox of God's strength in weakness? When serious tension erupts over behavior as first century Christians live in a pagan culture, Paul writes of "disputable matters" (Rom 14:1) that must never be allowed to separate Christian believers. For example, some are sensitive about the food they eat, rejecting meat bought in the marketplace as spiritually inappropriate since it might have been sacrificed to idols. For such a person, Paul says, "faith is weak" (Rom 14:2).

---

11. Leas, *Discover Your Conflict Management Style*, iv.

Yet the responsibility of those who are "strong" (which includes himself) focuses on avoiding community breakdown on such disputable issues. In a strong plea for reconciliation he commands, "We who are strong ought to bear with the failings of the weak and not to please ourselves. Each of us should please his neighbor for his good, to build him up. Even Christ did not please himself" (Rom 15:1–2). Reconciliation in Christ's name by his Spirit offers profound motivation to resolving disputes. Similarly, when division threatens the early church over the Judaizers's demands—such as circumcision, the Council of Jerusalem works through to resolution by gracious debate. Discerning what is indisputable it concludes: "It seemed good to the Holy Spirit and to us not to burden you with anything beyond the following requirements" (Acts 15:28).

However, sometimes "weakness" requires not sensitive reconciliation but strong rebuke. Most famously, the "failings of the weak" are seen in Jesus's disappointment at his sleeping disciples in the Garden of Gethsemane. "The spirit is willing, but the flesh is weak" (Matt 26:41; Mk 14:38). His command, "Watch and pray lest you enter into temptation" confronts spiritual weakness. Hebrews 12:12 commands, "Therefore strengthen your feeble arms and weak knees." Jim Herrington, Mike Bonem and James Furr commend a model of church transformation, but describe as "momentum killers" those issues and people who block spiritual momentum for change.[12] For example, fatigue and resistance can kill God's vision and need careful attention and rebuke.

As Leas recommends studying conflict management before the need arises, so preacher/leaders need to preach on texts about handling disputes before difficulties emerge. Sermons on passages such as Matthew 18:15–20, Acts 15, Philippians 4:2–7 should help churches to be realistic about conflict as part and parcel of Christian life.

Another issue that needs careful treatment is leadership's stress on the need for rigorous evaluation and its strategic use. Gaining a clear picture of current reality is vital for progress. Unless you know the truth about a situation, untested assumptions can so readily promote complacency or prejudice. Leadership books offer a range of practical programs to audit the health of a local congregation within its wider community. For example, Kennon Callahan offers a diagnostic approach in his *Twelve*

---

12. Herrington, Bonem, Furr, *Leading Congregational Change*, 86.

Keys to an Effective Church and Christian Schwartz identifies eight vital signs in *Natural Church Development*.

But having discovered the facts, what happens next? Consider this advice I heard at a leadership conference. The speaker argued that many churches are in danger of concentrating on their problems instead of focusing on their successes to "build on islands of health and strength." Chastising denominations for pouring resources into sick churches and therefore concentrating on the most dysfunctional situations rather than on productive contexts, he posed as the essential question, "What is your church really good at doing?" This seems to make solid common sense. Why not start with strengths? However, the logic of this advice understands "failure" and "success" in "doing things" as the whole point of the exercise, assessing outcomes as though it is an entrepreneurial enterprise. It is in grave danger of encouraging self-help, self-reliance and self-congratulation.

The most important aspects of "being church" are not easily quantifiable. Qualities of holiness, righteousness, compassion, and mission can be cloaked by numbers and noise. George Barna comments, sadly, "We are more impressed by a church of 4,000 people who have no clue about God's character and His expectations than by a church of 100 deeply committed saints who are serving humankind in quiet but significant ways."[13] Is there any hope for churches that cannot respond impressively, and statistically, to the question: What is your church really good at doing? As you will see from my story below, God's gift of renewal can occur in the most apparently negative situations. To judge churches according to organizational success models is utter travesty. Consider the Lord's criteria as he walks among the seven churches (Rev 2–3) and assesses qualities such as perseverance, love, courage, and good deeds. Notably, the most positive letter commends the church in Philadelphia, "I know that you have little strength, yet you have kept my word and have not denied my name" (Rev 3:8).

Personal reflections

While writing this chapter I became aware of how potent the theme of "strength in weakness" has been in my life as preacher/leader. I testify to experiencing its paradox as illustrated by two significant events. The first, which I describe in more detail elsewhere,[14] concerns my call to the

---

13. Barna, *Barna Report*, 147.
14. See *360-Degree Leadership*, especially pages 168–72.

Strength in weakness

Baptist church in Cambridge, UK. When first approached to become its pastor in 1978, I gave an emphatic "No." I could not believe God would want me to walk away from my current ministry in Blackburn where there was so much strength—in numbers, buildings, staff, and mission. I found the prospect of the Cambridge church, which I had attended as a student some ten years earlier, utterly depressing. Set in a downtown situation, with a struggling elderly congregation, it looked virtually down and out. Frankly it represented "weakness" writ large. The question "What is this church really good at doing?" had no reply. But over the months following my first rejection of the invitation, subversive thoughts began unsettling me. Perhaps God might actually want me to go there. One denominational leader spoke strongly, "Michael, if God wants someone to go to Cambridge, why shouldn't it be you?" Could it be that I needed to be pushed into a situation of dire dependency in order to experience God's strength?

How I wrestled with the decision, with prayer and fasting. When eventually I agreed and arrived in 1980 the church seemed every bit as depressing as I imagined, though some faithful saints welcomed me. In this highly uncomfortable situation I had two foci for my preaching—the cross and prayer. On the first Sunday I preached a sermon entitled "Glory in the cross" (1 Cor 2:1–5; Gal. 6:11–16). I called people to go to the center of our faith—the cross. I knew that only by such "foolish" preaching could anything happen. But I also pleaded with the small congregation to join in corporate weekly prayer with me.

In an amazing response, the majority turned out two days later and began with me to make earnest prayer a priority. In our "weakness" we all seemed to recognize our need. Our asking God about basic needs and our future had nothing phony or artificial about it. Desperation meant dependency. For example, it was obvious that the church needed to grow. I recall a New Year's Eve prayer meeting at the end of 1980 when we focused on the need for more people to join our little fellowship. We even dared to pray that God would add 50 new people during 1981. This was patently absurd—it meant almost doubling our church. Yet we prayed expectantly every week through the year that God would add new believers, not sheep transferring from elsewhere. Dependency led to corporate prayer like I have never seen. Although it took 14 months, we were overwhelmed that in our weakness God answered prayer by adding 50 new members. Some came via amazing faith journeys. Many were baptized as believers. We experienced our own mini-Pentecost out of the frailest of contexts.

Out of this weakness and dependency in prayer, the church began to grow and develop its mission. Within ten years it would have many hundreds in worship and many tens working through its mission center that was built next door to serve the city, Sunday to Sunday. By many different resources—such as a restaurant, counseling rooms, club for the unemployed, youth work suite, accommodation for the homeless—the church reached out in what we termed "the laboratory working out our Sunday claims." However, being part of this church renewal was an easier experience of discovering "strength in weakness" than a devastating illness that befell me during this time.

In the summer of 1997, while vacationing in France, I suddenly began to feel my head twist around to the right pulling my body awkwardly out of shape. Until then I had always been fit and well. A typically activist pastor I had thrived on local church ministry, especially as it developed in Cambridge. My condition deteriorated sharply puzzling my own doctor. As basic tasks of dressing and walking becoming progressively difficult, I entered hospital for neurological scans and tests. The specialist announced the results with finality, "I know what you have—it's dystonia disease that has focused in your neck as spasmodic torticollis. It won't kill you, but there's no treatment. You will have to come to terms with the fact that you will not be able to do public ministry again."

For six months I was crushed in weakness compounded by depression, pain, and anxiety. In aching frustration every day I found praying so difficult. Dependency on the Spirit who helps in weakness was actually a dispiriting new experience. I felt my life and purpose had been taken away. Physically, emotionally, spiritually I was a wreck. Though writing was arduous I kept a limited daily journal trying to trace any signs of hope yet more often railing against the disease.

But every day the church held prayer meetings for my recovery. The eventual medical breakthrough that put me in the first British clinical trial for botulinum toxin injections interrupted my decline with glorious results. Though I need injections for the rest of my life, and the progress of the disease remains unknown, God has given me back my public ministry. I learned many lessons in my enforced weakness but supremely, I discovered God's promise of grace and strength. I returned to ministry a very different person. With humility, I realize that many prayers in weakness of health do not enjoy such spectacular results. Yet I also know the deep spiritual places that people undergoing weakness can experience.

Strength in weakness

As I was finalizing this chapter my telephone rang. It was a friend whose ministry nose-dived several months ago. Without a job, at a financially critical time for his family, he spoke about some new job possibilities that had just emerged. But then he said, "I have learned so much more about God's grace in this time than I have ever experienced before. I couldn't have learned this until I was in this uncomfortable weak place! But now I am trusting God in new ways. Honestly, money doesn't matter as much. Actually many things don't matter as much. I have learned to trust in his grace. And that's what life is all about." Indeed it is.

Bibliography

Achtemeier, P. J. "Gods Made With Hands: The New Testament and the Problem of Idolatry." *Ex Auditu* 15 (1999) 43–59.
Ackroyd, P. R. "The Book of Jeremiah—Some Recent Studies." *JSOT* 28 (1984) 47–59.
Akin, D. L. "Triumphalism, Suffering, and Spiritual Maturity: An Exposition of 2 Corinthians 12:1–10 in its Literary, Theological, and Historical Context." *CTR* 4 (1989–90) 119–44.
Allen, R. J. "Between Text and Sermon: 2 Corinthians 4:7–18." *Int* 52.3 (1998) 286–289.
Amichai, Y. "Young David." *Jewish Heritage Online Magazine*, 2005, www.ihom.com/topics/david. From: D. C. Jacobson, *Does David Still Play Before You? Israeli Poetry and the Bible*. Wayne State University Press, 1997.
Andrews, S. B. "Too Weak Not To Lead: The Form and Function of 2 Cor 11.23b–33." *NTS* 42 (1995) 263–76.
Astell, A. W. "Introduction." In *Divine Representations: Postmodernism and Spirituality*, edited by A. W. Astell, 1–18. New Jersey: Paulist, 1994.
Avioz, M. "The Call for Revenge" in Jeremiah's Complaints (Jer Xi–Xx)." *VT* 55.4 (2005) 429–38.
Bader-Saye, S. "The Emergent Matrix." *CC* 24 (2004) 20–26.
Bakhtin, M. M. *Problems of Dostoevsky's Poetics*. Translated by C. Emerson. Minneapolis: University of Minnesota, 1984.
———. *The Dialogic Imagination*. Translated by C. Emerson and M. Holquist. Austin: University of Texas, 1981.
Balserak, J. "The God of Love and Weakness: Calvin's Understanding of God's Accommodating Relationship with his People." *WTJ* 62 (2000) 177–95.
Barna, G. *The Barna Report 1994–95: Virtual America*. Ventura: Regal, 1994.
Barnett, P. *The Second Epistle to the Corinthians*. Grand Rapids: Eerdmans, 1997.
———. "Mark: Story and History". In *In the Fullness of Time: Biblical Studies in Honour of Archbishop Donald Robinson*, edited by D. Petersen and J. Pryor, 29–44. Homebush West, NSW: Lancer, 1992.
Barrett, C. K. *The Second Epistle to the Corinthians*. London: A&C Black, 1973.
Barth, K. "Action in Waiting for the Kingdom of God"." In *Action in Waiting*, edited by the Society of Brothers, 19–45. Rifton, NY: Plough, 1969.
———. *Church Dogmatics* III/4, "The Doctrine of Creation." Translated by A. T. Mackay, et al. Edited by G. W. Bromiley and T. F. Torrance. Edinburgh: T & T Clark, 1961.
———. *Der Römerbrief (Erste Fassung) 1919*, edited by H. Schmidt. Zurich: Theologischer-Verlag, 1985.
———. "Past and Future: Friedrich Naumann and Christoph Blumhardt." In *The Beginnings of Dialectic Theology*, edited by J. M. Robinson, 35–45. Richmond: John Knox, 1968.

Bibliography

———. *Protestant Theology in the Nineteenth Century: Its Background and History.* Translated by J. Bowden and B. Cozens. London: SCM, 2001.

———. *Theology and Church: Shorter Writings 1920–1928.* Translated by L. P. Smith. New York: Harper and Row, 1962.

———. *The Word of God and the Word of Man.* Translated by D. Horton. New York: Harper, 1956.

Barton, J. "'The Work of Human Hands' (Ps 115:4): Idolatry in the Old Testament." *Ex Auditu* 15 (1999) 63–72.

Basinger, D. and R. Basinger (eds). *Predestination and Free Will.* Downers Grove, IVP, 1986).

Baumgartner, W. *Jeremiah's Poems of Lament.* Translated by D. E. Orton. Decatur: Almond 1987.

Beeke, J. R. "Calvin on Piety." In *Cambridge Companion to John Calvin*, edited by D. K. McKim, 125–152. Cambridge: CUP, 2004.

Beerens, G. "Journey into Weakness: An exploration of servant leadership." *Sojourners* 9 (1980) 25–28.

Begrich, J. *Studien Zu Deuterojesaja.* Vol. 20, *Theologische Bücherei.* Munich: Chr. Kaiser Verlag, 1938. Reprint, 1963.

Beilby, J. K. and P. R. Eddy (eds). *Divine Foreknowledge: Four Views.* Downers Grove: IVP, 2001.

Bellah, R. N., R. Madsen, W. M. Sullivan, A. Swidler and S. M. Tipton, *Habits of the Heart: Individualism and Commitment in American Life.* New York: Harper and Row, 1986.

Belleville, L. L. *2 Corinthians.* Leicester: IVP, 1996.

Berger, P. L. *The Sacred Canopy: Elements of a Sociological Theory of Religion.* Garden City, N.Y.: Doubleday, 1969.

Berkhof, H. *Christian Faith: An Introduction to a Study of the Faith.* Grand Rapids: Eerdmans. 1979.

Bernier, O. *Louis the Beloved: The Life of Louis XV.* London: Weidenfeld and Nicholson, 1984.

Bernten, H. and R. Rivera. "Air Force Adds to Controversy with its Own Coffin Photos." http://seattletimes.nwsource.com/html/localnews/200190952_coffin22m.html. (accessed October 5, 2005).

Beuken, W. A. M. "The First Servant Song and Its Context." *VT* 22 (1972) 1–30.

Biddle, M. E. *Polyphony and Symphony in Prophetic Literature Rereading Jeremiah 7–20.* Macon, Georgia: Mercer University Press, 1996.

Birch, B. C. "The First and Second Books of Samuel." In *NIB*, volume 2, 947–1383. Nashville: Abingdon, 1998.

Bird, M. "The Crucifixion of Jesus as the Fulfillment of Mark 9:1." *TrinJ* 24 (2003) 23–36.

———. "Jesus is the Christ: Messianic Apologetics in the Gospel of Mark." *RTR* 64 (2005) 1–14.

Black, D. A. *Paul, Apostle of Weakness: Astheneia and its Cognates in the Pauline Literature.* New York: Peter Lang, 1984.

Black, M. *Models and Metaphors.* Ithaca: Cornell University Press, 1962.

Blackaby, H. and R. Blackaby. *Spiritual Leadership.* Nashville: Broadman & Holman, 2001.

Blenkinsopp, J. *Isaiah 40–55.* New York: Doubleday, 2002.

Bolognesi, P. "L'He[set acute accent over e]ritage The dù Calvinisme et les Protestants d'Europe." *EJT* 4 (1995) 121–29.

Bolt, P. G. *Jesus' Defeat of Death: Persuading Mark's Early Readers.* Cambridge: CUP, 2003.

Bibliography

———. *The Cross from a Distance: Atonement in Mark's Gospel.* Downers Grove: IVP, 2004.
Bonhoeffer, D. *Letters and Papers from Prison.* Translated by E. Bethge. London: Fontana, 1959.
Boorer, S. "The Prophetic Ministry? Jeremiah as a Paradigm." *Trinity Occasional Papers* 15.1 (1996) 5–30.
Boring, M. E. "The Kingdom of God in Mark." In *The Kingdom of God in 20th Century Interpretation*, edited by W. Willis, 131–45. Peabody, MA: Hendrickson, 1987.
Bouwsma, W. J. *John Calvin. A Sixteenth Century Portrait.* New York: OUP, 1989.
———. "The Spirituality of John Calvin." In *Christian Spirituality: High Middle Ages and Reformation*, edited by J. Raitt, 318–33. New York: Crossroad, 1987.
Boyd, G. A. *God at War: The Bible and Spiritual Conflict.* Downers Grove: IVP, 1997.
———. *Satan and the Problem of Evil: Constructing a Trinitarian Warfare Theodicy.* Downers Grove: IVP, 2001.
Brenner, A. *The Intercourse of Knowledge.* Leiden: Brill, 1997.
Bright, J. *Jeremiah.* New York: Doubleday, 1965.
———. "Jeremiah's Complaints: Liturgy, or Expressions of Personal Distress?" In *Proclamation and Presence*, 189–214. London: SCM, 1970.
Brown, A. R. *The Cross and Human Transformation.* Minneapolis: Fortress, 1995.
———. "The Gospel Takes Place: Paul's Theology of Power-in-Weakness in 2 Corinthians." *Int* 52.3 (1998) 271–85.
Brueggemann, W. *A Commentary on Jeremiah: Exile and Homecoming.* Grand Rapids, Eerdmans, 1998.
———. *Old Testament Theology.* Minneapolis: Fortress, 1992.
———. "The Book of Jeremiah: Portrait of the Prophet." In *Interpreting the Prophets*, 113–29. Philadelphia: Fortress, 1987.
Bultmann, R. *The Second Letter to the Corinthians.* Minneapolis: Augsburg, 1985; German orig. 1976.
Busch, E. *Karl Barth: His Life and Letters and Autobiographical Texts.* Translated by J. Bowden. Philadelphia: Fortress, 1976.
Büsser, F. "The Spirituality of Zwingli and Bullinger in the Reformation of Zurich." In *Christian Spirituality. High Middle Ages and Reformation*, edited by J. Raitt, 300–317. New York: Crossroad, 1987.
Callahan, K. *12 keys to an effective church.* San Francisco: Jossey-Bass, 1983.
Calvin, J. *A Harmony of the Gospels. Matthew, Mark and Luke*, edited by D. W. Torrance and T. F. Torrance. Grand Rapids: Eerdmans/ Carlisle: Paternoster, 1994.
———. *Commentary on Acts*, edited by D. W. Torrance and T. F. Torrance. Grand Rapids: Eerdmans/ Carlisle: Paternoster, 1995.
———. *Commentary on 2 Timothy*, edited by D. W. Torrance and T. F. Torrance. Grand Rapids: Eerdmans/ Carlisle: Paternoster, 1996.
———. *Institutes of the Christian Religion*, edited by J. T. McNeill. Philadelphia: Westminster, 1960.
———. *Institutionis Christianae religionis 1559* in *Johannis Calvini Opera Selecta*, volumes 3–5, edited by P. Barth and D. Scheuener. Munich: Kaiser, 1952.
———. *Letters of John Calvin*, 4 volumes, edited by J. Bonnet. Philadelphia: Presbyterian Board, 1858.
———. *Sermons on Galatians*, translated by Kathy Childress. Edinburgh: Banner of Truth, 1997.
Campbell, W. "Art, Sin and Salvation: The Aesthetics of Salvation." *Interface* 5 (2002) 17–22.

Bibliography

Carroll, R. P. *From Chaos to Covenant: Uses of Prophecy in the Book of Jeremiah*. London: SCM, 1981.
———. *Jeremiah*. Old Testament Guides. Sheffield: Sheffield Academic, 1989.
———. *When Prophecy Failed*. London: SCM, 1979.
Childs, B. S. *Isaiah. The Old Testament Library*. Louisville, KY: WJKP, 2001.
Chilton, B. D. *God in Strength: Jesus' Announcement of the Kingdom*. Sheffield: JSOT, 1987.
———. *The Isaiah Targum: Introduction, Translation, Apparatus and Notes*, edited by K. Cathcart, M. Maher, and M. McNamara. Vol. 11, *The Aramaic Bible*. Collegeville, MN: Liturgical, 1987.
Chul-Ha, H. "A Comparison between Calvin and Karl Barth on Prayer." *ATA* 1 (1993) 65–76.
Clayton, P. and A. Peacocke (eds). *In Whom We Live and Move and Have our Being: Panentheistic Reflections on God's Presence in a Scientific World*. Grand Rapids: Eerdmans, 2004.
Clifford, R. J. *Fair Spoken and Persuading: An Interpretation of Second Isaiah*. Theological Inquiries. Ramsey, NJ: Paulist, 1984.
Clines, D. J. A., Gunn, D. M. "'You Tried to Persuade Me' And 'Violence! Outrage!' In Jeremiah Xx 7–8." *VT* 28 (1978) 20–27.
Collinson, S. and B. Hill. *Making Disciples: The Significance of Jesus' Educational Methods for Today's Church*. London: Paternoster, 2007.
Copan, P. and W. L. Craig. *Creation out of Nothing: A Biblical, Philosophical, and Scientific Exploration*. Grand Rapids: Baker Academic, 2004.
Craigie, P. C., P. H. Kelley, J. F. Drinkard Jr., *Jeremiah 1–25*. Dallas, Texas: Word, 1991.
Dawn, M. J. *Powers, Weakness, and the Tabernacling of God*. Grand Rapids: Eerdmans, 2001.
Dearman, A. "YHWH's House: Gender Roles and Metaphors for Israel in Hosea." *JNSL* 25.1 (1999) 97–108.
DeSilva, D. *An Introduction to the New Testament: Contexts, Methods and Ministry Formation*. Downers Grove: IVP, 2004.
Diamond, A. R. *The Confessions of Jeremiah in Context*. Sheffield: Sheffield Academic, 1987.
———. "Deceiving Hope: The Ironies of Metaphorical Beauty and Ideological Terror in Jeremiah." *SJOT* 17.1 (2003) 34–48.
Dick, M. B. "Prophetic *Poiesis* and the Verbal Icon." *CBQ* 46 (1984) 226–46.
Dillenberger, J. "The Visual and the Verbal: One Reality, Two Modalities." *RevExp* 87 (1990) 563–65.
Dodd, B. J. *Empowered Church Leadership: Ministry in the Spirit According to Paul*. Downers Grove: IVP, 2003.
Donne, J. "No man is an island entire of . . ." *The Columbia World of Quotations*. Ed. Robert Andrews, Mary Biggs, and Michael Seidel. Columbia University Press, 2006. http://www.enotes.com/famous-quots/no-man-is-an-island-entire-of-itself-every-man-is (15 Dec, 2007).
Donnelly, K. "Hasta la vista to literature." *Weekend Australian* September 17 (2005) 19.
Dunn, J. D. G. *Baptism in the Holy Spirit*. Philadelphia: Westminster, 1970.
Dyrness, W. "A Turn to the Visual." http://www.cornerstonemag.com/page/show_page.asp?442. Accessed 10th October 2005.
Edwards, D. *Breath of Life: A Theology of the Creator Spirit*. Maryknoll, NY: Orbis, 2004.
Edwards, M. U. "The Power of a Picture." *CC* 122 (2005) 31–32.
Eidevall, G. *Grapes in the Desert*. Stockholm: Almqvist & Wiksell International, 1996.

Bibliography

Eire, C. M. N. *War Against the Idols. The Reformation of Worship from Erasmus to Calvin.* Cambridge: CUP, 1989.

Ekblad jr., E. R. *Isaiah's Servant Poems According to the Septuagint: An Exegetical and Theological Study.* Leuven: Peeters, 1999.

Ellul, J. "Notes on the Humiliation of the Word." *Cross Currents* 35 (1986) 54–64.

———. *The Humiliation of the Word.* Grand Rapids: Eerdmans, 1985.

Erickson, M. *The Word Became Flesh: A Contemporary Incarnational Christology.* Grand Rapids: Baker, 1991.

Evans, M. *The Message of Samuel* Leicester: IVP 2004.

Fahy, T. "St. Paul's 'Boasting' and 'Weakness.'" *ITQ* 31 (1964) 214–27.

Fallon, F. T. "Self-Sufficiency or God's Sufficiency: 2 Corinthians 2:16." *HTR* 76 (1983) 369–74.

Fitzgerald, J. T. *Cracks in an Earthen Vessel: An Examination of the Catalogues of Hardships in the Corinthian Correspondence.* Atlanta: Scholars, 1988.

Foucault, M. *Discipline and Punish: The Birth of the Prison.* Translated by A. Sheridan. London: Penguin, 1977.

Fraser, A. "God's flock corralled to a rock beat." *Australian* August 15 (2005) 3.

Fretheim, T. E. *God and World in the Old Testament.* Nashville: Abingdon, 2005.

———. *Jeremiah.* Macon, Georgia: Smyth and Helwys, 2002.

———. *The Suffering of God: An Old Testament Perspective.* Minneapolis: Fortress, 1984.

Furnish, V. P. *II Corinthians*; New York: Doubleday, 1984.

———. "Paul and the Corinthians: The Letters, the Challenges of Ministry, the Gospel." *Int* 52.3 (1998) 229–45.

Ganssle, G. (ed.). *God and Time: Four Views.* Downers Grove: IVP, 2001.

Garland, D. E. "Paul's Apostolic Authority: The Power of Christ Sustaining Weakness (2 Corinthians 10–13)." *RE* 86 (1989) 371–89.

———. *2 Corinthians.* Nashville: Broadman & Holman, 1999.

George, T. *Theology of the Reformers.* Nashville: Broadman, 1988.

Gerstenberger, E. "Jeremiah's Complaints: Observations of Jeremiah 15:10–21." *JBL* 82.4 (1963) 393–408.

Girard, R. *My Weakness: His Strength.* Grand Rapids: Zondervan, 1981.

Gitay, Y. *Prophecy and Persuasion: A Study of Isaiah 40–48.* Bonn: Linguistica Biblica, 1981.

Goldingay, J. *The Message of Isaiah 40–55.* London: T & T Clark, 2005.

Gooch, G. P. *Louis XV: The Monarchy in Decline.* London: Longmans Green, 1956.

Gorringe, T. J. *Against Hegemony.* Oxford: OUP, 1999.

———. "Eschatology and Political Radicalism: The Example of Karl Barth and Jürgen Moltmann." In *God will be All in All: The Eschatology of Jürgen Moltmann*, edited by R. Bauckham, 87–114. Edinburgh: T & T Clark, 1999.

Greenspahn, F. E. "Syncretism and Idolatry in the Bible." *VT* 54 (2004) 480–94.

Grenz, S. J. "Die Begrenzte Gemeinschaft ('The Boundaried People') and the Character of Evangelical Theology." *JETS* 45 (2002) 301–16.

———. *Revisioning Evangelical Theology: A Fresh Agenda for the Twenty First Century.* Downers Grove: IVP, 1993.

———. *Theology for the Community of God.* Nashville: Broadman and Holman, 1994.

———. *The Social God and the Relational Self: A Trinitarian Theology of the Imago Dei.* Louisville: WJKP, 2001.

———. (and J. R. Franke) *Beyond Foundationalism: Shaping Theology in a Postmodern Context.* Louisville: WJKP, 2001.

Bibliography

Griffin, D. R. *Evil Revisited: Responses and Reconsiderations*. New York: Suny, 1991.
Griffith, H. "'The First Title of the Spirit': Adoption in Calvin's Soteriology." *EQ* 73 (2001) 135–53.
Gundry, R. H. *Mark: A Commentary on His Apology for the Cross*. Grand Rapids: Baker, 1993.
Habel, N. *The God of Jeremiah. The Australian Biblical Project*. Homebush, St Pauls, 1996.
Hafemann, S. J. *Paul, Moses, and the History of Israel: The Letter/Spirit Contrast and the Argument from Scripture in 2 Corinthians 3*. Peabody: Hendrickson, 1995.
———. *Suffering and Ministry in the Spirit: Paul's Defence of His Ministry in II Corinthians 2:14–3:3*. Grand Rapids: Eerdmans, 1990.
———. "The Comfort and Power of the Gospel: The Argument of 2 Corinthians 1–3." *RE* 86 (1989) 325–49.
———. *2 Corinthians*. Grand Rapids: Zondervan, 2000.
Hallman, J. M. *The Descent of God: Divine Suffering in History and Theology*. Minneapolis: Fortress, 1991.
Hanson, A. T. *The Paradox of the Cross in the Thought of St. Paul*. Sheffield: JSNT, 1987.
Harris, B. S. *Of Tall Poppies, Mateship and Pragmatism: Spirituality in the Australasian Context*. Mexico City: Theological Education Commission: Baptist World Alliance, 2006.
Harris, M. J. *The Second Epistle to the Corinthians*. Grand Rapids: Eerdmans, 2005.
Harvey, A. E. *Renewal Through Suffering: A Study of 2 Corinthians*. Edinburgh: T. & T. Clark, 1996.
Hays, R. B. "'Why do you stand looking up toward heaven?' New Testament Eschatology at the Turn of the Millennium." In *Theology and Eschatology at the Turn of the Millennium*, edited by J. J. Buckley and L. G. Jones, 113–31. Oxford: Blackwell, 2002.
Hebart, F. "The Role of the Lord's Prayer in Luther's Theology of Prayer." *LTJ* 18 (1984) 6–17.
Helm, P. *John Calvin's Ideas*. Oxford: OUP, 2004.
Hendrix, S. "Martin Luther's Reformation of Spirituality." In *Harvesting Martin Luther's Reflections on Theology, Ethics, and the Church*, edited by T. J. Wengert, 240–60. Grand Rapids: Eerdmans, 2004.
Henry, C. F. H. *God, Revelation and Authority*, volume 1. Waco: Word, 1976.
Henry, D. P. *The Early Development of the Hermeneutic of Karl Barth as Evidenced by his Appropriation of Romans 5:12–21*. Macon, Ga: Mercer University Press, 1985.
Herrington, J., M. Bonem and J. Furr. *Leading Congregational Change*. San Francisco: Jossey-Bass, 2000.
Heschel, A. J. *The Prophets*. New York: Harper and Row, 1962.
Hiebert, P. G. *Anthropological Reflections on Missiological Issues*. Grand Rapids: Baker, 1994.
Hoffman, Y. "A North Israelite Typological Myth and a Judean Historical Tradition: The Exodus in Hosea and Amos." *VT* 39.2 (1989) 169–81.
Holloway, J. Y. (ed.) *Barth, Barmen and the Confessing Church Today*. Lewiston, NY: Edwin Mellen, 1992.
Hughes, P. E. *The Second Epistle to the Corinthians*. Grand Rapids: Eerdmans, 1962.
Hunsinger, G. "Conclusion: Toward A Radical Barth." In *Karl Barth and Radical Politics*, edited by G. Hunsinger, 181–233. Philadelphia: Westminster, 1976.
Hurtado, L. *The Lord Jesus Christ*. Grand Rapids: Eerdmans, 2003.
Janzen, J. G. "Metaphor and Reality in Hosea 11." *Semeia* 24 (1982) 7–44.
Johnson, R. K. *Reel Spirituality: theology and film in dialogue*. Grand Rapids: Baker Academic, 2000.

Bibliography

Johnson, S. B. W. "Strength Revealed as Weakness." *CC* 114 (1997) 75.

Johnston, G. *Preaching to a Postmodern World: A Guide to Reaching Twenty-First-Century Listeners.* Grand Rapids: Baker, 2001.

Johnston, W. *The Mystical Way.* London: Harper Collins, 1993.

Jones, D. R. *Jeremiah.* Grand Rapids: Eerdmans, 1992.

Kaminouchi, A. de Mingo. *'But It Is Not So Among You': Echoes of Power in Mark 10.32-45.* London: T. & T. Clark, 2003.

Keefe, A. A. *Woman's Body and the Social Body in Hosea.* Sheffield: Sheffield Academic, 2001.

Kelsay, J. "Prayer and Ethics: Reflections on Calvin and Barth." *HTR* 82 (1989) 169-84.

Kingsbury, J. D. "The Significance of the Cross within Mark's Story." In *Gospel Interpretation: Narrative and Social-Scientific Approaches,* edited by J. D. Kingsbury. Harrisburg, PA: Trinity, 1997.

Kistemaker, S. J. *II Corinthians.* Grand Rapids: Baker, 1997.

Kleiner, F. S. and C. J. Mamiya (eds). *Gardner's Art Through the Ages,* 12th ed. Belmont: Wadsworth Thomson, 2005.

Koch, T. "Luthers reformatorisches Versta[set umlaut over a]ndis des Gebets." In *Das Gebet. Veöffentlichungen der Luther-Akademie,* edited by V. Ratzeburg, 47-66. Erlangen: Martin-Luther-Verlag, 2002.

Kroon, M. de. *The Honour of God and Human Salvation. Calvin's Theology According to his Institutes.* Edinburgh: T. & T. Clark, 2001.

Kusukawa, S. "Melanchthon." In *Cambridge Companion to Reformation Theology,* edited by D. Bagchi and D. C. Steinmetz, 57-67. Cambridge: CUP, 2004.

Lambrecht, J. *Second Corinthians.* Collegeville: Liturgical, 1999.

———. "Strength in Weakness: A Reply to Scott B. Andrews' Exegesis of 2 Cor 11.23b-33." *NTS* 43 (1997) 285-90.

———. "The Fool's Speech and Its Context: Paul's Particular Way of Arguing in 2 Cor 10-13." *Biblica* 82 (2001) 305-24.

Landy, F. *Hosea.* Sheffield: Sheffield Academic, 1995.

———. "In the Wilderness of Speech: Problems of Metaphor in Hosea." *BibInt* 3.1 (1995) 35-59.

Leas, S. B. *Discover your conflict management style.* Bethesda: Alban Institute, 1997.

Lee-Pollard, D. A. "Powerlessness as Power: A Key Emphasis in the Gospel of Mark." *SJT* 40 (1987) 173-88.

Lejeune, R. *Christoph Blumhardt and his Message.* Translated by H. Ehrlich and N. Maas. Rifton, NY: Plough, 1963.

Lenski, R. C. H. *The Interpretation of St. Paul's First and Second Epistles to the Corinthians.* Minneapolis: Augsburg, 1937.

Levenson, J. D. *Creation and the Persistence of Evil.* Princeton: Princeton University Press, 1987.

Lohfink, N. "Distribution of the Functions of Power: The laws concerning public offices in Deuteronomy 16:18—18:22." In *A Song of Power and the Power of Song,* 336-54. Winona Lake: Eisenbrauns, 1993.

Lohrey, A. "Voting for Jesus: Christianity and Politics in Australia." *Quarterly Essay* 22 (2006) 1-79.

Lohse, B. *Martin Luther. An Introduction to his Life and Work.* Edinburgh: T & T Clark, 1987.

Lundbom, J. R. "The Double Curse in Jeremiah 20:14-18." *JBL* 104.4 (1985) 589-600.

Bibliography

Luther, M. *Luther's Works*. St Louis: Concordia/Philadelphia: Fortress, 1955–86.
Lyon, D. *Jesus in Disneyland: religion in postmodern times*. Cambridge: Polity, 2000.
Lyotard, J. F. "Defining the Postmodern." In *Cultural Studies Reader*, edited by S. During, 170–73. London: Routledge, 1993.
MacLachlan, G. and I. Reid. *Framing and Interpretation*. Melbourne: Melbourne University Press, 1994.
Martin, R. P. *2 Corinthians*. Dallas: Word, 1986.
Matera, F. J. *The Kingship of Jesus: Composition and Theology in Mark 15*. Chico: Scholars, 1982.
Matheson, P. *The Imaginative World of the Reformation*. Edinburgh: T. & T. Clark, 2000.
Matthews, V. H., and D. C. Benjamin. *Social World of Ancient Israel 1250–587 BCE*. Peabody: Hendrickson, 1993.
May, G. *Creatio Ex Nihilo: The Doctrine of "Creation out of Nothing" in Early Christian Thought*. Edinburgh: T. & T. Clark, 1994.
McCartney, D. G. "No Grace Without Weakness." *WTJ* 61 (1999) 1–13.
McConville, J. G. *Deuteronomy*, Leicester: IVP, 2002.
———. *Judgment and Promise: An Interpretation of the Book of Jeremiah*. Winona Lake, Indiana: Eisenbrauns, 1993.
McCredden, L. "Popular Culture/Sacredness." *Interface* 5 (2002) 114–26.
McKane, W. *A Critical and Exegetical Commentary on Jeremiah*. Edinburgh: T & T Clark, 1986.
McKnight S. *Jesus and His Death: Historiography. The Historical Jesus, and Atonement Theory*. Waco: Baylor University Press, 2005.
McLaren, B. D. *A Generous Orthodoxy*. Grand Rapids: Zondervan, 2004.
McLeod, W. T. (ed.), *The New Collins Thesaurus*. London: Collins, 1984.
Melanchthon, P. *Loci Communes (1543)*. Translated by J. A. O. Preus. St Louis: Concordia, 1992.
Melugin, R. F. *The Formation of Isaiah 40–55*. Berlin: de Gruyter, 1976.
Miller, G. J. "Huldrych Zwingli (1484–1531)." In *Reformation Theologians. An Introduction to Theology in the Early Modern Period*, edited by C. Lindberg, 157–69. Oxford: Blackwell, 2002.
Miller, M. R. *The Millennium Matrix: Reclaiming the Past, Reframing the Future of the Church*. San Francisco: Jossey-Bass, 2004.
Miller, P. D. "The Book of Jeremiah." In *NIB*, 6: 555–926. Nashville: Abingdon, 2001.
Moeller, P. A. *Calvin's Doxology*. Allison Park: Pickwick, 1997.
Moltmann, J. *Theology of Hope. On the Ground and Implications of Christian Eschatology*. Translated by J. W. Leitch. London: SCM, 1967.
———. *The Trinity and the Kingdom of God. Doctrine of God*. Translated by M. Kohl. San Francisco: Harper & Row, 1981.
Morris, C. *Epistles to the Apostle—Tarsus please forward*. London: Hodder and Stoughton, 1974.
Morris, K. and J. Lyons. "The Word Made Visual." *Your Church* 48 (2002) 14.
Muggeridge, M. *Christ and the Media: London Lectures in Contemporary Christianity*. London: Hodder and Stoughton, 1977.
Muilenburg, J. "The Book of Isaiah, Chapters 40–66: Exegesis." In *The Interpreter's Bible (5)*, edited by George Arthur Buttrick, 422–793. Nashville: Abingdon, 1956.
Nevin, T. R. *Simone Weil: Portrait of a Self-Exiled Jew*. London: University of North Carolina Press, 1991.

Bibliography

Neuman, M. "Ministry, Weakness, and Spirit in II Corinthians." *Clergy Review* 59 (1974) 647–60.
Newall, R. "Blumhardt, Johann Christoph (1805–80) and Christoph Friedrich (1842–1919)." In *Dictionary of Historical Theology*, edited by T. A. Hart, 76–77. Grand Rapids: Eerdmans, 2000.
Newbigin, L. *The Gospel in a Pluralist Society*. London: SPCK, 1989.
Newsom, C. A. *The Book of Job: A Contest of Moral Imaginations*. Oxford: OUP, 2003.
North, C. R. *The Second Isaiah: Introduction, Translation and Commentary to Chapters 40–55*. Oxford: Clarendon, 1964.
Nouwen, H. J. M. *In the Name of Jesus: Reflections on Christian Leadership*. New York: Crossroad, 1989.
Oakes, E. T. "Icons and Kitsch." *First Things* 111 (2001) 37–44.
Oberman, H. A. *Luther: Man between God and the Devil*. Translated by E. Walliser-Schwarzbart. German original 1982. New Haven: Yale University Press, 1989.
O'Brien, B. "Image and Purpose." *RevExp* 87 (1990) 586–93.
O'Collins, G. G. "Power Made Perfect in Weakness: 2 Cor 12:9–10." *CBQ* 44 (1971) 528–37.
O'Connor, K. M. *The Confessions of Jeremiah: Their Interpretation and Role in Chapters 1–25*. Atlanta, Georgia: Scholars, 1988.
———. "The Prophet Jeremiah and Exclusive Loyalty to God." *Int* 59.2 (2005) 130–40.
Olson, R. E. *The Mosaic of Christian Belief: Twenty Centuries of Unity and Diversity*. Downers Grove: IVP, 2002.
Ozment, S. E. *The Age of Reform 1250–1550. An Intellectual and Religious History of Later Medieval and Reformation Europe*. New Haven: Yale University Press, 1980.
Pannenberg, W. "The Appropriation of the Philosophical Concept of God as a Dogmatic Problem of Early Christian Theology." In *Basic Questions in Theology*, volume 2, 119–83. Philadelphia: Fortress, 1971.
Parker, T. H. L. *Calvin. An Introduction to his Thought*. London: Geoffrey Chapman, 1995.
Parsons, M. *Calvin's Preaching on the Prophet Micah: The 1550–51 Sermons in Geneva*. Lewiston, NY: Edwin Mellen, 2006.
———. *Luther and Calvin on Old Testament Narratives. Reformation Thought and Narrative Text*. Lewiston, NY: Edwin Mellen, 2004.
Paterson, R. M. "Reinterpretation in the Book of Jeremiah." *JSOT* 28 (1984) 37–46.
Peterson, B. K. "Conquest, Control, and the Cross: Paul's Self-Portrayal in 2 Corinthians 10–13." *Int* 52 (1998) 258–70.
Peterson, E. *Christ Plays in Ten Thousand Places. A Conversation in Spiritual Theology*. London: Hodder and Stoughton, 2005.
Petrosillo, O. *Vatican City*. Translated by E. Rizzo and L. Dansteel. Vatican City: Ufficio Vendita, 2002.
Pinnock, C. "Constrained by Love: Divine Self-Restraint according to Open Theism." In *Perspectives in Religion*, edited by R. E. Olson (forthcoming).
———. "God limits his knowledge." In *Predestination and Free Will*, edited by D. Basinger and R. Basinger, 141–62. Downers Grove, IVP, 1986.
———. *Most Moved Mover: A Theology of God's Openness*. Grand Rapids: Baker Academic, 2002.
Pinsky, M. I. *The Gospel According to the Simpsons*. Philadelphia: Westminster, 2001.
Piper, J. *Brothers, We Are Not Professionals: A Plea to Pastors for Radical Ministry*. Nashville, TN: Broadman & Holman, 2002.

Bibliography

Pipkin, H. W. "Resonating with Zwingli." In *Huldrych Zwingli, 1484–1531: A Legacy of Radical Reform. Papers for the 1984 International Zwingli Symposium*, edited by E. J. Furcha, 99–106. Montreal: McGill University, 1985.

Poland, L. W. "Christ and Culture: The Christian and the Media." In *God and Culture: Essays in Honor of Carl F. H. Henry*, edited by D. A. Carson and J. D. Woodbridge, 254–74. Grand Rapids: Eerdmans, 1993.

Polk, T. *The Prophetic Persona*. Sheffield: Sheffield Academic, 1984.

Polkinghorne, J. (ed). *The Work of Love: Creation as Kenosis*. Grand Rapids: Eerdmans, 2001.

Potter, G. R. *Zwingli*. Cambridge: CUP, 1976.

Provence, T. E. "'Who Is Sufficient for These Things?' An Exegesis of 2 Corinthians ii15—iii18." *NT* 24 (1982) 54–81.

Quart, A. *Branded: The Buying and Selling of Teenagers*. London: Arrow, 2003.

Quicke, M. J. *360-Degree Leadership: Preaching to Transform Congregations*. Grand Rapids: Baker, 2006.

———. *360-Degree Preaching: Hearing, Speaking and Living the Word*. Grand Rapids: Baker, 2003.

Resner, A. Jr. *Preacher and Cross—Person and Message in Theology and Rhetoric*. Grand Rapids: Eerdmans, 1999.

Rohr, R. *Job and the Mystery of Suffering*. New York: Crossroad, 1996.

Sanders, J. *The God Who Risks: A Theology of Providence*. Downers Grove: IVP, 1998.

Savage, T. B. *Power Through Weakness: Paul's Understanding of the Christian Ministry in 2 Corinthians*. Cambridge: CUP, 1996.

Scheible, H. "Philip Melanchthon (1497–1560)." In *Reformation Theologians. An Introduction to Theology in the Early Modern Period*, edited by C. Lindberg, 67–82. Oxford: Blackwell, 2002.

Schmidt, T. E. "Mark 15.16–32: The Crucifixion Narrative and the Roman Triumphal Procession." *NTS* 41 (1995) 1–18.

Schoors, A. *I Am God Your Saviour: A Form-Critical Study of the Main Genres in Is. XL–LV*. Leiden: E.J. Brill, 1973.

Schwartz, C. A. *Natural Church Development: A Guide to Eight Essential Qualities of Healthy Churches*. Carol Stream, IL: Churchsmart Resources, 1996.

Seitz, C.R. "How is the Prophet Isaiah Present in the Latter Half of the Book?" In *Word Without End: The Old Testament as Abiding Theological Witness*, 168–93. Waco, TX: Baylor University, 2004.

———. "The Book of Isaiah 40–66." In *NIB (6)*, 309–552. Nashville: Abingdon, 2001.

Shoemaker, H. S. "2 Corinthians 11:1–21." *RE* 86 (1989) 407–11.

Smart, J. D. *The Divided Mind of Modern Theology: Karl Barth and Rudolph Bultmann, 1908–1933*. Philadelphia: Westminster, 1967.

Smith, D. A. "Kinship and Covenant in Hosea 11:1–4." *HBT* 16.1 (1994) 41–53.

Smith, M. S. *The Laments of Jeremiah and Their Contexts*. Atlanta, Georgia: Scholars, 1990.

Sockman, R. W. *The Paradoxes of Jesus*. Nashville: Abingdon, 1940.

Sommer, B. D. *A Prophet Reads Scripture: Allusion in Isaiah 40–66. Contraversions: Jews and Other Differences*. Stanford: Stanford University Press, 1998.

Soskice, J. M. *Metaphor and Religious Language*. Oxford: Clarendon, 1985.

Spykerboer, H. C. *The Structure and Composition of Deutero-Isaiah: With Special Reference to the Polemics Against Idolatry*. Meppel: Krips Repro B.V, 1976.

Bibliography

Spykman, G. J. *Reformational Theology. A New Paradigm for Doing Dogmatics.* Grand Rapids: Eerdmans, 1992.

Standing, R. *Finding the Plot: Preaching in Narrative Style.* Peabody: Hendrickson, 2004.

Stephens, M. *the Rise of the Image the Fall of the Word.* New York: OUP, 1998.

Stephens, W. P, *Zwingli. An Introduction to his Thought.* Oxford: Clarendon Press, 1994.

———. "The Theology of Zwingli." In *Cambridge Companion to Reformation Theology*, edited by D. Bagchi and D. C. Steinmetz, 80–99. Cambridge: CUP, 2004.

Stevenson, K. W. *The Lord's Prayer. A Text in Tradition.* London: SCM, 2004.

Stewart, A. "The Simpsons, Scripture and Postmodern Youth." *Zadok Perspectives* 81 (2003) 6–10.

Stott, J. *Basic Christian Leadership: Biblical Models of Church, Gospel and Ministry.* Downers Grove: IVP, 2002.

Stuhlmueller, C. *Creative Redemption in Deutero-Isaiah.* Rome: Biblical Institute, 1970.

Sumney, J. L. "Paul's 'Weakness': An integral part of his conception of Apostleship." *JSNT* 52 (1993) 71–91.

Tannehill, R. C. *Dying and Rising with Christ: A Study in Pauline Theology.* Berlin: Alfred Töpelmann, 1967.

Taylor, V. *The Gospel According to St. Mark.* London: MacMillan, 1953.

Thomas, N. E. "Radical Mission in a Post-9/11 World: Creative Dissonances." *IBMR* 29 (2005) 2–8.

Thompson, M. D. "Luther on Despair." In *The Consolations of Theology*, edited by B. S. Rosner. Grand Rapids: Eerdmans, 2007.

Thomson, J. A. *The Book of Jeremiah.* Grand Rapids: Eerdmans, 1980.

Thrall, M. E. *A Critical and Exegetical Commentary on Paul's Second Epistle to the Corinthians.* Edinburgh: T & T Clark, 1994, 2000.

Tonkin, J., "Word and Image: Luther and the Arts." *Colloquium* 17 (1985) 47–53.

Torrance, T. F. *Karl Barth: An Introduction to his Early Theology 1910–1931.* Edinburgh: T & T Clark, 1962.

———. *Space, Time and Incarnation.* New York: OUP, 1969.

Tull, P.K. "One Book, Many Voices: Conceiving of Isaiah's Polyphonic Message." In *"As Those Who Are Taught": The Interpretation of Isaiah From the LXX to the SBL*, edited by C. Mathews and P. K. Tull, 279–314. Atlanta: SBL, 2006.

Tupper, E. F. *A Scandalous Providence: The Jesus Story of the Compassion of God.* Macon: Mercer University Press, 1995.

Ugolnik, A., "The Orthodox and the Icon." *ReflJ* 38 (1998) 16–22.

Vanhoozer, K. J. *First Theology: God, scriptures and hermeneutics.* Downers Grove: IVP, 2002.

———. *Is There a Meaning in This Text? The Bible, the Reader, and the Morality of Literary Knowledge.* Grand Rapids: Zondervan, 1998.

———. "The Trials of Truth: Mission, Martyrdom, and the Epistemology of the Cross." In *To Stake a Claim: Mission and the Western Crisis of Knowledge*, edited by J. A. Kirk and K. J. Vanhoozer, 120–56. New York: Orbis, 1999.

———. "The Voice and the Actor: A Dramatic Proposal about the Ministry and Minstrelsy of Theology." In *Evangelical Futures: A Conversation on Theological Method*, edited by J. G. Stackhouse, 63–106. Grand Rapids: Baker, 2000.

Vincent, S. http://occhronicle.blogspot.com/2005/08/steven-vincent.rip.hotmail. Accessed September 19, 2005.

Bibliography

Volf, M. *After Our Likeness: The Church as the Image of the Trinity*. Grand Rapids: Eerdmans, 1998.

von Rad, G. "The Confessions of Jeremiah." In *A Prophet to the Nations: Essay in Jeremiah Studies*, 339–47. Winona Lake, Indiana: Eisenbrauns, 1984.

Wallace, R. S. *Calvin's Doctrine of the Christian Life*. Grand Rapids: Eerdmans, 1959.

Walsh, B. J. and S. C. Keesmaat. *Colossians Remixed: Subverting the Empire*. Downers Grove: IVP, 2004.

Watson, D. *Death Sentence: The Decay of Public Language*. Sydney: Random House, 2003.

Watson, N. M. "'To Make Us Rely Not on Ourselves but on God who Raises the Dead'—2 Cor 1:9b as the heart of Paul's Theology" in *Die Mitte des Neuen Testament: Einheit und Vielfalt neutestamentlicher Theologie*, edited by U. Luz and H. Weder, 384–98. Göttingen: Vandenhoeck und Ruprecht, 1983.

———. *The Second Epistle to the Corinthians*. London: Epworth, 1993.

Watts, J. D. W. *Isaiah 34–66*, edited by B. M. Metzger, D. A. Hubbard, and G. W. Barker. Nashville, TN: Nelson, 2005.

Watts, R. E. "Consolation or Confrontation? Isaiah 40—55 and the Delay of the New Exodus." *TB* 41 (1990) 31–59.

———. *Isaiah's New Exodus and Mark*. Tübingen: Mohr/Siebeck, 1997.

Webber, R. E. *Ancient-Future Faith: Rethinking Evangelicalism for a Postmodern World*. Grand Rapids: Baker, 1999.

Weeden, T. "The Heresy That Necessitated Mark's Gospel." *ZNW* 59 (1968) 145–58.

———. "The Cross as Power in Weakness (Mark 15:20b–41)." In *The Passion in Mark: Studies in Mark 14–16*, edited by W. H. Kelber, 115–134. Philadelphia: Fortress, 1974.

Wegener, M. I. "Reading Mark's Gospel Today: A Cruciforming Experience." *CurTM* 20 (1993) 462–70.

Weil, S. *Gravity and Grace*. Translated by E. Craufurd. London: Routledge and Kegan Paul, 1952.

———. *Waiting on God*. Translated by E. Craufurd. London: Routledge and Kegan Paul, 1951.

Westermann, C. *Isaiah 40–066*. Translated by David M.G. Stalker. London: SCM, 1969.

Westhead, N. "Adoption in the Thought of John Calvin." *SBET* 3 (1995) 102–115.

Wheeler, G. "Visual Art and the Reformed Tradition: Jerome Cotton's Contribution to Its Re-appraisal." *Interface* 5 (2002) 41–54.

Whitlock, G. http://www.theaustralian.com.au. Accessed October 10, 2005.

Williams, R. *Christ on Trial: How the Gospel Unsettles Our Judgement*. London: Harper Collins, 2000.

Witherington, B. (III), *Conflict and Community in Corinth: A Socio-Rhetorical Commentary on 1 and 2 Corinthians*. Grand Rapids: Eerdmans / Carlisle: Paternoster, 1995.

———. *The Christology of Jesus*. Minneapolis: Fortress, 1990.

Wright, N. T. "How Can The Bible Be Authoritative?" *VE* 21(1991) 7–32.

———. *Jesus and the Victory of God*. London: SPCK, 1996.

———. *Mark for Everyone*. London: SPCK, 2001.

Yancey, P. *I Was Just Wondering*. Grand Rapids: Eerdmans, 1989.

Zachman, R. C. *The Assurance of Faith*. Minneapolis: Fortress, 1993.

Zimmerli, W. "Visionary Experience in Jeremiah." In *Israel's Prophetic Tradition*, 95–118. Cambridge: CUP, 1982.

Zwingli, H. *Latin Works of Huldreich Zwingli*, translated by S. M. Jackson. Philadelphia: Heidelberg, 1922.

www.ingramcontent.com/pod-product-compliance
Lightning Source LLC
Chambersburg PA
CBHW070248230426
43664CB00014B/2439